Women in the United States Military

Women's participation in the United States armed forces has grown over time in response to national need for their services. Throughout each era of American history, patriotic women have volunteered to serve their country in a wide variety of officially and unofficially sanctioned capacities. When there has been a call to duty, the United States armed forces have always relied upon women to be a part of the effort. *Women in the United States Military: An Annotated Bibliography* is the most complete and up-to-date listing of resources to help students and scholars understand the effect women have had on the wars that have shaped the United States. Covering everything from the American Revolution to operations in Iraq, *Women in the United States Military* is essential for all academic and research libraries.

Routledge Research Guides to American Military Studies provide concise, annotated bibliographies for the major areas and events in American military history. With the inclusion of brief critical annotations after each entry, the student and researcher can easily assess the utility of each bibliographic source and evaluate the abundance of resources available with ease and efficiency. Comprehensive, concise, and current – **Routledge Research Guides to American Military Studies** are an essential research tool for any historian.

Judith Bellafaire Ph.D. is a historian with Science Applications International Corporation, currently assigned to the Defense Intelligence Agency. For ten years she served as Chief Historian of the Women In Military Service For America Memorial Inc. Prior to that she was a historian with the U.S. Army Center of Military History.

Routledge Research Guides to American Military Studies

America and World War I
David R. Woodward

The War of 1812
John Grodzinski

The United States in the Vietnam War, 1954–1975
Louis A. Peake

The Western European and Mediterranean Theaters in World War II
Donal J. Sexton

The Korean War
Keith D. McFarland

The Spanish-American War and Philippine Insurrection, 1898–1902
Mark Barnes

The Small Wars of the United States, 1899–2009
Benjamin R. Beede

Women in the United States Military
Judith Bellafaire

Women in the United States Military
An Annotated Bibliography

Judith Bellafaire

Routledge
Taylor & Francis Group
NEW YORK AND LONDON

First published 2011
by Routledge
270 Madison Avenue, New York, NY 10016

Simultaneously published in the UK
by Routledge
2 Park Square, Milton Park, Abingdon, Oxon OX14 4RN

Routledge is an imprint of the Taylor & Francis Group, an informa business

© 2011 Taylor & Francis

The right of Judith Bellafaire to be identified as author of this work has been asserted by her in accordance with sections 77 and 78 of the Copyright, Designs and Patents Act 1988.

Typeset in Times NR MT by RefineCatch Limited, Bungay, Suffolk
Printed and bound in the United States of America on acid-free paper by IBT Global

All rights reserved. No part of this book may be reprinted or reproduced or utilized in any form or by any electronic, mechanical, or other means, now known or hereafter invented, including photocopying and recording, or in any information storage or retrieval system, without permission in writing from the publishers.

Trademark Notice: Product or corporate names may be trademarks or registered trademarks, and are used only for identification and explanation without intent to infringe.

Library of Congress Cataloging in Publication Data
Bellafaire, Judith, 1954–
  Women in the United States military: an annotated bibliography/Judith Bellafaire.
    p. cm. -- (Routledge research guides to American military studies)
  1. United States —Armed Forces—Women—History—Bibliography. 2. Women soldiers—United States—History—Bibliography. I. Title.
  27963.S55B45 2011
  [UB418.W65]
  016.3550082'0973—dc22

ISBN 13: 978-0-415-80146-1 (hbk)
ISBN 13: 978-0-203-83509-8 (ebk)

Contents

	Introduction	1
I	**Women in Defense of the Nation Across the Centuries**	5
	A. General Histories	5
	B. Thematic and Service-Specific Histories Covering Multiple Eras	7
	C. Guides to Sources	10
	D. Encyclopedias	10
	E. Journal Articles	11
II	**Early Patriots: Military Women from the American Revolution to the Civil War**	12
	A. Books	13
	B. Journal Articles	16
	C. Official Records	16
	D. Archival Records	17
III	**Women and the American Civil War: More Than Expected**	19
	A. Scholarly Monographs on Women and the Civil War	20
	B. Memoirs and Biographies	25
	C. Journal Articles	33
	D. Arlington National Cemetery Website	34
IV	**Women on the Western Frontier: Few and Far Between**	35
	A. Books	35
V	**Spanish American War Nurses: Proving Themselves of Value**	38
	A. Books	40
	B. Journal Articles	40
	C. Website	41
VI	**World War I: Women Volunteers Establish Parameters of Service**	42
	A. Books	44
	B. Journal Articles	48
	C. Archival Sources	50
	D. Official Records	51
VII	**World War II Women: Bedpans, Typewriters, and Lipstick**	52
	A. General Histories of Women and World War II	53
	B. The Army and Navy Nurse Corps	54
	C. The Women's Army Auxiliary Corps and the Women's Army Corps	63
	D. The Navy WAVES	68

	E. The Coast Guard SPARs	71
	F. Women Marines	71
	G. Women Airforce Service Pilots	72
	H. Unit Histories	76
	I. Journal Articles	76
	J. Reports and Theses	78
VIII	**The Korean War: Women Serving Under the Protection of Uncle Sam**	79
	A. Books	81
	B. Journal Articles	83
IX	**The Vietnam War: The Nurse Heroine and Her Forgotten Sister**	85
	A. Books	86
	B. Journal Articles	88
	C. Official Histories	89
	D. Unpublished Oral Histories and Memoirs	89
	E. Unpublished Thesis	90
X	**The All Volunteer Force Through the 1980s: How Many Women Is Too Many Women?**	91
	A. Books	95
	B. Journal Articles	98
	C. Reports	100
	D. Oral History	100
	E. Periodicals Devoted to Women in the Military	101
	F. Archival Collections	101
XI	**Operations Desert Shield and Desert Storm and the 1990s**	102
	A. Women in the Gulf	102
	A1. Books	104
	A2. Journal Articles	106
	A3. Government Reports	108
	B. Dismantling Combat Exclusion Regulations and 1990s Military Operations	108
	B1. Books	111
	B2. Journal Articles	112
	B3. Theses	114
	B4. Government Reports	115
	C. Gender Discrimination and Sexual Harassment	117
	C1. Books	118
	C2. Journal Articles	122
	C3. Unpublished Conference Papers	123
	C4. Theses	123
	C5. Government Reports	123
	D. Gender and Military Academies	124
	D1. Books	124
	D2. Journal Article	125
	D3. Government Reports	126

XII	**The All Volunteer Force and the War on Terror**	127
	A. Books	128
	B. Theses and Academic Papers	131
	C. Journal Articles	132
	D. Official Reports and Policies	137
Conclusion		139
Index		140

Introduction

Throughout this nation's history, the extent of women's military participation has been directly tied to society's ideas of women's place. The changing definition of women's proper roles has frequently, but not always, been affected by the national need for their services; the number of nurses who served in official and unofficial capacities during the Civil War and the Navy's sudden utilization of women in uniform in the midst of the manpower shortage during World War I are perfect examples of this phenomenon. As this bibliography demonstrates, many of women's contributions to defense remain unexplored. Scanty surviving records tell us little about women's military roles during the American Revolution, the War of 1812 and the Mexican American War of 1846–1848. Although we know that revolutionary era women aided their menfolk in whatever ways they could, accompanying their soldier-husbands to the battlefield to cook for them, nursing the wounded, carrying information across enemy lines and even dressing as men so that they could participate directly in battle, we can document only a few individual women who did these things, the names of many others are unrecorded and unremembered. Although the War of 1812 did not directly impact as large a segment of the American population as the Revolution, battles were fought on American soil, soldiers were wounded, and we must assume that some of these men were cared for by women. However, very few of their names survive. Women's contributions to the Mexican American War are even more problematical. Very scanty documentation of the activities of information-gatherer Anne Chase exists, although Texans appear to have granted her a place in local history. The other almost mythological woman of that era, Sarah Bowman, remains a subject of debate among historians and is not remembered by the public.

The paucity of documentation for women's military service ends with the Civil War, an era when writing was an art as well as a form of communication and recordkeeping. Many of the women who journeyed to the battlefields to nurse wounded soldiers saw fit to record their experiences for friends, family and posterity, and numerous memoirs and collections of letters have been and continue to be published. Among these are the letters of Sarah Rosetta Wakeman, who served as a soldier in New York State's 153d Volunteer Regiment, which participated in the Mississippi Campaign. Although Wakeman's letters do not explain why she chose to dress and live as a man in the Army or how she managed to keep her gender a secret for three years in uniform, they provide a fascinating picture of Army life and provide feminist historians with proof that such disguises were possible, at least until the military services began conducting complete professional examinations at the turn of the twentieth century.

The Spanish American War of 1898 convinced the Army and Navy of the need for permanent nursing corps, and official records of the Army and Navy Nurse Corps begin with their establishment in 1901 and 1907, respectively. It was during the twentieth century's first great war, World War I, that the Armed Services first placed non-nursing women in uniform, gave them the same rank and pay as men (albeit on a temporary basis) and put them to work behind desks and on the homefront so that more men could be sent overseas to fight. This startling innovation was first tried by the Navy, with the Marines following suit. From this era onward, it is possible to trace women's military service through official records. An increasing number of private records such as letters home, diaries and memoirs are being edited and commercially published and reprinted.

World War II is the most written about and documented of America's wars, and the role women played in the war is no exception. The 50th anniversary of the war saw an explosion of published memoirs and "letters home," of Army and Navy nurses who had served in locations around the world; of young women who had defied the wishes of their parents and joined the WACS, WAVES, SPARs and Women Marines; and of women who defied convention and learned to fly military aircraft as members of the WAF and WASP. Scholars remain fascinated with this era and have written extensively about the numerous jobs that opened up to women during the war and whether or not women reverted back into homemakers once the war was over.

The Korean War, dubbed the "Forgotten War," gets less play amongst historians and publishers, although at least 50,000 women served in uniform during the war (as compared to 150,000 during World War II). It was during this era, however, that the official foundations for women's military service were established, with the passage of the controversial 1948 Women's Armed Services Integration Act, Executive Order 10240 of 1951, the establishment of the Defense Advisory Committee on Women in the Service (DACOWITS) that same year, and the Army's now forgotten attempt to keep its nurses safe in Korea by using only male medics in field hospitals. These understudied events continue to have a great deal to tell historians about women's place in 1950s America.

Unlike their counterparts of the Korean War, the military nurses of the Vietnam War have achieved a heroine-like status in the public consciousness. Less well known are the thousands of servicewomen assigned to military bases in the United States and Europe during the 1960s and 1970s. This period cries out for more scholarly studies. The feminist movement was gaining ground during the 1960s and emerged in full flower during the 1970s, and this liberal movement seemed to ignore women in uniform, even though they were fighting the same battles as their civilian sisters. For example, in 1971, a female Air Force First Lieutenant, incensed because the Air Force refused to consider her husband to be her dependant (wives of Airmen were automatically considered dependants of their husbands) sued the Secretary of Defense. The case went all the way to the

Supreme Court, and the lawyer arguing on behalf of the female lieutenant was none other than Columbia Law Professor Ruth Bader Ginsburg, who later became a member of the Supreme Court. At the time Ginsburg argued the case in 1973, the court was solely male. However a plurality of eight justices agreed with the plaintiff that the preferential treatment given to military men in the form of pay and benefits was unconstitutional. The sole holdout was William Rehnquist, who later served as Chief Justice of the Supreme Court.

During this same period servicewomen also challenged the common practice of firing a woman who became pregnant. When the Army notified a Reserve nurse that she would have to resign her commission because she had given birth to a son, she filed suit in a California court, claiming that she was still ready and able to fulfill her Reserve duties. The court issued an injunction ordering the Army to stop the discharge proceedings. Defense Department lawyers concluded that if servicewomen chose to challenge the automatic discharge for pregnancy policy in the courts, the military services would find the cases unwinnable. The lawyers believed that the policy violated the Fifth Amendment because no other temporary physical disabilities resulted in mandatory discharge. In 1975, DOD ordered the services to drop the waiver policy and allow those women who wanted to remain in uniform after giving birth to a child to remain in the service as a matter of course.

The Navy also found itself in an untenable legal position during this period when a female interior communications technician recommended for assignment to the U.S. Naval Survey Ship *Michaelson* saw the assignment disapproved because the Navy's Judge Advocate believed it would be in violation of the Women's Armed Services Integration Act, which prohibited Navy women from serving aboard any vessels other than transports and hospital ships. The female technician and six other Navy women took the Navy to court in a class action suit. In 1978, Judge John J. Sirica of the U.S. District Court in Washington, D.C., ruled on behalf of the plaintiffs and ordered the Navy to proceed with "measured steps" and make individualized decisions regarding women's capabilities with respect to their roles in the Navy. Although the judge did not order the Navy to take immediate action, he did indicate that the courts would no longer tolerate automatic blanket exclusions based on gender alone.

The Navy, realizing that if it did not quickly begin assigning women to sea it would soon be ordered to, and undoubtedly told how to do it as well, decided to proceed at its own chosen pace. In 1978, the Navy assigned women to the *Vulcan*, a repair ship. The women comprised 10 percent of the ship's crew. When few problems occurred, the Navy began to move a bit faster. By the end of 1979, 17 ships had women serving aboard them. Integration continued without fanfare, and in 1987 there were 248 women aboard the USS *Acadia* when it was deployed to the mined waters of the Persian Gulf to repair the crippled USS *Stark*, damaged by Iraqi missiles.

Obviously, the status of servicewomen during this time could tell historians a great deal about the place of American women in society. However, the above court cases have been all but forgotten by historians. Unfortunately the study of servicewomen throughout the 1980s, when their numbers were growing exponentially in the Armed Forces, fares little better. During the 1980s women participated in Operation Urgent Fury (the invasion of Grenada in 1983) and Operation Just Cause (the invasion of Panama in 1989), but not without hesitation and confusion on the part of military commanders, some of whom were uncertain of the legality of sending women into the battle theater along with the units with which they had trained. Although official records and oral histories pertaining to these military operations are available to researchers, very little has been written on the military women who deployed during Urgent Fury and Just Cause, and these women have been disinclined to write about and publish their experiences.

The same cannot be said about the women who deployed to Southwest Asia during Operations Desert Shield and Desert Storm. By 1991 women represented more than 11 percent of the U.S. Armed Forces, and this statistic was reflected in the number of women soldiers, sailors, airmen and Marines who deployed to Saudi Arabia with their units. Women began writing about their experiences in the desert as soon as they returned home, and memoirs from this historic and pivotal period are still being published. Historians interested in this era also have at their disposal numerous newspaper and magazine articles featuring women service members. The press, reflecting the American public's fascination with uniformed women who deployed to the Gulf during the war, wrote prolifically about the women who toiled alongside their male colleagues building hospitals and latrines, guarding perimeters and driving convoys and maintaining aircraft. Press and public were also inordinately interested in uniformed mothers forced to leave their children behind when they deployed. Much attention was focused on family care plans, single mothers in uniform, and dual military parents.

Although the sexual harassment cases of the 1990s also received scrutiny and have been much written about, servicewomen's contributions during the numerous contingency operations of the 1990s, including those to Somalia, Haiti and the Balkans, have failed to receive much attention. This lapse is particularly unfortunate because during this period military commanders were attempting to navigate the vague, confusing and sometimes contradictory Combat Exclusion Laws created by the Department of Defense and the individual services to keep servicewomen safe in the combat theater.

To date, military women's participation in the current War on Terror appears to be receiving significant press, and already a good number of memoirs have appeared in print. Although it is far too early to assess how history will view women's contributions to national defense during this period, it appears that there will be no lack of material for historians to work with. Whether scholars will continue to view servicewomen as a separate subset of the Armed Forces is a fair question to ask at this point in time. In the eyes of this historian at least, as long as servicewomen are treated differently from servicemen during selection, assignment and promotion processes, they must be viewed as a distinct part of the U.S. Armed Forces. Women's place in the military continues to be driven by their place in society as a whole. Although in recent eras tremendous progress has been made in achieving legal, economic and social parity for women, today both servicewomen and civilian women remain separate and unequal under American law and within both American society and its military services.

I
Women in Defense of the Nation Across the Centuries

This section includes general histories of women's service in and with the Armed Forces of the United States. These works are not confined to a single era or to a single service or type of work but encompass several time periods and all or several different services or jobs.

A. General Histories

1. Breuer, William. *War and American Women: Heroism, Deeds and Controversy*. Westport, CT: Praeger, 1997.

    An easy reading, general introduction to the concept of women in military uniform from World War I through the first Gulf War. Although not a scholarly history, this book may surprise the average reader with its discussions of women on the front lines.

2. De Pauw, Linda Grant. *Battle Cries and Lullabies: Women in War from Prehistory to the Present*. Norman, OK: University of Oklahoma Press, 1998.

    One of the "founding mothers" of the academic study of women's military history, De Pauw looks at women's participation in war from a world history perspective. De Pauw's examples of women warriors from fighting Greeks to combat pilots underscore her theme that today's controversy over women in combat is both historically ignorant and foolishly outdated.

3. Fortin, Noonie. *Women at Risk: We Also Served*. Bloomington, IN: IUniverse, 2002.

    Fortin profiles over 60 women who served in the U.S. military or in civilian positions supporting the military from World War II forward.

The women explain why they volunteered and describe their often life-changing experiences.

4. Goldstein, Joshua. *War and Gender: How Gender Shapes the War System and Vice Versa.* New York: Cambridge University Press, 2003.

As Goldstein's title suggests, this book is an academic look at how society's perceptions of the different roles men and women should play influences that society's ways of war. Like De Pauw, Goldstein reaches across historical eras from ancient civilizations to modern day.

5. Holm, Jeanne, Major General, U.S. Air Force (Ret.). *Women in the Military: An Unfinished Revolution.* Novato, CA: Presidio Press, 1987, 1992.

Holm's book is the single most important publication to trace women's military contributions over the course of American history. The book begins with the American Revolution, but its strength lies in its later chapters, which cover World War II through the 1990s. Holm, who began her military service as a member of the Women's Army Corps during World War II and ended her career as the first woman two-star general officer in the U.S. Armed Forces, writes from her own experiences and the knowledge of women's issues she gained as an Air Force officer and leader of military women during the 1950s, 1960s and 1970s.

6. Jones, David. *Women Warriors: A History.* Dulles, VA: Brassey's, 2000.

Written for popular consumption, Jones's book describes past heroines who demonstrated bravery on the field of battle. Although engagingly written, the book contains some disturbing errors. For example, in his discussion of the American Revolution, Jones describes the activities of both Molly Pitcher and Margaret Corbin, but confuses the timeline, placing the Battle of Monmouth (1776) before Margaret Corbin's battlefield experience in 1775. Jones also assigns equal weight to both episodes, although Molly Pitcher's exploits are obscured by myth and difficult to unravel and Corbin's are well documented in official records.

7. Lewis, Vickie. *Side by Side: A Photographic History of American Women in War.* New York: Stuart, Tabori and Chang, 1999.

Photographer Vickie Lewis has pulled together a group of wonderfully evocative photographs of women in uniform throughout American history. Lewis was granted access to the Women in Military Service Memorial Foundation Archives, allowing her to publish never-before-seen photographs of women in uniform. Just as important, however, are the first-hand accounts of the pictured women's experiences, often in their own words, pulled from the diaries and letters home now resting in the Memorial's underutilized archives.

8. Miles, Rosalind and Robin Cross. *Hell Hath No Fury: True Stories of Women at War from Antiquity to Iraq.* New York: Three Rivers Press, 2008.

This highly readable compilation includes short biographies of Air Force Colonel Martha McSally, helicopter pilots Tammy Duckworth and Marie

Rossi, World War II WASP Director Jackie Cochran, computer scientist Admiral Grace Hopper, Silver Star recipient Leigh Ann Hester, and numerous others.

9. Monahan, Evelyn and Rosemary Neidel-Greenlee. *A Few Good Women: America's Military Women from World War I to the Wars in Iraq and Afghanistan.* New York: Knopf, 2010.

   The authors of the acclaimed *All This Hell: U.S. Nurses Imprisoned by the Japanese* and *And If I Perish: Front line U.S. Army Nurses in World War II* turn their attention to a more general history of military women. Both Monahan and Greenlee are veterans, and their interpretation of women's service throughout the past century is compelling and true to life. Utilizing a wealth of archival sources and interviews, the authors chronicle the persistent if little acknowledged bravery of military women over time, society's slow but steady acceptance of uniformed women and the slowly expanding variety of jobs to which they can be assigned.

10. *Salute to Freedom: 100 Years of Women in Military Service.* Belleair, FL: Layfayette Marketing Group, 2008.

    A short, lively, and highly readable account of American women's volunteer service in wartime.

11. Smith, Jill Halcomb. *Dressed for Duty: America's Women in Uniform Volumes 1 and 2.* San Jose, CA: R. James Bender Publishing, 2004.

    Smith's two-volume study of military uniforms worn by American women from the nineteenth century forward is a one-of-a-kind examination of clothing worn by the wide variety of military and civilian women involved in war work over time. Smith's book covers both women who served in the military such as World War I Army and Navy nurses and those who served with it, including Red Cross nurses and World War I Army Signal Corps "Hello Girls." It is the only comprehensive study of women's twentieth century military uniforms currently available.

B. Thematic and Service-Specific Histories Covering Multiple Eras

This section includes monographs that focus on a single service or job over several eras, for example Navy women from World War I to the present or military nurses from the American Revolution through the Vietnam War. Here the reader will find many of the official histories that focus on the women of a single military service over time.

12. Aggles, Theodora B. *Answering the Call: Nurses of Post 122.* Bloomington, IN: Xlibris, 2007.

    The author gathered the individual stories of the military nurses of American Legion Post 122 of Tampa, Florida, called the Jane A. Delano Post, for the founder of the Red Cross Nursing Service. Included in this small publication are first-person accounts of women nurses from World War II, Korea and Vietnam.

13. Air Force Dietitians Association. *Fifty Years of Air Force Dietetics 1949–1999*. San Antonio, TX: Retired Air Force Dietitians Association, 2001.

    This fascinating, informal book consists of reminiscences and oral histories of Air Force dietitians, usually written in the first person.

14. Anderson, Robert, Colonel, U.S. Army, editor-in-chief. *The Army Medical Specialist Corps*. Washington, D.C.: Department of the Army, 1986.

    This history of the Army Medical Specialist Corps describes the contributions of female physical therapists and dietitians overseas during World War I and World War II, the eventual establishment of the Women's Medical Specialist Corps in 1947, and the contributions of Corps members during the Korean War.

15. Barber, Mary. *History of the American Dietetic Association 1917–1959*. Philadelphia: J.B. Lippincott Co., 1959.

    Although somewhat dated by old-fashioned prose, this small book contains some delightful first-person accounts and reminiscences of World War I and World War II military dietitians, which can be found nowhere else. Barber is also a valuable resource for scholars interested in tracing the evolution of Army dietitians from a "nice to have" luxury to an official part of the U.S. Army medical establishment.

16. Bellafaire, Judith and Mercedes Graf. *Women Doctors at War*. College Station, TX: Texas A&M University Press, 2010.

    Bellafaire and Graf trace the participation of women doctors in the Armed Forces during wartime from the Civil War forward into the twenty-first century. Limited initially to serving as nurses and then as civilians under contract, female doctors were utilized by the military services as needed; each limited step forward in status shaped by the needs of the Armed Forces.

17. Ebbert, Jean and Mary Beth Hall. *Crossed Currents: Navy Women in a Century of Change*. Dulles, VA: Potomac Books, 1999.

    This is the second edition of Ebbert and Hall's popular history of Navy women, the first being *Crossed Currents: Navy Women from World War I to Tailhook*. Ebbert and Hall focus on non-nursing Navy women. Their book is well written, engaging, and spot-on in its analysis of the disjunction between the official viewpoint of women's military service and the on-the-job realities of service experienced by the women themselves.

18. Godson, Susan. *Serving Proudly: A History of Women in the U.S. Navy*. Annapolis, MD: Naval Institute Press, 2002.

    An excellent, official, scholarly history of women in the U.S. Navy from World War I through the 1990s. Godson's overview includes both Navy nurses and non-nursing personnel.

19. Graf, Mercedes. *On the Field of Mercy: Women Medical Volunteers from the Civil War to the First World War*. Humanity Books, 2006.

This book details the efforts of little-known and forgotten volunteer female medical workers who stepped up to help the American Army handle unexpectedly large numbers of ill and wounded soldiers during the American Civil War, the Spanish American War, and World War I. Graf tells the stories of female nurses, physicians, and others who frequently without official status, rank, pay or even uniform sacrificed their time, health and in some cases their lives to aid soldiers in need of their services.

20. Lacey, Linda Cates. *We Are Marines: World War I to the Present.* Swansboro, NC: Tar Heel Chapter, North Carolina Women Marines Association, 2004.

A fun-to-read history loaded with lively quotes by and about "Women Marines," and filled with first-person accounts of women's experiences from World War I forward. The book also features over 60 historical photographs, chronologies, quick facts and the words to many of the songs women trainees sang during boot camp and drill.

21. Morden, Bettie, Colonel, U.S. Army (Ret.). *The Women's Army Corps: 1945–1978.* Washington, D.C: U.S. Army Center of Military History, 1990.

Colonel Morden was the official Army historian of the WAC. Her careful, detailed, comprehensive story of the WAC, from its creation during World War II through its eventual disestablishment in 1978 is the starting point for every student interested in women's Army service. Mixing official records with her own personal knowledge of the women involved in the growth of and eventual disestablishment of the WAC, Morden created the foundation for all following studies of this groundbreaking organization.

22. Sarnecky, Mary, Colonel, U.S. Army (Ret.). *History of the Army Nurse Corps.* Philadelphia: University of Pennsylvania Press, 1999.

This is the definitive study of the history of the Army Nurse Corps from its founding in 1901 through to the war in Vietnam. The official historian of the U.S. Army Nurse Corps, Colonel Sarnecky's exhaustive research through government archives and the personal papers of Army nurses is illuminated in this comprehensive yet highly readable history. Although many scholarly works have been published on the Army Nurse Corps during World War II, this volume remains the most important source for anyone interested in looking at the Corps during the Spanish American War, World War I and the years between major wars.

23. Sterner, Doris. *In and Out of Harm's Way: A History of the Navy Nurse Corps.* Seattle, WA: Peanut Butter Publishing, 1998.

Although lacking an index, Sterner's history is lively, chatty, and chock full of wonderfully detailed information, including a large number of personal accounts unavailable elsewhere.

24. Stremlow, Mary V., Marine Colonel, U.S. Marine Corps Reserve. *A History of Women Marines 1946–1977.* Washington, D.C.: History and Museums Division, Headquarters U.S. Marine Corps, 1986.

Stremlow's history of Women Marines after World War II through to disestablishment of the women as a separate branch of the Marine Corps in 1977 provides readers with a clear look at the official philosophy behind the idea of the Woman Marine and the important but limited ways in which women contributed to the mission of the Marine Corps during the 1950s, 1960s and 1970s.

C. Guides to Sources

25. Freidel, Vicki. *Women in the United States Military, 1901–1996.* Westport, CT: Greenwood Press, 1996.

    Although excellent, and certainly worth consulting, this annotated bibliography has been overtaken by recent events and the considerable lists of books and articles that have been published on military women over the past 14 years.

26. Seeley, Charlotte Palmer, Virginia C. Purdy and Robert Gruber. *American Women and the U.S. Armed Forces: A Guide to the Records of Military Agencies in the National Archives Relating to American Women.* Washington, D.C.: U.S. Government Printing Office, NARA 1992.

    The National Archives has revised their filing system since this book was written; however, when shown a page of this volume, archivists working at NARA can usually locate the records in question. The book is still a valuable resource for pinpointing particular records of interest, and will also help researchers identify the types of records they would like to utilize.

D. Encyclopedias

27. Cook, Bernard A. *Women and War: A Historical Encyclopedia from Antiquity to the Present.* Santa Barbara, CA: ABC Clio, 2006.

    An excellent resource for students hoping to learn more about individual military women, the activities of women during specific wars, or topics such as military medicine, the Holocaust and other atrocities, the U.S. homefront, peace movements, resistance movements, service organizations and numerous other war-related topics. Cook emphasizes that while women have often participated in war, they have as often been its victims.

28. Dever, John P. and Maria C. Dever. *Women and the Military: Over 100 Notable Contributors, Historic to Contemporary.* Jefferson, NC: McFarland, 1994.

    The authors pulled together 100 biographies of women they believe are particularly significant in the history of women's military service. Although the majority of these biographies feature U.S. women, a few represent women from other countries.

29. Pennington, Reina and Robin Higham. *Amazons to Fighter Pilots: A Biographical Dictionary of Military Women. 2 Volumes.* Westport, CT: Greenwood Press, 2003.

Pennington and Higham describe the actions and significance of individual women across time and around the world who have been involved in war, combat, military medicine, revolution, rebellion, flight, war-related politics and other numerous controversial themes and subjects. The book also includes bibliographies on subtopics such as "women, medicine and the military" and "women as prisoners of war." This is an outstanding work that deserves a spot on every military historian's bookshelf.

30. Salmonson, Jessica Amanda. *The Encyclopedia of Amazons: Women Warriors from Antiquity to the Modern Era.* New York: Paragon House, 1991.

    Containing over 1,000 entries, this book covers all eras back through antiquity to the twentieth century. The author covers only those women who participated in combat; she does not attempt to discuss women who engaged in adjunct missions such as spying, smuggling or nursing.

31. Sherrow, Victoria. *Women and the Military: An Encyclopedia.* Denver, CO: ABC-CLIO 1996.

    This encyclopedia covers notable individual women, topics and themes pertaining to women's military service up to the Gulf War. It also includes a good bibliography up through that era.

E. Journal Articles

32. Mets, David R. "True Confessions of an Ex-Chauvinist: Fodder for Your Professional Reading on Women and the Military." *Air and Space Power Journal* (Fall 2007) Vol. 21, Issue 3: 89–104.

    This even-handed account of women's increasing military participation does a good job of connecting the rise of the modern feminist movement with political efforts to expand women's military roles.

33. Michael, Sara. "The Face of Courage on the Battlefield." *Defense Standard Quarterly* (Fall 2008): 12–18.

II

Early Patriots: Military Women from the American Revolution to the Civil War

Throughout the eighteenth and early nineteenth centuries thousands of American women accompanied their husbands to war, following them from camp to camp and serving with and without compensation as cooks, laundresses and nurses. While many nurses worked in military hospitals for pay, many more nursed unofficially in volunteer capacities. Women also provided skilled services as seamstresses and ammunition makers and served unofficially as volunteer message carriers and spies. A small number of women, Deborah Sampson being the most famous, served on the battlefield disguised as men; others such as Margaret Corbin served on the battlefield beside their husbands as helpmeets.

One of the most common ways women could aid the American cause was to nurse sick and wounded soldiers. During the American Revolution, nurses were civilian employees of the Army and were paid a standard wage. War orders issued from Washington's Headquarters at Valley Forge during the winter of 1778–1779 stated, "The Commanding Officers of the Regiments will assist the Regimental Surgeons in procuring as many Women of the Army as can be prevailed on to serve as nurses . . . who will be paid the usual price." While the regulations remain and can be studied to this day, most of the lists of women who served as nurses and information about their specific duties have been lost to time. Only small tantalizing references remain. For example, in 1776, nurse Alice Redman petitioned the Maryland Council of Safety. She stated that she was paid $2.00 a month and had 16 men for whom to cook and care for. Her rations did not include tea or coffee, which she longed for, and, out of her two-dollar salary, she was obliged to buy brooms and to keep her ward clean.

It was also possible to directly aid the war effort without actually going out onto the field of battle. Seamstress Rebecca Flower Young made the flag General Washington raised over his headquarters in Cambridge, Massachusetts, in 1776. Women also crossed enemy lines to carry messages to American military forces involving battle plans and troop movements. For example, when British officers requisitioned one of the rooms in her house for a strategy session, Lydia Darragh listened and learned of a plan to attack Washington's Army at Whitemarsh. She obtained a pass allowing her to leave Philadelphia and travel to a flourmill, left her flour at the mill, continued down the road to Whitemarsh and told the first American officer she met what she had heard. She then went home, and when General William Howe led 12,000 soldiers to Whitemarsh several days later, the American Army was expecting them and the British were unable to dislodge them from their entrenched position.

A. Books

34. Berkin, Carol. *Revolutionary Mothers: Women in the Struggle for America's Independence.* New York: Knopf, 2005.

    Berkin examines women's political and legal status during the Revolutionary era and contrasts this with women's efforts on behalf of the Revolutionary cause. She describes the activities of such diverse women as Esther Reed, Catharine Greene and Molly Brant and discusses the lives of women from all walks of society, including Loyalists, African Americans and Native Americans.

35. Claghorn, Charles E. *Women Patriots of the American Revolution.* Metuchen, NJ: Scarecrow Press Inc., 1994.

    Using the archives of the Daughters of the American Revolution, author Claghorn pulled together more than 600 biographies of active female participants in the Revolution. Claghorn lists the women who collected money and food for soldiers, those who helped nurse the sick and wounded, those who manufactured and stored ammunition, those who spied for the Revolutionary Army and other women who participated in the Revolutionary cause in a myriad of ways. This is an outstanding resource for scholars interested in documenting women's participation in the Revolution.

36. Clement, Jesse. *Noble Deeds of American Women: With Biographical Sketches of Some of the Most Prominent.* Buffalo, NY: George E. Derby and Co., 1851. Reprinted by Corner House in 1974.

    Although dated by Victorian language, the author offers a unique perspective on the Revolutionary activities of such well-known women as Abigail Adams, Martha Washington, Lydia Darragh and Margaret Corbin. Not all the "noble deeds" discussed pertain to Revolutionary contributions; however a careful reader will discover numerous interesting allusions to forgotten Revolutionary heroines.

37. Cohen, Daniel. *The Female Marine and Related Works: Narratives of Cross-Dressing and Urban Vice in America's Early Republic.* Amherst, MA: University of Massachusetts Press, 1997.

    Cohen explores the myth of "Molly Marine," the young New England woman who supposedly served aboard an American naval vessel disguised as a man during the War of 1812. Although in the course of tracing the evolution of the "Molly Myth" Cohen proves that the story was just that, the product of a romanticized "dime novel," he provides readers with an excellent idea of the limitations women faced during this era.

38. Dann, John C., ed. *The Revolution Remembered: Eyewitness Accounts of the War for Independence*. Chicago: University of Chicago Press, 1980.

    The vast majority of these eyewitness accounts are those of men. However, this book contains one unique and very important account of a Revolutionary era woman, Sarah Osborn. In 1837, when Osborn was 81 years old, she gave a legal deposition to authorities of Wayne County, Pennsylvania. The purpose of the deposition was to enable Osborn to receive Revolutionary War pensions for two husbands, both Revolutionary War veterans. Osborn describes her experiences as a cook for American Forces at the Battle of Yorktown, working under British cannon fire serving coffee, bread and soup to American troops.

39. Ellet, Elizabeth F. *The Women of the American Revolution*. Baker and Scribner, 1848.

    This valuable three-volume historic study has been reprinted several times and is available in paperback from several publishers. Writing approximately 70 years after the Revolution, Ellet benefited by being able to interview individuals who had personally known the women under discussion. Ellet also had access to a wealth of archival material that has since either disappeared or has fallen into private collections. Although Ellet's prose is dated and quaint, the information contained within this volume is extremely valuable for its insights and is unavailable elsewhere.

40. Freeman, Lucy and Alva Bond, Ph.D. *America's First Woman Warrior: The Courage of Deborah Sampson*. New York: Paragon House, 1992.

    Tells the story of Deborah Sampson Gannett, the first woman (as far as we know) to disguise herself as a male to enlist in the American Army.

41. Gunderson, Joan R. *To be Useful to the World: Women in Revolutionary America 1740–1790*. Twayne, 1996; revised edition University of North Carolina Press, 2006.

    Examines the forces that shaped the world Revolutionary women grew up in; looks at their values, beliefs, and expectations. The final two chapters, "Daughters of Liberty" and "Mothers of the Republic," discuss the impact of the Revolution itself on the women who lived through it. The book contains some interesting tidbits on women's activities that directly impacted on the war; for example a New York woman named Elizabeth Burgin helped 200 American prisoners of war escape from the British, who offered a $2,000 award for her capture.

42. Hendricks, William. *A Journal of the March of a Party of Provincials from Carlisle to Boston and from Thence to Quebec, Begun the 13th of July and Ended the 31st of December 1775*. Glasgow, R. Chapman and A. Duncan, 1776. Reprinted in the Pennsylvania Archives, 2nd Series 15, 21–58, and Oscar H. Stroh, *Thompson's Battalion, and/or the First Continental Infantry*. Harrisburg: Graphic Services, 1975, 47–51.

The diary of William Hendricks documents the actions of Jemima Greer and Susanna Green, who accompanied their husbands on General Benedict Arnold's 1775–1776 expedition to Quebec, and may have been the first two American women to die by gunfire while involved in a military campaign.

43. Kerber, Linda. *Women of the Republic: Intellect and Ideology in Revolutionary America.* University of North Carolina Press, 1997.

    The author looks at the Revolution through the eyes of colonial women, who if not direct participants were nonetheless directly affected by the war. Some women accompanied their husbands to war and served as cooks, laundresses and nurses; others remained at home and tried to maintain the family farm or business. Most accepted new responsibilities on top of old expectations. The author mined numerous primary source accounts in the course of writing her volume: looking at letters, diaries, and official records for hints of the impact of the Revolution on women's lives.

44. Mayer, Holly A. *Belonging to the Army: Camp Follower and Community during the American Revolution.* University of South Carolina Press, 1999.

    Mayer does an excellent job of clearing up misconceptions behind the term "camp followers." She points out that women were integral elements of both the British and American armies throughout the American Revolution. It was not unusual or unwelcome for women to accompany their soldier husbands on military campaigns during the eighteenth century when armies had no organized food or medical services, and women could make themselves very useful. Soldiers on campaign appreciated the hot food and clean clothes women provided, and commanders realized that these were not trivial amenities but often influenced the overall health of the troops. The American Army put women on the payroll as cooks, laundresses, seamstresses, and nurses.

45. Mann, Herman. *The Female Review.* Dedham, MA, 1797.

    A "memoir" of Deborah Sampson, by printer Herman Mann, who supposedly interviewed Sampson about her experiences while disguised as a male soldier during the American Revolution. This publication is considered a primary source by historians because it is the only surviving representation of Sampson's own words. It was reprinted several times during the nineteenth century and is readily available today.

46. Norton, Mary Beth. *Liberty's Daughters: The Revolutionary Experience of American Women 1750–1800.* Ithaca, NY: Cornell University Press, 1996. First published in 1980 by Little, Brown and Company, New York.

    A classic, one of the first books to take an in-depth look at women's social, intellectual, political, and economic lives during the Revolution and how the fighting affected their families, properties, and even their own bodies.

47. Roberts, Cokie. *Founding Mothers: The Women Who Raised Our Nation.* New York: Harper Collins, 2004.

    Roberts examines the sometimes surprising impact the wives, mothers, and sisters of America's Founding Fathers had on the policies, decisions, and actions of these military men and politicians throughout the Revolutionary period and beyond.

48. Young, Alfred F. *Masquerade: The Life and Times of Deborah Sampson, Continental Soldier.* New York: Alfred A. Knopf, 2004.

Young's innovative biography of Deborah Sampson does an excellent job of using a wide variety of unconventional sources, including architecture and artifacts, to complement scarce documentary sources and fill out gaps in Sampson's life, character and motivations. Sampson, one of the most famous women of the Revolutionary era, disguised herself as a man so that she could enlist in the Massachusetts militia and fight for her country. Sampson joined the Fourth Massachusetts Regiment of the Continental Army under the name "Robert Shurtleff," and remained in the Army approximately 18 months before her disguise was discovered. During that time, Sampson's regiment was based at West Point, New York, and ordered to clear out roving bands of Loyalist guerrillas plaguing the area. When Sampson's regiment saw battle for the first time, she acquitted herself well, firing her musket until the battle became a hand-to-hand affair, and then swinging her bayoneted musket at the enemy at close quarters. She received a saber slash across the right side of her head. The regimental surgeon treated it without noticing her gender. During the regiment's next skirmish, a musket ball grazed Sampson's thigh. She treated the wound herself, and was eventually sent to Philadelphia to serve as a clerk to Major General John Paterson. In Philadelphia, she caught a fever and was sent to a doctor, who discovered her gender. She was then honorably discharged. After the war, Sampson returned to Massachusetts, married a farmer, and had three children. She eventually received a pension from the federal government, the records of which historians have used to document her service.

B. Journal Articles

49. Cornetta, Elizabeth. "Women of the American Revolution." *The New England Quarterly* (September 1947) Vol. 20, No. 3: 329–346.

50. Erkkila, Betsy. "Revolutionary Women." *Tulsa Studies in Women's Literature* (Autumn 1987) Vol. 6, No. 2: 189–223.

51. Graf, Mercedes. "Standing Tall with Sarah Bowman: The Amazon of the Border." *Minerva: Quarterly Report on Women in the Military* (Fall Winter 2001) 19: 27–38.

52. Leonard, Patrick J. "As Private Robert Shurtliff, Deborah Sampson Served 18 Months in the Continental Army." *Military History* (April 2001) 18: 16–18.

C. Official Records

53. Documents of the Assembly of the State of New York, Vol. 18, New York State Legislature Assembly, 1917.

Newlywed Margaret Corbin was with her husband John, an artilleryman, during the battle of Fort Washington in November 1776 when the American Army was defending the fort against the British. Margaret was at her husband's side helping him load his cannon when he was killed by enemy fire. She took control of his gun, loading and firing it until she too was wounded. When the fort fell, she was captured near the gun by the British and taken to a hospital in nearby New York City, which at the time was under British control. The British did not hold Corbin as a prisoner of war, and in 1777 she left New York and went to Philadelphia, where she was assigned to the Continental Invalid Corps until formally mustered out of the Army in 1783. In July 1779, the Continental Congress voted to pay her a military pension totaling half her dead husband's pay and a new suit of clothing each year. The 26-year-old war widow was the first American woman to receive a pension for her military service.

54. Colonel Records of Pennsylvania, Volume 15, 1853, p. 566.

Eleanor Hitchcock, who lived near Cape Henlopen, Pennsylvania, put up a flagpole that could be seen by American ships in Delaware Bay, and signaled the ships by hoisting up special flags warning them of the enemy's approach.

D. Archival Records

The historian's files for the War of 1812 at the Women in Military Service for American Memorial Foundation in Arlington, Virginia, contain information on seamstress and flag maker **Mary Pickersgill** of Baltimore, Maryland, who made the Fort McHenry during the War of 1812. Pickersgill learned her craft from her mother, flag maker Rebecca Flower Young. The Army paid Pickersgill to make a large flag for Fort McHenry near Baltimore. When the British attacked the fort in 1814, it was the flag made by Pickersgill that Francis Scott Key saw as he watched the battle from a warship in Baltimore harbor. Key was inspired to write a song about the flag waving defiantly over Fort McHenry. Today that song, known as "The Star Spangled Banner," is our national anthem.

The above files also have copies of payment records for contract nurse **Mary Ann Cole**, who worked as a hospital matron during the siege of Fort Erie from July through November of 1814, during which time 1,800 Americans were killed or wounded in action. As the Americans inside the fort tried desperately to hold out against British bombardment, nurse Cole went about her duties caring for sick and wounded soldiers in the fort's makeshift hospital. She prepared meals, dispensed medications and kept medical records for the regimental surgeon. As the siege continued, the number of wounded increased and medical supplies grew short. Finally, in early November, the Americans surrendered and abandoned the fort. Nurse Cole left the fort with the troops but was not taken prisoner by the British. She made her own way back to Buffalo, New York, where she is lost to history.

The historian's files for the Mexican American War of 1848 at the Women's Memorial hold copies of the records and legal proceedings initiated by **Elizabeth Newcom.** Newcom enlisted as Private Bill Newcom in Company D of the Missouri Volunteer Infantry in hopes of receiving the "bounty land" that the state was promising all men who joined up. "Bill" and his unit marched from Fort

Leavenworth, Kansas, 600 miles to an area near Pueblo, Colorado. After a period of from three to four months, "Bill" was discovered to be a woman and was discharged from the Army. We know about her service because some five years after her discharge, Newcom, by that time a married woman urged on by her husband, applied to the Missouri courts to receive her promised land. Missouri initially refused to grant Newcom and her husband the land, but they petitioned the federal government. Congress eventually found that Newcom had indeed served and granted her the standard allotment of 160 acres of land.

The above files also contain information on **Anne Chase**, who provided the U.S. Navy with important information on the fortifications of the Mexican city of Tampico, giving U.S. forces the advantage they needed to seize the town. Ann Chase was married to an American diplomat stationed in Tampico, Mexico, when the war broke out. Ann's husband left the country, but Chase remained because she did not want to leave the family property. As part of Tampico's upper class, Chase attended social gatherings and dinner parties with Mexican Army officers. She made a point of listening carefully to their conversations and reported all the tidbits of information she obtained about the size of their forces and their movements to her American contacts. When Mexican officials began to get suspicious of Ann and threatened to confiscate the family property, she decided to take more decisive action. She told several Mexican officers that the Americans planned to attack Tampico with 30,000 troops. The Mexicans believed her and abandoned the city, allowing the American forces to enter the city and take it without a shot. It was an important city to the United States military because they used it as a staging port from which to launch an attack on the Mexican stronghold of Veracruz.

III

Women and the American Civil War: More Than Expected

In 1861, the issue of slavery, which had been festering for decades, finally split the nation. It was assumed by both sides that women's role in the dispute would remain home based; politicians, government officials and military officers did not envision women taking any part in a war, which both sides believed would be of short duration. Although a few women inquired about volunteering as nurses, Army officers assured the public that wounded soldiers would be well cared for by Army doctors and medics.

Once the war started, however, it quickly became evident that the tiny Army Medical Departments of both sides were overwhelmed by unexpectedly large numbers of casualties. Furthermore, military and political leaders realized that the war would not end quickly but drag on, with ever-increasing casualties on both sides. Reluctantly, the Union Army decided to hire female nurses to help male doctors and medics handle the growing numbers of sick and wounded soldiers. But who should select and supervise these women? Army leaders decided to entrust one of the most respected women of that time, Dorothea Dix, to hire and oversee the efforts of women nurses working under contract to the Army.

Dix, a 60-year-old spinster and social reformer from Massachusetts, was credited with convincing Massachusetts' legislators to provide more humane services and asylums for the mentally ill. Her well-publicized altruistic efforts on behalf of the poor, blind and insane had made her a heroine in many circles. Dix hired several hundred nurses for the Army. In addition to the nurses Dix appointed, however, thousands of other women simply volunteered unofficially and worked as needed on battlefields and in military hospitals. Some had originally applied to Dix for official appointments, but Dix had very firm ideas about the type of women she wanted as her nurses. She made a point of selecting plain, sturdy, middle-aged women so that soldiers would not be tempted to fall in love with their nurses. That way, everyone would keep their minds on work rather than on romance, and no questions pertaining to the morality of her nurses would develop.

Southern women also volunteered to nurse the sick and wounded, often defying the wishes of family and friends to work in makeshift military hospitals. Women who left their homes to nurse were usually widowed or single women who were not responsible for young children or other dependants, and had control over their own destinies. Those tethered to home by husbands, children, elderly parents or farms had to content themselves with helping to gather food, medicines and medical supplies for soldiers in need.

Although most women who left home to involve themselves in the Civil War worked as nurses, smaller numbers dressed themselves as men and volunteered for duty with the Union and Confederate Armies. Only recently have historians, delving into private and official records, realized the fairly significant number of women who served on the battlefield during the war. Women also involved themselves in war by serving as volunteer and official spies. This was an extremely literary era, and numerous excellent memoirs, diaries and collections of letters written by contract and volunteer nurses who worked in Union and Confederate hospitals are readily available as are a smaller number of writings of women spies and soldiers.

A. Scholarly Monographs on Women and the Civil War

55. Andrews, Matthew Page. *Women of the South in War Times*. The Norman Remington Company, 1920.

    Andrews, writing 50 years after the Civil War, accessed a large number of now rare and hard-to-find personal accounts of women's war experiences. Although his prose and perspective will appear quaint and dated to modern readers, some first-person narratives in his volume appear nowhere else. Andrews focus is on women who supported fathers, husbands and brothers against federal and military authority, even at the cost of imprisonment.

56. Attie, Jeanie. *Patriotic Toil: Northern Women and the American Civil War*. Ithaca, NY: Cornell University Press, 1998.

    Attie discusses the women who volunteered with the U.S. Sanitary Commission during the war, and links their successful work within that organization to their later efforts in the suffrage and temperance movements.

57. Blanton, DeAnn and Lauren Burgess Cook. *They Fought Like Demons: Women Soldiers in the American Civil War*. Baton Rouge: Louisiana State University Press, 2002.

    Delving through long lost private and public archives, the authors describe documentary proof of hundreds of women on both sides of the conflict who disguised themselves as men to participate in battle. The case of Irish immigrant Jennie Hodgers provides a perfect example. Hodgers' service is documented because of an investigation carried out by the U.S. Pension Bureau 40 years after the Civil War. Hodgers enlisted in the 95th Illinois Volunteer Infantry as Albert D. J. Cashier. Private Cashier's unit commander found him to be quick-witted, courageous and dependable and often selected him for scouting and foraging duties. Cashier served from 1862–1865 and participated in at least 40 battles. After the war, a demobilized Hodgers, still dressing as a man, settled down in Saunemin, Illinois, as a general handyman. In 1890 the so-called Cashier applied for a veteran's pension and received it. Cashier's true gender wasn't discovered until 1911, when she was taken to a local veteran's hospital after an accident. Believing the woman must have committed fraud, the Pension Bureau investigated the case and brought several of Cashier's old Army buddies to see her. The veterans all testified that the individual in question was indeed the person they had served with for three years. Hodgers/Cashier died shortly after, traumatized by the discovery of her gender. Her case records are housed in the National Archives.

58. Brocket, L.P. and Mary C. Vaughn. *Women at War: Civil War Heroines*. Originally published in 1867, reprinted in 1993 by Long Meadow Press, Stamford, CT.

   This classic volume contains detailed stories of famous as well as forgotten women active in war work. The famous include Dorothea Dix and Clara Barton; less well-known women profiled are Helen Louise Gilson, Eliza Porter, Amy Bradley and many more.

59. Campbell, Edward D.C. and Kym S. Rice, eds. *Southern Women, the Civil War and the Confederate Legacy*. Charlottesville, VA: Museum of the Confederacy, 1996.

   The result of an exhibition on the impact of the Civil War on the lives of Confederate Women at the Museum of the Confederacy in the 1990s, this volume is loaded with interesting photographs of art and artifacts that illustrate the changes in women's lives brought on by the war.

60. Clinton, Catherine and Nina Silber, eds. *Battle Scars: Gender and Sexuality in the American Civil War*. Oxford University Press, 2006.

   In a series of related essays, Clinton, Silber and their contributors look at the variety of ways gender impacted on the roles assigned to women during the Civil War. Some of the types of women they look at include nursing nuns, freed black women, and female abolitionists.

61. Eggleston, Larry F. *Women in the Civil War: Extraordinary Stories of Soldiers, Spies, Nurses, Doctors, Crusaders and Others*. Jefferson, NC: McFarland and Co., 2003.

   Includes short profiles of a wide variety of women activists including Clara Barton, Mary Ann Bickerdyke, Anna Ella Carroll, Harriet Tubman, Elizabeth Van Lew, Frances Hook and many others.

62. Frank, Lisa Tendrich, ed. *Women in the American Civil War*. Santa Barbara, CA: ABC-CLIO, 2007.

   This excellent two-volume encyclopedia includes biographies, topical essays, a bibliography, photographs and excerpts from primary source materials. It emphasizes the multiple roles women held during the war and details the lives of hundreds of women who participated in the war effort on both sides.

63. Giesberg, Judith. *Civil War Sisterhood: The U.S. Sanitary Commission and Women's Politics in Transition*. Boston: Northeastern University Press, 2000.

Giesberg connects women's experiences with the local and regional efforts of the U.S. Sanitary Commission with their later activism in the temperance and suffrage movements. It was with the Sanitary Commission and its works, Giesberg points out, that women learned how to organize their efforts towards a common goal, and they learned what it was possible to accomplish through cooperation and organization.

64. Greenbie, Marjorie Barstow. *Lincoln's Daughters of Mercy.* New York: GP Putnam's Sons, 1944.

An excellent, often overlooked examination of many of the women, young through middle-aged, who served as nurses and/or coordinated food and supplies destined for northern hospitals. Although the author's interpretation is somewhat dated, Greenbie does an excellent job bringing to life the personalities of the women she describes, and is very good at illuminating the network of connections many of these middle-class women utilized to get the job done.

65. Hall, Richard. *Patriots in Disguise: Women Warriors of the Civil War.* Marlowe & Co., 1994.

Although an interesting read at the time of its publication, Hall's work has been eclipsed by the efforts of authors Blandon and Cook, who have done a better job of documenting women's battlefield exploits and of separating fact from fiction.

66. Hall, Richard. *Women on the Civil War Battlefront.* University Press of Kansas, 2006.

Hall's second work is a well-documented study of the battlefield experiences of more than 400 women who served as scouts, spies, saboteurs, nurses, and smugglers, many in disguise.

67. Harper, Judith E. *Women during the Civil War: An Encyclopedia.* New York: Routledge, 2004.

Harper discusses the experiences of women during the war as well as those who participated in it, and shows that many women were directly affected by the war even if they and their families did not participate in it. For example, she explains the draft riot in New York City in 1863, as well as life for the average woman of the American west, far from the war itself. Her use of primary source material to illuminate her discussions and biographies is exceptionally deft.

68. Kinchen, Oscar A. *Women Who Spied for the Blue and Gray.* Philadelphia: Dorrance, 1972.

A somewhat dated examination of the female spies of the Civil War, including Belle Boyd and Rose Greenhow among others less well known.

69. Leonard, Elizabeth. *All the Daring of the Soldier: Women of the Civil War Armies.* New York: WW Norton, 1999.

Leonard's groundbreaking work examines the motivations behind the actions of women who opted to undertake nontraditional wartime roles and fight in disguise (often alongside husbands and brothers) or spy or smuggle for the Union or Confederate armies. Leonard's discussion of Sarah Emma Edmonds is a good example of the even-handed methods this excellent historian uses to get as close as possible to the truth.

70. Lowry, Thomas. *Confederate Heroines: 120 Southern Women Convicted by Union Military Justice*. Baton Rouge, LA: Louisiana State University Press, 2006.

Lowry mined heretofore forgotten official records in the National Archives to document the surprising activities of Confederate women captured and tried by the Union Army during the Civil War. Although some women were convicted for failing to respect Union authority, others were caught taking direct and significant action against the Union, such as cutting telegraph lines, smuggling medicine and percussion caps, and aiding fugitives.

71. Maher, Sister Mary Denis. *To Bind Up the Wounds: Catholic Sister Nurses in the U.S. Civil War*. Baton Rouge, LA: Louisiana State University Press, 1989.

Maher's often forgotten but immensely interesting look at Catholic nuns' nursing contributions to the war includes information on the contributions of African American women nurses as well as nuns. Although little is known about them, many African American women worked aboard Union hospital steamships that plied up and down the Mississippi River during the war. In most cases, these women were hired to help the Catholic nuns assigned to these vessels. Maher points out that both the Union and Confederate Armies accepted the nursing services of hundreds of Catholic nuns during the war because convent trained nuns were the sole source of "professionally" trained nurses at the time (nursing schools were not established in the United States until years after the war) and that the sisters and their African American helpers who worked aboard the steamboats transporting wounded soldiers from southern battlefields to northern cities along the Mississippi River frequently came under enemy fire.

72. Massey, Mary Elizabeth. *The Bonnet Brigade: American Women and the Civil War*. New York: Knopf, 1966.

An excellent examination of the lives of northern and southern women during the war; the foundation on which modern historians Attie, Giesberg and Silber have built. Among those women Massey singles out for in-depth treatment are the "infamous" spies Pauline Cushman and Belle Boyd as well as those history has treated more kindly, the "saintly" Clara Barton and Mary Livermore, who subscribed more closely to the feminine standards of their day.

73. McDevitt, Theresa. *Women and the American Civil War: An Annotated Bibliography*. Westport, CT: Praeger, 2003.

McDevitt describes approximately 800 published books and articles pertaining to American women and the Civil War. She groups her materials topically and considers women in medicine, women as spies, women who served disguised as men, and a variety of other subjects.

74. Moore, Frank. *Women of the War.* Hartford, CT: S.S. Scranton, 1866, reprinted by Blue and Gray Books, NC, 1997.

    Includes descriptions of the wartime activities of Kady Brownell, Pauline Cushman, Mary Ann Byckerdyke, Myra Breckinridge, Rebecca Usher, Charlotte McKay, Elida Rumsey Fowle, Isabella Fogg and numerous others. Because Moore was writing immediately after the end of the war, his work is valuable to scholars interested in seeing how Civil War society perceived the women who had made names for themselves during the war.

75. Schultz, Jane E. *Women at the Front: Hospital Workers in Civil War America.* Chapel Hill, NC: University of North Carolina Press, 2004.

    The author looks at the motivations and experiences of the thousands of women who left their homes to nurse in military hospitals during the Civil War. Schultz uses both personal memoirs of individual nurses as well as hospital records to paint a detailed and comprehensive picture of the hardships these women faced and the heroism they exhibited.

76. Silber, Nina. *Daughters of the Union: Northern Women Fight the Civil War.* Boston: Harvard University Press, 2005.

    Silber emphasizes how tightly constrained to home, hearth, and male domination women remained throughout the course of the war. Even as nurses and volunteers in local charitable organizations and sanitary commissions, the majority of women's efforts remained dominated by male physicians, officers, local leaders, and bureaucrats. If men always led, however, women did much of the work in hospitals and on commissions and in doing so learned a great deal about their abilities, and this knowledge served as an important basis for later efforts long after the war ended.

77. Silber, Nina and Catherine Clinton, eds. *Divided Houses: Gender and the Civil War.* New York: Oxford University Press, 1992.

    In 18 essays, scholars examine the meaning of gender, race, and class in Civil War era America. The authors use primary source documents to illustrate the immense hold expectations pertaining to gender, race, and class had on the perceptions, interpretations, attitudes, and actions of Civil War men and women, whether idealistic abolitionists, defeated soldiers, freed black slaves, or divorced women.

78. Tsui, Bonnie. *She Went to the Field: Women Soldiers of the Civil War.* Guilford, CT: Two Dot, 2006.

    An examination of women who served on the Civil War battlefield disguised as men. Tsui profiles Jennie Hodgers, Loreta Velazquez, Sarah Rosetta Wakeman, Sarah Emma Edmonds and numerous others.

79. Young, Agatha. *The Women and the Crisis: The Women of the North and the Civil War.* New York: McDowell Obolensky, 1959.

    Although over 50 years old, Young's vibrant and perceptive writing style makes readers feel they really know and understand the women described in this book. She includes numerous small details about her subjects' lives, but she is never boring; her interpretation remains fresh.

80. Wiley, Bell Irvin. *Confederate Women*. Westport, CT: Greenwood Press, 1975.

Wiley focuses on three wealthy Southern women who left considerable writings behind them, all of which demonstrate hidden strengths of will and determination that the author believes were reflective of a good portion of their cohort group. The worlds of Mary Boykin Chesnut, Virginia Tunstall Clay, and Varina Howell Davis were destroyed by the war; but each woman understood where her duty lay and vowed to carry on to the best of her ability.

B. Memoirs and Biographies

81. Alcott, Louisa May. *Civil War Hospital Sketches*. Bedford, MA: Applewood Books, 1993, originally published in 1863 by J. Redpath, Boston.

Future famous author Louisa May Alcott was one of many applicants chosen to work in Northern Civil War hospitals by Dorothea Dix. Alcott was forced to return home after only a few weeks because she contracted pneumonia. Alcott's small memoir is written in a series of sentimental vignettes of the type one would expect from this author.

82. Baker, Nina Brown. *Cyclone in Calico*. Boston: Little Brown and Co., 1952.

An often overlooked but excellent biography of Civil War nurse and relief organizer Mary Ann Bickerdyke. Much like Clara Barton, the middle-aged Mary Ann Bickerdyke began collecting food and medicine for hospitalized soldiers and ended up nursing in Army hospitals throughout the war. General Ulysses Grant was impressed with Bickerdyke's accomplishments in the military hospitals under his command and usually sanctioned whatever she wanted to do to make things more comfortable for injured troops. Her influence and authority was resented by many Army doctors and military officers used to quiet, hardworking nurses who meekly took orders, but her ability to organize and administer clean, comfortable hospitals could not be disputed. She was the only woman the irascible General William T. Sherman would allow in his camp during the war.

83. Beers, Fannie. *Memories*. Philadelphia, PA: Press of J.B. Lippincott Company, 1888.

Beers was born in the North and met a young southern gentleman named A.P. Beers while he was a student at Yale. When they married she went with him to his home, and when Civil War started, Beer's husband enlisted in the Confederate Army. Fannie, with one small child and pregnant, initially visited her own family, but "unhappy feelings" persuaded her to return to the South and accompany her husband. While with the Confederate Army, Beers nursed at field hospitals in Virginia, Georgia and Alabama.

84. Berlin, Jean, ed. *The Confederate Nurse: The Diary of Ada W. Bacot 1860–1863*. University of South Carolina Press, 1994.

Bacot, a childless widow of independent means, who owned a plantation in South Carolina, left her home to nurse Confederate soldiers at a hospital in Charlottesville, Virginia. Her diary describes her working and social relationships with fellow nurses and doctors at the hospital. Much of her work involved cooking and laundry rather than patient care, which was usually administered by ward men. Bacot left nursing before the end of the war and returned home, although the diary does not explain why; she eventually married an officer whom she may have met in Charlottesville.

85. Blackman, Ann. *Wild Rose: Rose O'Neale Greenhow, Civil War Spy, A True Story*. New York: Random House, 2005.

Confederate spy Rose Greenhow, the widow of a Washington, D.C., politician, moved in the best social circles in the capital and gleaned information from her dinner party conversations with Union officers. She then encoded the information and sent it to Confederate Army officers in Richmond, Virginia. Eventually, the federal government arrested Greenhow and deported her to Richmond. Greenhow then traveled to England in an attempt to obtain support for the Confederacy. While in England, she published her memoirs and received royalties of about $2,000. On her way home, her ship was pursued by a Yankee vessel and ran aground near Cape Fear, North Carolina. Fearing recapture, Greenhow asked to be put overboard in a small boat. When the boat sank in heavy surf, Greenhow, weighted down by gold meant for the Confederate treasury sewn into her clothes, drowned.

86. Boyd, Belle. *Belle Boyd in Camp and Prison*. Baton Rouge, LA: Louisiana State University Press, 1998.

Boyd's memoir has been published and republished numerous times. In this particular edition, historians Drew Gilpin Faust and Sharon Kennedy-Nolle examine Boyd's words from a feminist perspective. Boyd describes her motivations for spying for the Confederacy and her many activities in support of her cause. Although few historians dispute the facts of Belle's story, the overall significance of her efforts is still under discussion.

87. Burgess, Lauren Cook, ed. *An Uncommon Soldier: The Civil War Letters of Sarah Rosetta Wakeman Alias Private Lyons Wakeman*. Pasadena, MD: The Minerva Center, 1994.

Editor Cook Burgess discovered a treasure trove of letters in an old farmhouse in upstate New York. The letters turned out to be from Rosetta Wakeman to her family. Rosetta, disguised as a man, enlisted in the 153d New York Volunteer Regiment under the name of Lyons Wakeman. She served from August 1862 until her death from disease in a hospital in New Orleans in June 1864. Before her death, she saw combat during the four-hour battle of Pleasant Hill, part of the Mississippi Campaign. The Army buried Wakeman without discovering her gender.

88. Christian, William J. *Pauline Cushman: Spy of the Cumberland*. Roseville, MN: Edinborough Press, 2006.

Pauline Cushman's story has long been cloaked in myth, and for many years historians believed her story to be fiction. Christian spent more than

10 years of meticulous research tracking down Cushman's experiences, and has been able to fill in much about her character, motivations and the things she actually did on behalf of the Union cause.

89. Clinton, Catherine. *Harriet Tubman: The Road to Freedom.* New York: Little Brown and Co., 2004.

One of the most famous African American women who took a direct part in the war was Harriet Tubman, who had run away from a Maryland plantation to freedom in 1849 and found her way on foot to Philadelphia. Tubman made it her mission to rescue as many slaves as possible by helping more than 140 reach the Underground Railroad in the years prior to the Civil War. When the war started, Tubman worked informally with the Union Army as a scout and spy in South Carolina, passing into enemy territory to guide slaves to Union encampments, and leading raids on plantations along the Comcahee River. During the winter of 1862–1863 Tubman was attached to the all black Second South Carolina Volunteers and commanded a small reconnaissance unit comprising nine men and several riverboat pilots. The unit's mission was to slip behind enemy lines and determine Confederate troop movements and strength. In June 1863, Tubman led 150 African American troops upriver to remove underwater mines and destroy bridges and railroad tracks to disrupt Confederate supply lines. The raiding party also seized several plantations and freed about 700 slaves on them. Clinton is a deft biographer and has crafted a well-documented and highly readable account of this legendary woman.

90. Conklin, E.F. *Exile to Sweet Dixie: The Story of Euphemia Goldsborough: Confederate Nurse and Smuggler.* Gettysburg, PA: Thomas Publications, 1998.

Goldsborough was a Maryland woman and nurse at Gettysburg who volunteered as a nurse at a Union-run camp for Confederate prisoners of war. A Confederate sympathizer, Goldsborough smuggled contraband materials in to the prisoners. Eventually, Goldsborough was caught, arrested, and exiled back to Confederate-held territory. Conklin does an excellent job of bringing her heroine to life.

91. Coryell, Janet. *Neither Heroine nor Fool: Anna Ella Carroll of Maryland.* Kent, OH: Kent State University Press, 1990.

An interesting, even-handed examination of the life of Anna Ella Carroll that tries to separate fiction from fact and determine the true significance of this forgotten woman writer's pamphlets supporting Lincoln's assumption of war powers and on her plan for a military invasion of the Cumberland and Tennessee River Valleys.

92. Creighton, Margaret. *The Colors of Courage: Gettysburg's Forgotten History: Immigrants, Women and African Americans in the Civil War's Defining Battle.* New York: Basic Books, 2005.

Although women's experiences at Gettysburg are not the author's sole concern in this interesting volume, her descriptions of individual women's reactions to the battle, their attempts to keep their families and properties safe, and the aid they provided to soldiers of both sides illuminate important lost perspectives of that historic battle.

93. Cumming, Kate and Richard Barksdale Harwell. *Kate: The Journal of a Confederate Nurse*. Louisiana State University Press, 1998.

   Cumming was a gently reared Southern "lady" who felt compelled to leave home and nurse in Confederate hospitals, against the wishes of her family. Cumming's journal details the hard work she never shirked and the short supplies that fueled her bitterness against the hated Yankees, whom she blamed for all the war's suffering.

94. De Leeuw, Adel. *Civil War Nurse Mary Ann Bickerdyke*. J. Messner, 1973.

   A biography of Civil War organizer and nurse Mary Ann Bickerdyke, whose formidable skills brought her respect rarely accorded women of her era.

95. Edmonds, Sara Emma. *Memoirs of a Soldier, Nurse and Spy in the Union Army: A Woman's Adventures in the Union Army*. Diggory Press, 2006.

   The memoirs of a Canadian woman and cross-dresser who enlisted in the Union Army and served disguised as "Frank Thompson" in a variety of assignments: as a male nurse, as a messenger, and as a spy. When Edmonds originally published her memoir immediately after the Civil War it caused a sensation, many readers refusing to believe it could be a true story. Edmonds, who had fallen in love with a fellow soldier during the war, eventually married a man she met after the war and had children.

96. Galbraith, William and Loretta, eds. *A Lost Heroine of the Confederacy: The Diaries and Letters of Belle Edmondson*. Jackson, MS: University Press of Mississippi, 1990.

   The authors bring to light Edmondson's activities against the Union detailed in her numerous letters to family and friends. Edmondson acted as a courier of information as well as a gatherer of intelligence and smuggler.

97. Garrison, Nancy Scripture. *With Courage and Delicacy: Civil War on the Peninsula: Women and the U.S. Sanitary Commission*. Mason City, IA: Savas Publishing Company, 1999.

   The letters and journals of Georgeanna Woolsey, Katharine Wormeley, Eliza Howland, three well-to-do, literate and intelligent sisters who volunteered with the U.S. Sanitary Commission during the war.

98. Graf, Mercedes. *A Woman of Honor: Dr. Mary E. Walker and the Civil War*. Gettysburg, PA: Thomas Publications, 2001.

   A handful of women physicians volunteered their services to the Union and Confederate armies but were automatically turned down because the military wanted only male doctors. Dr. Mary Edwards Walker succeeded in her efforts to work as a physician only because she bypassed the Army Medical Department hierarchy and went directly to regiments in the field and volunteered with the regimental surgeon. One beleaguered, overworked and practical gentleman accepted the help offered him by a qualified physician. After serving for years in a volunteer capacity, Walker was appointed assistant surgeon to the 52nd Ohio Volunteers in early 1864. On April 10, while answering a call for help close to enemy lines, Walker was taken prisoner by a Confederate sentry. She was imprisoned in Castle Thunder, a military jail in Richmond, Virginia, and released in a prisoner exchange on August 12. She was then assigned to the Louisville, Tennessee Female Prison to care for the inmates there. After the war, President Andrew Johnson granted Walker the Medal of Honor for her "untiring efforts" on behalf of the government and her "devotion and patriotic zeal to sick and wounded soldiers both in the field and in hospitals to the detriment of her own health." To date, Dr. Mary Walker is the sole woman to have received this prestigious award. Graf has done a wonderful job of documenting Walker's service and bringing the character of this unique woman to light.

99. Hancock, Cornelia, Henrietta Stratton Jacquette and Jean V. Berlin. *Letters of a Civil War Nurse*. Bison Books, 1998.

Many young, attractive, idealistic women, whom Dix had rejected, such as the young Quaker Cornelia Hancock, simply journeyed to the battlefields and began nursing without a contract and no anticipation of payment. Because their services were desperately needed, field commanders were not inclined to turn volunteer nurses away. Hancock served as a volunteer nurse at the battles of Gettysburg, Brandy Station, Fredericksburg, and the Wilderness.

100. Hanson, Kathleen J. *Turn Backward, O Time: Civil War Diary of Amanda Shelton*, Roseville, MN: Edinborough Press, 2008.

Shelton worked in a special diet kitchen; she and her peers opened the door for the World War I era dietitians. Hanson provides the reader with Shelton's original diary, written while she worked as a member of the Christian Commission between 1864 and 1866. Shelton was eventually sent home by her supervisor for attending a dance at the hospital where she worked, an episode that illuminates how carefully nurses, especially young and unmarried ones, had to comport themselves to remove any taint of suspicion pertaining to their morals or reasons for working away from their homes.

101. Hoisington, Daniel John. *My Heart toward Home: Letters of a Family during the Civil War*. Roseville, MN: Edinborough Press, 2001.

The letters of family members Georgeanna Woolsey Bacon, Eliza Woolsey Howland and Jane Stuart Woolsey, gently reared women, all of whom served as nurses in Northern Civil War hospitals.

102. Holland, Mary Gardner. *Our Army Nurses: Stories from Women in the Civil War*. Roseville, MN: Edinborough Press, 1998.

This outstanding collection of firsthand accounts and mini-biographies of rank and file Civil War nurses was first published in 1889. Holland collected firsthand reminiscences of 100 of the 5,000 women who had served as Army nurses in the Civil War. This book is an invaluable primary source. While it represents only a fraction of the women who served as nurses during the Civil War, it is enough to depict the variety and scope of the women who volunteered and their numerous and varying experiences.

103. Humez, Jean McMahon. *Harriet Tubman: The Life and Life Stories.* University of Wisconsin Press, 2004.

    Because Harriet Tubman could neither read nor write, primary sources dealing with her life were scarce and for years there existed a dearth of biographies of this famous woman. Then in 2004, three scholars published landmark works on Tubman: Catherine Clinton, Jean M. Humez and Kate Clifford Larson. Humez emphasizes that every contemporary account of Tubman is filtered through another individual's eyes, and must be read with care. Consequently, her biography of Tubman emphasizes Tubman's relationships with the people who wrote about her, including Frederick Douglass, John Brown and Sojourner Truth.

104. Larson, Kate Clifford. *Bound for the Promised Land: Harriet Tubman: Portrait of an American Hero.* New York: Ballantine, 2004.

    Although biographies of Tubman by Jean M. Humez and Catherine Clinton also appeared in 2004, Larson's was the first book to see print and was consequently hailed as the first "adult" biography of Tubman to appear in over 50 years. This well-researched volume uses a wide variety of documentation (contemporary newspaper accounts, census data, everything except Tubman's own words, for she was illiterate) to develop an amazingly detailed biography of the woman "Arminta Ross," known to the world as Harriet Tubman.

105. Livermore, Mary A. *My Story of the War: The Civil War Memoirs of the Famous Nurse, Relief Organizer and Suffragette.* Da Capo Press, 1995.

    Livermore served with the U.S. Sanitary Commission during the Civil War, nursing wounded soldiers at the front and organizing events that raised more than a million dollars for the commission's relief work. During the course of the war she met Abraham Lincoln, Ulysses Grant, Mary Ann Bickerdyke and Dorothea Dix, and recorded her impressions of all of them.

106. Oakes, Sister Mary Paulinus. *Angels of Mercy: An Eyewitness Account: A Primary Source by Sister Ignatius Sumner of the Civil War and Yellow Fever.* Baltimore, MD: Cathedral Foundation Press, 1998.

    Few people know the contributions Catholic sisters made to Civil War nursing. This first-person account by one of the Sisters of Mercy describes nursing activities of Catholic nuns during the Battle for Vicksburg.

107. Oates, Stephen. *Woman of Valor: Clara Barton and the Civil War.* Free Press, 1995.

    Oates is perhaps the first biographer of Clara Barton to emphasize that Barton, who would become famous for starting the American Red Cross in the 1880s, nursed on the battlefield under fire during the Civil War. Initially Barton's fear that she would shame her family prevented her from trying to get to the front. Finally, her 80-year-old father, a veteran of the War of 1812, freed his daughter of her worries. On his deathbed, he instructed her to go and do what she could to help the wounded. "The soldiers will know you are a decent woman as soon as they lay eyes on you," he said. During the Battle of Antietam, Barton worked in a surgery set up in a farmhouse close to the front lines that was under fire much of the time. Rebel shells burst overhead, crashed into the surrounding trees and exploded in the nearby barn and outbuildings while stray bullets peppered the walls. One bullet ripped through the sleeve of Barton's dress. The farmhouse floor shook so much that the operating table jarred and rolled and Barton and the doctor struggled to keep their patients on the table. Barton's first battle did nothing to discourage her; she continued to nurse at the battles of Marye's Heights, the Wilderness Campaign, Hilton Head and Battery Wagner.

108. Ropes, Hannah, edited by John R. Brumgardt. *Civil War Nurse: The Diary and Letters of Hannah Ropes.* Knoxville, TN: University of Tennessee Press, 1993.

Maine native and anti-slavery activist Hannah Ropes served under very poor conditions in Army hospitals in Washington, D.C. Long hours working with little rest in overcrowded wards packed with patients suffering from rampant contagious diseases broke down the health of many nurses. Ropes, the matron in charge of nurses at the Union Hotel Hospital, died of typhoid in 1863.

109. Ryan, David D., ed. *A Yankee Spy in Richmond: The Civil War Diary of "Crazy Bet" Van Lew.* Mechanicsburg, PA: Stackpole Books, 1996.

Elizabeth Van Lew is perhaps the most thoroughly documented female spy of the Civil War. Van Lew was a member of a wealthy, respected Richmond, Virginia, family who had been educated in Philadelphia, where she learned to abhor slavery. When the war started, Van Lew used her social connections to collect information she thought would be of interest to the Northern Army, and devised a code by which to pass it along. She recruited her African American servants (the Van Lew family had legally freed their former slaves) to the cause, and placed one woman, Mary Bowser, as a servant in Confederate President Jefferson Davis's Richmond mansion. Documents indicate that Van Lew's information was read and valued by General Benjamin Butler, General George Meade and Secretary of War Edwin Stanton. After the war, Van Lew's neighbors ostracized her for helping the North. The grateful northern government gave her a well-paying job as postmistress for several years (this was before the advent of the civil service system), but the job was taken from her after President Grant left office.

110. Schwartz, Gerald, ed. *A Woman Doctor's Civil War: Esther Hill Hawk's Diary.* Columbia, SC: University of South Carolina Press, 1986.

The Hawks were New England abolitionists driven by moral duty to help suffering former slaves. Hawk worked primarily as her physician husband's assistant (nurse) as well as a teacher of former slaves and African

American soldiers in a Hilton Head Island, South Carolina, hospital during and after the war.

111. Sigaud, Louis A. *Belle Boyd: Confederate Spy*. Richmond, VA: Dietz Press Inc., 1944.

    The classic story of Confederate spy Belle Boyd. Although Sigaud's analysis has recently been called into question by modern historians, his work remains the defining foundation for other studies of Boyd and the significance of her activities on behalf of the South.

112. Stearns, Amanda Akin. *The Lady Nurse of Ward E*. The Baker and Taylor Co., 1909.

    The memoir of a Confederate nurse.

113. Taylor, Susie King, ed. by Patricia Romero. *A Black Woman's Civil War Memoirs: Reminiscences of My Life in Camp with the 33rd U.S. Colored Troops, Late 1st South Carolina Volunteers*. M. Wiener Publishing, 1988.

    Many African American women worked as nurses in the North and South during the Civil War, but only a few were literate, and the King Taylor memoir is unique. Susie King Taylor was a slave in Savannah, Georgia, when the Civil War started. Taylor had been taught to read and write, which was against the law in Georgia at that time. Taking advantage of the social disruption caused by the war, Taylor's uncle took her and his own children to freedom on St. Simons Island, which was controlled by Union forces. The Army originally hired Taylor as a laundress, but she also served as a nurse throughout the war and, in her spare time, taught many black soldiers how to read and write.

114. Tucker, Phillip Thomas. *Cathy Williams: From Slave to Female Buffalo Soldier*. Mechanicsville, PA: Stackpole Books, 2002.

    Considering the paucity of primary source material on Williams, a former slave who left no words of her own for posterity explaining her decision to dress as a man and join the Army at the end of the Civil War, Tucker does an excellent job reconstructing her life. He weaves together a few surviving military records from unit infirmaries, and a few local records from towns where Williams resided, to craft a fascinating if hazy portrait of Williams and the forces that shaped her destiny.

115. Varon, Elizabeth. *Southern Lady, Yankee Spy: The True Story of Elizabeth Van Lew, A Union Agent at the Heart of the Confederacy*. New York: Oxford University Press, 2003.

    Rather than let Van Lew's papers speak for themselves, as her previous biographer did, Varon's interpretation paints a full and nuanced portrait of this exceptional and clever woman and the times and town in which she lived. Varon demonstrates that it was not Van Lew's eccentricity that protected her from suspicion for so long, but Southern society's incomprehension that a Southern "lady" would ever stoop to consorting with the types of people (African Americans and poor whites) who supported the Union.

116. Velazquez, Loreta Janeta. *The Woman in Battle: The Civil War Narrative of Loreta Janeta Velazquez, Cuban Woman and Confederate Soldier.* Madison, WI: University of Wisconsin Press, 2003.

To date, historians have been unable to ascertain whether Velazquez's autobiography is fact, embroidered fact, or fiction. Details mentioned such as the names of other officers, place names and dates remain illusive and unverifiable.

117. Woolsey, Jane Stuart. *Hospital Days: Reminiscence of a Civil War Nurse.* Edinborough Press, 1996.

Jane was a member of the extensive, idealistic, and literate Woolsey family; she and several of her siblings volunteered for hospital work during the Civil War. Jane worked not as a nurse but as a hospital administrator, supervising nurses, laundresses and cooks and seeing to it that the hospital ran smoothly.

C. Journal Articles

118. Bartlett, Sara. "Kady Brownell, a Rhode Island Legend." *Minerva: Quarterly Report on Women in the Military* (Summer 2001) 19: 30–58.

119. Fetterly, Judith. "Little Women: Alcott's Civil War." *Feminist Studies* (Summer 1979) Vol. 5, No. 2: 369–383.

An examination of the famous author Louisa May Alcott's brief nursing career during the Civil War.

120. King, Lisa Y. "In Search of Women of African Descent Who Served in the Civil War Navy." *Journal of Negro History* (Autumn 1998) Vol. 83, No. 4: 302–309.

Through patient examination of official archived Naval records, King has identified several African American women who served in the Navy during the Civil War.

121. Maggiano, Ron. "Captain Sally Tompkins: Angel of the Confederacy." *OHA Magazine of History* (Winter 2002) 16.

Prominent society matron Sally Louisa Tompkins used her own fortune to establish and run a hospital for Confederate soldiers in Richmond, Virginia. Her institution quickly gained a reputation for the lowest mortality rate of any Southern hospital. Historians, wondering how she achieved this, have come to the conclusion that it was a combination of her beliefs in absolute cleanliness and a healthy diet. When the Confederate government placed all hospitals under military control, they granted Tompkins a commission as a captain in the Army so that she could continue to direct her successful hospital. This was the only commission granted to a woman by the Confederate Army. During and after the war, Tompkins was known affectionately as "Captain Sally."

122. Sartin, Jeffrey S. "Commissioned by God: Mother Bickerdyke during the Civil War." *Military Medicine* (2003) Vol. 168, Issue 10.

123. Schultz, Jane E. "The Inhospitable Hospital: Gender and Professionalism in Civil War Medicine." *Signs: The Journal of Women in Culture and Society* (1992) Vol. 17, No. 2.

124. Wells, Cheryl A. "Battle Time: Gender, Modernity, and Confederate Hospitals." *Journal of Social History* (Winter 2001) Vol. 35, Issue 2: 409–429.

    The author argues that the special exigencies of war placed Confederate nurses in a unique situation, "Battle Time," during which doctors were forced by special circumstances to grant them more autonomy and authority than they otherwise would have. Once these special circumstances passed, however, so did the special status the nurse had enjoyed.

D. Arlington National Cemetery Website

125. www.arlingtoncemetery.net/jhopkins.htm

    Alabama native and Confederate nurse Juliet Ann Opie Hopkins was assisting a severely injured officer onto a stretcher during the Battle of Seven Pines on June 1, 1862, when a bullet shattered a bone in her left leg. For the rest of her life, Hopkins walked with a limp.

IV

Women on the Western Frontier: Few and Far Between

The American Army of the frontier west was for the most part an all-male institution. Although many units paid for the services of a civilian laundress (often the wife of an enlisted soldier), they did not employ significant numbers of female nurses. The only women connected to these frontier units were the wives and family members of the soldiers and officers. Because officers' wives were more likely to be literate, theirs form the bulk of published letters and memoirs of life with the frontier Army.

The majority of officers' wives, however, did not choose to accompany their husbands to the far flung, primitive and desolate frontier forts to which they were assigned. Much like the wives of today's deploying soldiers, they remained home with their families back East, saw their absent husbands only on furloughs, and hoped that they would be able to accompany their husbands on the next assignment. Only a relatively small number of women experienced life in the frontier forts. Many of those whose letters survived have been published, and together they paint a vivid if somewhat skewed (due to inherent prejudices of class) picture of every-day life in the Frontier Army.

Certain themes appear in almost all these women's letters, diaries and memoirs; the difficulty of the journey, the isolation of the post, the poor quality of the quarters, the lack of skilled household help, and above all the lack of congenial companionship due to the scarcity of other wives. Numerous women were unable to adapt to this spartan lifestyle and returned to their families back East. Those who remained used imagination, ingenuity, and adaptability to create homes for their husbands and families, and thrived on the challenge.

A. Books

126. Biddle, Ellen McGowan. *Reminiscences of a Soldier's Wife*. Mechanicsville, PA: Stackpole Books, 2002.

Biddle followed her husband across the west, from Texas to California to Colorado and Nebraska.

127. Chartier, JoAnn, and Chris Enss. *She Wore a Yellow Ribbon: Women Soldiers and Patriots of the Western Frontier.* Guilford, CT: Two Dot, 2004.

128. Convis, Charles L. *Women of the Frontier Army.* Pioneer Press, 2004.

    The author profiles 16 women connected with the frontier Army.

129. Custer, Elizabeth Bacon. *Boots and Saddles, or Life in Dakota with General Custer.* University of Oklahoma Press, 1994.

    This final book in Elizabeth Bacon Custer's trilogy discusses her life with her husband to his death at the Battle of Little Bighorn in 1876.

130. Custer, Elizabeth Bacon. *Following the Guidon.* University of Oklahoma Press, 1994.

    Although Bacon Custer wrote and published her memoirs in an attempt to make certain that posterity would view her husband in a favorable light, her books can also be read for the valuable information they provide on the lives of the wives of Army officers on the frontier during this period.

131. Custer, Elizabeth Bacon. *Tenting on the Plains or General Custer in Kansas and Texas.* University of Oklahoma Press, 1994.

    The second book in Elizabeth Bacon Custer's trilogy about her life with her husband. This book covers Custer's activities against the Plains Indians between the Arkansas and Platte Rivers starting in 1867.

132. Eales, Anne Bruner. *Army Wives on the American Frontier: Living by the Bugles.* Boulder, CO: Johnson Printing Company, 1996.

    Eales examines the journals, letters and memoirs of officers' wives. Many of these gently reared ladies had a hard time adapting to the isolation and primitive conditions of frontier life.

133. Foote, Cheryl. *Women of the New Mexico Frontier 1846–1912.* University of New Mexico Press, 2005.

    Foote describes the lives of a wide variety of women who called New Mexico home prior to 1912: Army laundresses, the wives of Army soldiers and officers, missionaries' wives and prostitutes.

134. Grierson, Alice Kirk, ed. by Shirley Leckie. *The Colonel's Lady on the Western Frontier: The Correspondence of Alice Kirk Grierson.* University of Nebraska Press, 1989.

    Grierson followed her husband from frontier Army post to frontier Army post while raising seven children, three of whom did not survive childhood. Although her life was hard, she did not do too much complaining in her letters. A thoughtful woman, she came to believe in women's rights. Her husband Benjamin commanded the 10th Cavalry, one of the Army's two black units (the famous Buffalo Soldiers). Alice Grierson believed her husband was repeatedly passed over for promotion because of the Army's lack of respect for its black soldiers.

135. Leckie, Shirley. *Elizabeth Bacon Custer and the Making of a Myth.* University of Oklahoma Press, 1998.

"Libbie" Bacon married the flamboyant Brigadier General George Armstrong Custer in 1864. Through 12 years of marriage, she accompanied him to a series of frontier Army outposts. During this period, the Army was engaged in attempting to push Cheyenne and Sioux Indians into reservations so their former hunting grounds could be settled by Americans flocking west. After Custer's death at the Battle of Little Bighorn in 1876, Bacon Custer supported herself through writing and lecturing about her husband. In her writings, she attempted to salvage her husband's reputation after his critics accused him of disobeying orders and leading his men into certain death. Bacon Custer did an effective job of mythologizing her undeniably brave but headstrong and ambitious husband.

136. Nacy, Michele. *Members of the Regiment: Army Officers' Wives on the Western Frontier.* Westport, CT: Greenwood Press, 2000.

137. Stallard, Patricia Y. *Glittering Misery: Dependents of the Indian-Fighting Army.* University of Oklahoma Press, 1992.

Stallard was one of the first scholars to study Frontier Army wives through the lens of Women's Studies, and her book is considered to be a classic among feminist historians and others interested in the history of the American West. Although many of the sources Stallard used in her study have since been published in their own right, her book remains an excellent foundation upon which to build a specialized knowledge of this still vital topic.

138. Summerhayes, Martha. *Vanished Arizona: Recollections of the Army Life of a New England Woman.* University of Nebraska Press, 1979.

In 1874 Martha left life on the East Coast behind to follow her Cavalry officer husband first to Wyoming and then to the wilds of Arizona Territory. Martha was one of a few Army wives to brave the Arizona wilderness (the Army's Fort Apache Arizona). Martha gave birth to a baby son on the way to her home in Fort Apache. Her husband, a lieutenant, was very cognizant of the dangers his wife and son were exposed to, and warned her to shoot herself and her son if they were attacked and the unit overrun. Summerhayes' husband was eventually assigned to California, Nevada and Texas, and his wife faithfully followed him to each assignment.

V

Spanish American War Nurses: Proving Themselves of Value

In the 30-odd years after the Civil War, the Army forgot the medical lessons of that war, and once again assumed that the Medical Corps could handle the few casualties expected from America's fight with Spain. Women nurses, it was believed, would be unable to handle primitive field conditions and would give Army doctors more trouble than they were worth. Once the fighting started, however, it was not battle casualties that posed the problem but disease. Typhoid, malaria, and yellow fever, all of which demanded intensive nursing care if the patient was to survive, quickly overwhelmed the Army Medical Department. Army Surgeon General George Sternberg appointed socially connected Washington D.C. physician Anita Newcomb McGee to the rank of Assistant Surgeon General and placed her in charge of selecting women qualified to serve as contract nurses. McGee, who was secretary of the Daughters of the American Revolution (DAR), asked that organization to help her professionally vet the nurses. McGee wanted to send the Army the best trained and most morally upright women she could find. She and her fellow DAR matrons collected applications, checked personal and professional references, and selected 1,500 of the best-qualified nurses out of 5,000 applicants.

The contracts the women signed stipulated that they work where they were assigned for a specified salary until the Army dissolved the contract at its convenience. Contract nurses were sent to Army hospitals in Cuba, Florida, Georgia, Long Island, Puerto Rico, and the Philippines. The Army assigned Rose Heavren of Connecticut to Montauk Point, Long Island, with 12 other contract nurses and a group of Catholic sisters. When Heavren's group arrived at Montauk, the colonel in charge had the 12 women line up, and called in his doctors, allowing them to pick their nurses out of the line-up. The men pointed their fingers and said, "I'll take that one," and then, "I'll take this one," and "well, I guess that leaves her." Heavren's response to the selection process was to get the giggles, leaving one doctor stuck with "the giggler." Montauk had about 1,500 patients in any given day, said Heavren in her memoir, "running temperatures from 103 to

106, and dying like flies. It was not possible to get enough supplies of any kind . . . we were always running out of medicine. We worked from 5 am to 8 at night. Breakfast was black coffee and some sort of mush, dinner was boiled cabbage and black coffee." In letters written to her family, Heavren explained that the nurses had to pay to have their uniforms laundered, and that they also had to pay $10.00 a month out of their $30.00 a month salary to supplement their meals or they would get only half rations. Heavren was eventually sent to Havana, Cuba, where she came down with yellow fever. She recovered, returned home to her mother in Connecticut and continued her career as a nurse. Heavren's letters are available at the Women in Military Service for America Memorial Foundation Archives in Arlington, Virginia.

The Army sent nurse Helena Maria Gottschalk Arendt to Manila in the Philippines, where she was assigned to a field hospital on the outskirts of town. Moro snipers fired on the hospital from the jungle at night, forcing the staff to black out the hospital with blankets despite the tropical heat. Arendt was released from her contract when the war ended and was happy to be able to return to the U.S. Arendt's story as well as those of numerous other Spanish American War contract nurses can be found in the memoirs of individual nurses published in DAR journals between 1900 and the start of the First World War.

Several nurses who served aboard hospital transport ships during the war later joined the newly established Navy Nurse Corps. The following reminiscences are included in Doris Sterner's *In and Out of Harm's Way: A History of the Navy Nurse Corps*. Esther V. Hasson of the hospital ship *Relief*, who would later serve as Chief of the Navy Nurse Corps, wrote in her memoirs, "We were immensely proud of our beautiful ship. The crowning glory of the operating room on the *Relief* was the big x-ray machine, at that time new to medical science. After reaching Cuba, it was in constant use in cases of gunshot wounds, because it located bullets and enabled us to avoid the prolonged painful probing which so bothered patients." Hasson distinctly remembered how upset her fever patients got when they were placed on liquid diets while others around them were eating real food. "Big men broke down and cried," she wrote.

Beatrice Von Homrigh Stevenson worked aboard the Army transport ship *Lampasas*. "The ship was so crowded and it was so hot that the patients were laid on the decks," wrote Stevenson. "Their uniforms were woolen and they were miserable. We had no medicine but plenty of fresh water because the ship had its own distilling plant. So we gave the patients plenty of baths, and only lost 6 (of 130)."

The contract nurses performed so well in primitive and field conditions that the Army and Navy realized that it might be a good idea to have established corps of nurses ready for rapid mobilization in the event of another war. In 1901, Congress authorized the establishment of the Army Nurse Corps, and in 1908 established the Navy Nurse Corps. For the first time in American history, women became official, uniformed members of the U.S. Armed Forces.

However, the members of the Army and Navy Nurse Corps found themselves in a peculiar position, one that wasn't noticed until military nurses and medical corpsmen were working side by side under the battlefield conditions of World War I. Army and Navy Nurses held a unique position in the military – they held neither officer nor enlisted rank but were designated simply as nurses. As such, any authority they wielded on the wards was very much subject to question. Nurses were outside the military chain of command, and many medical corpsmen felt no compunction to obey their orders. Thus although the military expected their nurses to maintain order on their wards, they had no authority to do so. The military services wrestled with this question of female authority over men for several decades, and it wasn't until World War II that female military nurses were given officer status commensurate with that of male military officers.

A. Books

139. Sarnecky, Mary, Colonel, U.S. Army Nurse Corps Ret. *History of the Army Nurse Corps.* Philadelphia: University of Pennsylvania Press, 1999.

    Sarnecky's overall history of the Army Nurse Corps remains the best source for scholars interested in the Army contract nurses of the Spanish American War.

140. Stewart, George C. *Marvels of Charity: History of American Sisters and Nuns.* Huntington, IN: Our Sunday Visitor Publishing, 1994.

    This history of the nursing efforts of American Nuns contains one of the few accounts of a group of Native American Nursing Sisters from Fort Berthold, North Dakota who journeyed south to nurse for the American Army during the Spanish American War.

B. Journal Articles

141. Graf, Mercedes. "Band of Angels: Sister Nurses in the Spanish American War." *Prologue* (Fall 2002) Vol. 34, No. 3.

    Graf describes the contributions of nursing nuns during the Spanish American War.

142. Graf, Mercedes H. "Women Nurses in the Spanish American War." *Minerva: Quarterly Report on Women and the Military* (Spring 2001).

    An excellent description of the women selected to serve as contract nurses and the jobs they performed during the war. The author emphasizes the influence of Dr. Anita Newcomb McGee on the nurses and their assignments. Graf reviewed rating cards kept on individual contract nurses to determine what characteristics and actions were most valued by supervisors and which were unappreciated.

143. Graf, Mercedes. "Women Physicians in the Spanish American War." *Army History* (Fall 2002). No. 56: 4–15.

    The author discusses the small number of women physicians who served under contract during the Spanish American War. Other than Dr. Anita Newcomb McGee, whom the Army Surgeon General placed in charge of hiring contract nurses, most of the small number of women physicians served as nurses because the Army was uninterested in their services as physicians.

144. Hasson, Esther V. "The Navy Nurse Corps." *The American Journal of Nursing* (Jan. 1909) Vol. 9, No. 4: 267–268.

C. Website

145. www.nativewomenveterans.org/naanpic1.htm

    Four women from the Sioux tribe near Fort Berthold, South Dakota, answered the Army's call for nurses during the war and served under contract. Their forgotten story as well as several photographs of them can be seen at the website above.

VI

World War I: Women Volunteers Establish Parameters of Service

When the U.S. Navy experienced a manpower shortage during World War I, it became the first service in the U.S. Armed Forces to enlist non-nursing women for administrative and desk duties, with the idea of releasing men for shipboard service. The Navy enlisted 12,000 Yeoman (F) on a temporary basis for the duration of the war only and gave them the same pay as male sailors of comparable rank. The Marine Corps followed suit, enlisting only 300 of the fastest and most accurate typists available to serve at Marine Headquarters.

Thousands of Army and Navy nurses served overseas and on U.S. military bases without any kind of rank during World War I. Official Army Nurse Corps historian Colonel Mary Sarnecky has pointed out that two U.S. Army nurses were the first American military personnel killed in the war. It happened aboard one of the first troop ships to sail for France, the USS *Mongolia*. As the ship left New York's harbor on May 20, 1917, three Army nurses of Base Hospital # 12 stood on deck watching the ship's crew practice firing the deck guns, which would be used if the ship encountered enemy submarines. One of the guns misfired and spewed shrapnel across the deck, killing Edith Ayres and Helen Wood. The ship returned to dock so the third nurse, who was badly injured, could be taken to a hospital.

Once they arrived in France, a different type of danger faced the nurses. Some nurses were assigned to casualty clearing stations very near the front lines. Sarnecky tells the story of Army Nurse Helen McClelland, serving in France with U.S. Base Hospital # 10. McClelland was part of a surgical team assigned to Casualty Clearing Station # 61 near the Convent of St. Sixte. Although in theory each team was supposed to be at the front a total of 48 hours, McClelland's group ended up staying 11 weeks. One night, enemy planes bombed the camp, and McClelland's tent-mate, nurse Beatrice MacDonald, was wounded. McClelland later wrote that when the bombing occurred the women were asleep in their tent. The sound of enemy planes overhead woke both women and they reached for their "tin hats." McClelland rolled up into a ball on her cot and placed her hat so that it covered her head and the side of her face. MacDonald was slightly raised on one elbow when two bombs hit nearby, and pieces of shrapnel ripped through the tent. One piece hit her in the eye and the other piece hit the side of her face. McClelland said "Our tent was 25–30 feet from where the bombs hit. Even with my eyes closed I saw the flashes from the explosion. My uniform hanging on the bedpost was full of holes. My mattress was full of shrapnel." Before the bombing stopped, McClellan got off her bed and ran across the tent to stop MacDonald's hemorrhage. This action earned her the Distinguished Service Cross. Miss MacDonald lost her sight in one eye, but returned to duty with her unit.

Navy Nurse Corps historian Doris Sterner tell the story of several dozen Navy nurses who served in Brest, France, where the U.S. Navy established a hospital to care for soldiers and sailors who had been gassed. Sterner quotes Navy Nurse Esther Hunter, who wrote "Gassed patients cannot stand any light, cough a great deal and their hearing is poor. Many may lose their voices entirely. Some have been burnt around their abdomen and the inside of their hands. Luckier the man who loses his leg or arm than those who are gassed."

Towards the end of the war, the Spanish Influenza swept across Europe and the United States, killing over 400 military nurses. After the war, in acknowledgement of the dedication and sacrifice demonstrated by these exemplary women, Congress granted Army Nurses (but not Navy Nurses) "relative rank," ranks that paid less and conveyed less authority than those of male commissioned officers but which allowed nurses some authority over enlisted men. Navy nurses continued to serve in limbo, neither officer nor enlisted until after the start of World War II.

Much to its surprise, the U.S. Army realized in the middle of the war that it needed women who could operate telephone switchboards and typewriters. It took too long to train male soldiers to operate these essential machines, and the young men resented it, calling it "women's work." In a watershed moment, the Army Commander in Europe, General John Pershing, frustrated by the difficulties his soldiers encountered while attempting to send orders over French telephone lines, requested that the War Department send to him 200 women to work with the Signal Corps as telephone operators. Back in the United States, the Army attempted to fill Pershing's request. Women telephone operators were recruited, brought to New York City, given uniforms, and sent overseas to AEF headquarters. The "Hello Girls," as they were called, saw to it that messages from headquarters reached the troops in the field and vice versa. This was extremely important and sensitive work, involving orders to attack, move, and aim guns at specific locations. Several of the switchboards were located close to the front lines, where the women worked behind sandbags under blackout conditions. When the Quartermaster Corps and the Ordnance Corps commanders saw the Signal Corps women, they decided that they should requisition American women as secretaries, dictation takers and file clerks. The French women they were trying to use could not speak English well enough to work as quickly as necessary. The Army recruited about 20 women for each Corps. These women were civilians working as contract employees for the Army. They were not given uniforms and were never "sworn in," as many of the Hello Girls had been. This was an important distinction, because 50 years later, the Hello Girls were given veteran's status, while the secretaries were not.

A. Books

146. Anonymous. *Mademoiselle Miss: Letters From a World War I Nurse at an Army Hospital Near the Marne.* Diggory Press, 2006.

    The war in Europe compelled many upper-class, idealistic American women to venture overseas in a volunteer capacity to ease the suffering in France years before the United States officially entered the war. Although the majority of these women were not professionally trained, they pitched in doing whatever needed to be done, whether it was working in a Salvation Army kitchen or driving ambulances. The American author of *Mademoiselle Miss* served as a nurse in French and English Army hospitals.

147. Budreau, Lisa and Richard Prior, Lt. Col, U.S. Army, eds. *Answering the Call: The U.S. Army Nurse Corps 1917–1919: A Commemorative Tribute to Military Nursing in World War I.* U.S. Army Surgeon General's Office, Department of the Army, 2008.

    A fine collection of official photographs and records given life through the use of first-person quotes and accounts.

148. Byerly, Carol. *Fever of War: The Influenza Epidemic in the U.S. Army During World War I.* New York: New York University Press, 2005.

    Byerly's is the first book to take an in-depth look at the effects of the 1918–1919 influenza epidemic on the U.S. Army in the World War I era. Towards the end of the war this devastating epidemic put military personnel everywhere, on the homefront and overseas, both male and female, at grave risk. The influenza epidemic of 1918 and 1919 swept around the world, killing millions of people. Known as "swine flu," this particular strain of influenza was dangerous because it frequently segued into pneumonia, and there were no antibiotics with which to battle the disease at that time. Because the flu was highly contagious, people living and working in crowded conditions such as military camps and urban port cities were especially vulnerable.

149. Dessez, Eunice C. *The First Enlisted Women 1917–1918.* Philadelphia, PA: Dorrance and Co. Inc., 1955.

    Although somewhat dated, Dessez's account, written by a former Navy Yeoman (F), includes descriptions of the service experience of numerous women as well as significant and hard-to-find official records pertaining to Yeoman (F) issued by the Navy.

150. Ebbert, Jean and Marie Beth Hall. *The First, the Few and the Forgotten: Navy and Marine Corps Women in World War I.* Annapolis, MD: U.S. Naval Institute Press, 2002.

    Ebbert and Hall's account of the Navy and Marine Corps women of World War I uses memoirs, first-person accounts and official documents to look at who these women were, how they were recruited and the jobs to which they were assigned. The book includes a fascinating glimpse of a unit of black women who served with the Navy's Muster Roll office in Washington, D.C., during the war. Unbeknownst to many Navy officials, the chief clerk of the muster roll section in Washington, D.C., who was black, took it upon himself to hire 14 African American Yeoman (F). They worked as a segregated unit (except for the chief yeoman, who was white) in the muster roll section, which kept track of the assignment and location of every sailor in the Navy.

Months after the Navy began enlisting women, the Marine Corps decided to do the same. It also needed personnel to hold down a myriad of clerical positions at Marine Corps headquarters in Washington, D.C., and in district headquarters across the country. Marine Corps leaders decided to selectively recruit exceptionally highly skilled women. Although women flocked to enlist, Marine recruiters devised extremely tough typing and shorthand tests and accepted only those that scored the highest. In New York City, 2,000 applicants lined up the first day and only the five fastest typists with a 100 percent accuracy rate were selected. In the end, the Marines accepted only 305 women. Marine women, like Navy Yeoman (F), received the same pay as enlisted men of corresponding rank. Both the Navy and Marine Corps enlisted women only for the duration of the wartime emergency; these women's components were never meant to be permanent. Once the war was over, the women were quickly demobilized and sent home with the nation's profound thanks but no veteran's benefits.

151. Flikke, Julia O., Colonel U.S. Army Nurse Corps. *Nurses in Action.* Philadelphia, PA: J. B. Lippincott Company, 1943.

Written in the midst of the Second World War to inspire young women to enlist in the Army Nurse Corps, this book describes the activities of Army and Red Cross nurses in the European Theater during the First World War.

152. Gavin, Lettie. *American Women in World War I: They Also Served.* University of Colorado Press, 1997.

An excellent general treatment of women's World War I experiences, covering both nurses and non-nursing military and civilian women who volunteered for service during World War I. A former newspaper reporter, Gavin used a journalist's skills to bring to life the stories of military and civilian nurses, Yeoman (F) and Marine Corps women, the women of the Army Signal Corps and Red Cross and Salvation Army women as well as the women physicians who served overseas in volunteer capacities.

153. Goldenberg, Gary. *Nurses of a Different Stripe: A History of Colombia University School of Nursing.* Columbia University, 1992.

The author examines the relationship between Colombia's nursing school and the U.S. Army during two world wars, mining first-person accounts and school records.

154. Halvorson, Clara Elizabeth Bickford. *A Heart for Healing: A Memoir of the Life of Elizabeth Campbell Bickford.* Portland, OR: Binford and Mort Publishing, 2003.

Elizabeth Campbell Bickford served in the European Theater during World War I.

155. Hewitt, Linda L., Capt. USMCR. *Women Marines in World War I.* Washington, DC: History and Museums Division, Headquarters, U.S. Marine Corps, 1974.

This officially sanctioned history of the 300 women selected to serve as Women Marines during World War I describes the decision to recruit women, the selection process and the various types of assignments uniformed women held during the war. Although an official history, this slender volume nicely balances the official record with numerous first-person accounts.

156. Higonnet, Margaret R. *Nurses at the Front: Writing the Wounds of the War.* Northeastern University Press, 2001.

The author edits and discusses the writings of two American women who traveled to Europe to nurse during World War I. Both women later published accounts of their experiences during the war.

157. Hine, Darlene Clark. *Black Women in White Racial Conflict and Cooperation in the Nursing Profession 1890–1950.* Bloomington: Indiana University Press, 1989.

Hine's book contains an interesting section on black nurses and the U.S. Army Nurse Corps.

158. Jensen, Kimberly. *Mobilizing Minerva: American Women in the First World War.* University of Illinois Press, 2008.

Jensen connects American women's participation in World War I to women's activism of the late nineteenth and early twentieth centuries. Although many of the idealistic women who worked for the causes of women's suffrage, prohibition and progressivism were deeply involved in the peace movement, other similarly inclined women volunteered for war work, believing that this particular war would lead to worldwide, permanent peace. Jensen demonstrated how women's war work paved the way for women's suffrage and discusses how women doctors and nurses volunteered for service overseas with both civilian organizations (ie the Red Cross, Salvation Army and American Women's Hospitals) and with the U.S. Army as unranked nurses and doctors under contract.

159. Melosh, Barbara. *"The Physician's Hand": Work, Culture and Conflict in American Nursing.* Philadelphia: Temple University Press, 1982.

The author looks at the professional status of nurses, including military and Red Cross nurses, during the World War I era and beyond. Melosh describes nurses' search for professional status during this period.

160. Reverby, Susan. *Ordered to Care: The Dilemma of American Nursing 1850–1945.* New York: Cambridge University Press, 1987.

Includes an interesting discussion of the problems faced by military nurses during World War I due to their lack of official status or military rank and examines the political efforts of nursing leaders to acquire "relative rank."

161. Saltonstall, Nora, ed. by Judith S. Graham. *"Out Here at the Front": The World War I Letters of Nora Saltonstall.* Northeastern University Press, 2004.

Saltonstall, like so many idealistic, gently reared turn-of-the-century young women, wanted to do her part to ease suffering in Europe's Great War. This Junior League member who had "come out" in Boston only the year before served in a variety of volunteer capacities including nurse, canteen worker, ambulance driver, and even mechanic. Saltonstall returned home after the war only to die of typhoid on a cross-country trip across the United States.

162. Schneider, Dorothy and Carl. *Into the Breach: American Women Overseas during World War I.* toExcel, 2000, first published in 1991.

This illustrated edition provides readers with an excellent survey of the numerous groups of women who volunteered for overseas service during World War I, many in unofficial civilian organizations, just as many in government-sponsored civilian organizations such as the Red Cross, and others, from Army and Navy nurses to Army Signal Corps telephone operators and Ordnance Corps clerks as ad hoc members of the American military.

163. Stevenson, Sarah Sand. *Lamp for a Soldier: The Touching Story of an American Nurse in World War I.* North Dakota State Nurses Association, 1976.

The poignant memoir of a North Dakota nurse who traveled overseas during World War I as an Army nurse.

164. Stimson, Julia. *Finding Themselves: The Letters of an American Army Chief Nurse in a British Hospital in France.* First published in 1918, reprinted several times.

During the war Julia Stimson would rise to become the Chief Nurse of U.S. Army Nurses in France. The letters she sent home to her prominent New York family detail her relationships with the U.S. Army Medical hierarchy as well as individual chief nurses and the women who worked under them. Interestingly, Miss Stimson did not believe that giving Army nurses officer status would help them achieve professional status and respect in the Army. She preferred to believe that if each nurse conducted herself in a professional and morally upright manner, she would be treated as a professional by doctors, corpsmen and patients alike.

165. Rote, Nell Fairchild Hefty. *Nurse Helen Fairchild: World War I 1917–1918.* Lewisburg, PA: Fisher Fairchild Publishing Company, 2004.

Rote spent years researching the biography of Army Nurse Helen Fairchild, who served near the front lines in France. Fairchild's family believed Helen died from exposure to mustard gas while assigned near the front lines. Rote, a great niece of Helen Fairchild, has found material indicating that the family legend may well be correct.

166. Weaver, Emma Elizabeth. *Journal of E. Elizabeth Weaver, Army Nurse Corps, World War I.* Publisher unknown, 1996.

German submarines posed a grave danger to troop ships heading to Europe after the U.S. entered the war. Army nurse Elizabeth Weaver of Base Hospital #20 traveled to France in the *Leviathan*, a large ship capable of carrying 16,000 personnel that had already made numerous trips back and forth to the continent. Weaver wrote in her memoir that a member of the crew told her that the ship managed to evade enemy torpedoes because of the speed she could achieve—18 knots. Weaver could not help worrying a bit when the officer told her that the ship was carrying "two huge bombs with long fuses" in its cargo hold. If the ship was hit, wrote Weaver, it would be the end of everyone on board. Weaver described the utter darkness of the ship at night, when no lights were allowed anywhere on board, and wrote, "We go speeding and zigzagging along in utter darkness. . . . I can't help thinking that there is more of a danger of a collision than of submarines . . ."

On a lighter note, Weaver described the so-called "safety suits" that the nurses were supposed to don if the ship was hit. The nurses were told that the suits were unsinkable, and could be worn for any length of time in the coldest water. The suits had lead feet and "some material in the chest that increased buoyancy," so the women would bob about in the water while remaining upright. Immediately after her description of the safety suit, Weaver stated, "I made out my will."

167. Wigle, Shari Lynn. *Pride of America, We're With You: The Letters of Grace Anderson U.S. Army Nurse Corps World War I.* Seaboard Press, 2007.

Anderson served with Army Base Hospital 115 during the war as a nurse anesthetist. After the war, she remained with the U.S. Army in occupied Germany until 1925. Her letters home to family were discovered many years later during a home remodeling project.

168. Zeiger, Susan. *In Uncle Sam's Service: Women Workers with the American Expeditionary Force.* Ithaca, NY: Cornell University Press, 2000.

Zeiger focuses on those women who went to Europe during the war, including Army, Navy and Red Cross nurses, Army Signal Corps women, Salvation Army women, physicians, canteen workers, and many more. Zeiger emphasizes that although many of these volunteers were from upper- and middle-class families motivated by idealism, wage-earning, working-class women also felt moved by patriotism to serve. Zeiger's description of the "Hello Girls," working telephone operators, is a case in point.

B. Journal Articles

169. Banker, Grace Paddock. "I Was a Hello Girl." *Yankee Magazine* (March 1974).

Grace Paddock Banker recounts her experiences with the U.S. Army Signal Corps during World War I.

170. B.J.B. "A Letter from a Navy Nurse." *The American Journal of Nursing* (June 1921) Vol. 21, No. 9: 644–645.

171. B.M. "Letters from Navy Nurses." *The American Journal of Nursing* (September 1921) Vol. 21, No. 12: 901–902.

172. Bowman, Beatrice. "The History and Development of the Navy Nurse Corps." *The American Journal of Nursing* (May 1925) Vol. 25, No. 5: 356–360.

Although Army nurses gained relative rank after World War I, Navy nurses did not.

173. Cheatham, Paula M. "The Army's Forgotten Women." *Women's Overseas Service League Newsletter* (date unknown).

Contains first-person accounts of civilian and military women who served overseas during World War I.

174. Graf, Mercedes. "With High Hopes: Women Contract Surgeons in World War I." *Minerva: Quarterly Report on Women in the Military* (Summer 2002) 20: 16–28.

175. Higbee, Lenah S. "Letters from Navy Nurses." *The American Journal of Nursing* (December 1916) Vol. 17, No. 3: 248–249.

Higbee was the Superintendent Navy Nurse Corps during World War I.

176. Jensen, Kimberly. "A Base Hospital Is Not a Coney Island Dance Hall." *Frontiers* (2005) Vol. 26, No. 2: 206–238.

Jensen discusses the problems military nurses had during World War I due to their lack of status and describes their ultimately successful attempts to acquire rank after the war.

177. Kalisch, Philip A. "How Army Nurses Became Officers." *Nursing Research* (May–June 1976) 25: 164–177.

Tells the story of how Congress finally forced the Army to give its nurses relative rank after World War I.

178. "Letters from Navy Nurses." *The American Journal of Nursing* (June 1915) Vol. 15, No. 9: 760–763.

179. L.E. "Letters from Navy Nurses." *The American Journal of Nursing* (November 1913) Vol. 14, No. 2: 126–129.

180. L.E. "Letters from Navy Nurses III." *The American Journal of Nursing* (May 1914) Vol. 14, No. 8: 655–656.

181. L.E. "Letters from Navy Nurses IV." *The American Journal of Nursing* (August 1914) Vol. 14, No. 11: 987–988.

182. L.E. "Letters from Navy Nurses." *The American Journal of Nursing* (April 1915) Vol. 15, No. 7: 595–597.

183. L.E.M. "Letters from Navy Nurses." *The American Journal of Nursing* (Nov. 1914) Vol. 15, No. 2: 151–152.

184. McIsaac, Isabel. "The Army Nurse Corps." *The American Journal of Nursing* (December 1912) Vol. 13, No. 3: 172–176.

185. Meyers, Bertha I. "What the Navy Gives to and Expects from the Chelsea

Nurse." *The American Journal of Nursing* (May 1918) Vol. 18, No. 8: 700–703.

186. Miller, Richard E. "The Golden Fourteen: Black Navy Women in World War I." *Minerva: Quarterly Report on Women and the Military* (Fall Winter 1995) 13: 7–13.

187. More, Ellen S. "A Certain Restless Ambition: Women Physicians and World War I." *American Quarterly* (Dec. 1989) Vol. 41, No. 4: 636–660.

Describes the efforts of women physicians to serve in the Army Medical Corps during World War I. While most women physicians who went overseas were forced to enroll in civilian organizations such as the Women's Hospitals, a few women served with the Army as contract surgeons.

188. Murphy, Margaret McCloskey. "Experiences of an Army Nurse." *The American Journal of Nursing* (March 1914) Vol. 14, No. 6: 424–426.

189. Neil, Elizabeth Wells. "The Experiences of an Ex-Navy Nurse on Recruiting Duty." *The American Journal of Nursing* (May 1918) Vol. 18, No. 8: 625–626.

190. Prior, Richard M. and William Sanders Marble. "The Overlooked Heroines: Three Silver Star Nurses of World War I." *Military Medicine* (2008) Vol. 173, Issue 5: 493–499.

Discusses the battlefront experiences of Army nurses Jane Rignel, Linnie Leckrone and Irene Robar, who served under artillery fire at the front in France during July 1918.

191. "She's In the Navy Now." *The American Journal of Nursing* (December 1918) Vol. 19, No. 3: 168–170.

A brief discussion of the assignments of Yeoman (F) during the war.

192. Stack, James. "A Brand New Vet of WWI." *The Boston Globe* (April 25, 1980).

Discusses the political effort to grant Army Signal Corps women veteran's status during the 1970s.

193. Wood, Helen S. "From a Navy Nurse." *The American Journal of Nursing* (April 1923) Vol. 23, No. 7: 595–596.

C. Archival Sources

194. Letters and postcards of Rose Heavren, Women in Military Service for America Memorial Foundation, Arlington, Virginia.

When the United States entered World War I in April 1917, former Spanish American War contract nurse Rose Heavren was one of the first women to volunteer with the Army Nurse Corps. "I think you are crazy," said her mother. "I have been thinking that for quite some time," Heavren replied. Heavren was one of 10,000 Army nurses who ultimately served overseas in France during the war. If by "being crazy" Heavren's mother meant that she believed her daughter was exposing herself to grave danger, she was essentially correct. Army and Navy nurses who served during World War I did put themselves in harm's way, whether overseas or at home.

195. Lilliann Dial Collection, Women in Military Service for America Memorial Foundation, Arlington, Virginia.

   Army nurse Lilliann Dial was assigned to Mobile Hospital #1 in France. At Coulommiers, on the evening of June 26, Lillian experienced her first enemy raid. She wrote home, "The whirr-rr-rr of those planes, and then the guns! I had no idea the anti-aircraft could make the earth jump so! I expected to be popped right out of bed into eternity. . . ." The unit moved at least once a week, and Lilliann began to take the nighttime raids in stride. On July 4 she wrote, "The hospital is not the objective, it's Paris!" She obviously felt better knowing that she was not a target.

196. Charlotte Edith Anderson Monture Collection, Women in Military Service for America Memorial Foundation, Arlington, Virginia.

   Monture was one of perhaps two Native American women to join the Army Nurse Corps during World War I. Monture served overseas in France during the war.

197. The Signal Corps "Hello Girls" File, Historian's Office, Women in Military Service for America Memorial Foundation, Arlington, Virginia.

   This file contains Congressional testimonies and accounts taken during the 1970s when the U.S. Congress was considering giving the Army's World War I Signal Corps women veteran's status. One of the more interesting statements is from the young Army Lieutenant assigned to recruit the telephone operators.

D. Official Records

198. *Hearing Before the Committee on Military Affairs, House of Representatives, Sixty-Fifth Congress, Second Session, on Suggested Changes in Medical Reserve Corps, Nurse Corps, and Other Matters Relating to the Medical Department, April 16, 20 and June 7, 1918.* Washington, D.C.: Government Printing Office, 1918.

VII

World War II Women: Bedpans, Typewriters, and Lipstick

A wealth of individual memoirs and official histories are available for those interested in women's military contributions during World War II. Army nurses were sent overseas to all areas of the world in which U.S. servicemen were stationed, and 85 military nurses became POWs of the Japanese during the war. Six nurses died from enemy fire at Anzio, and another six died when a Japanese suicide plane crashed into the hospital ship *Comfort* off the Philippines. Nine flight nurses died when aircraft used in medical evacuations crashed due to mechanical failure or bad weather. Although the vast majority of Navy nurses served in naval hospitals in the United States, significant numbers served aboard hospital ships and as flight nurses in the Pacific Theater.

The Army formed the 150,000-strong Women's Army Auxiliary Corps (later the Women's Army Corps) early in the war so that women could perform non-combat-related military jobs such as typing, laboratory work, teaching, truck driving and turret gun and vehicle repair. The Navy quickly followed suit, creating the WAVES (Women Accepted for Volunteer Emergency Service). Unlike the WACs, who were sent overseas to the South Pacific and Europe, the 80,000 WAVES received home front assignments. Initially reluctant to include women, the Marine Corps finally acceded to putting 20,000 women into uniform for administrative jobs. The Coast Guard found jobs for 12,000 women. A small group of women, the Women's Airforce Service Pilots, were even trained to fly military aircraft in the United States so that pilots could be sent overseas. Ultimately 38 WASPs died in accidents caused by bad weather, mechanical failures and accidents. All told, some 350,000 women served in the Armed Forces "freeing" soldiers, sailors and airmen for combat duty during the war. Before the war was over, more than 500 uniformed women had given their lives in defense of the nation.

When Congress passed legislation enabling the Army, Navy, Coast Guard and Marine Corps to take women into the service, the laws establishing the Women's Army Auxiliary Corps (WAAC), the Navy WAVES, the Women's Reserve of the Coast Guard and the Marine Corps Women's Reserve were to exist only for the duration of the wartime emergency plus six months, at which point, Congress assumed, things would pretty much be back to normal. By normal, it meant that women, who had been engaged in war work in factories and who had been taking the places of men on farms and railroads and in banks, courtrooms and laboratories, would return to the home where they belonged.

Because women in uniform, subject to military discipline and barracks-style life was a unique and exciting concept, and because their wartime experiences were so eye-opening and important, this generation of women has inundated commercial, university and private presses with memoirs of all types. In addition to memoirs, official and scholarly histories abound for this time period.

A. General Histories of Women and World War II

199. Gruhzit-Hoyt, Olga. *They Also Served: American Women in World War II.* Seacaucus, NJ: Carol Publishing Group, 1995.

200. Holm, Jeanne, Major General, U.S. Air Force (Ret.) and Judith Bellafaire. *In Defense of a Nation: Military Women during World War II.* Arlington, VA: Vandamere Press, 1997.

    Chapter by chapter, this book examines the establishment and accomplishments of the World War II Women's Army Corps, Navy WAVES, Coast Guard SPARs, Women Marines and the WASP. It also devotes chapters to the Army and Navy Nurse Corps as well as Army dietitians, physical and occupational therapists, and finally looks at the many civilian organizations that supported the military that U.S. women joined during the war, including the Red Cross, the USO, Salvation Army and Public Health Service.

201. Larson, C. Kay. *Til I Come Marching Home: A Brief History of American Women in World War II.* Pasadena, MD: The Minerva Center, 1995.

    An overview of American women's participation in World War II.

202. Litoff, Judy Barrett and David Smith. *American Women in a World at War: Contemporary Accounts from World War II.* Wilmington, DE: Scholarly Resources Inc., 1997.

    This excellent history of women during World War II is portrayed through the words of the women themselves; published years ago and long out of print, many of which are described in this bibliography. Included are excerpts from Mary Lynne and Kay Arthur's *Three Years behind the Mast*, Juanita Redmond's *I Served on Bataan*, and Theresa Archard's *G.I. Nightingale*. Litoff also includes the words of many famous civilian women involved in war work, including Margaret Bourke White, Mary McCleod Bethune, and Susan B. Anthony II.

203. Litoff, Judy Barrett and David Smith. *We're in this War Too: World War II Letters from American Women in Uniform.* New York: Oxford University Press, 1994.

In this book Litoff and Smith focus on the letters home of women in uniform. Included are letters from Army and Navy nurses in far-flung areas of the world as well as those from members of the Women's Army Corps stationed in remote bases in the United States. The letters run the gamut of emotions, from exhausted to giddy to impatient to angry. They deal with a variety of subjects and concerns including racism and intolerance, and demonstrate that in many ways this war forced Americans to learn a measure of tolerance for fellow citizens shaped by experiences vastly different from their own.

204. Moore, Brenda. *Serving Our Country: Japanese American Women in the Military during World War II.* New Jersey: Rutgers University Press, 2003.

The author interviewed Japanese American nurses and WACs who served during World War II. Their stories remind readers of the patriotism felt by these women serving a nation that hated their very culture.

205. McIntosh, Elizabeth P. *Sisterhood of Spies: The Women of the OSS.* Annapolis, MD: Naval Institute Press, 1999.

Although the World War II OSS (Office of Strategic Services) is a fairly well-known organization, few people realize how many women the OSS employed in its Washington offices as well as overseas. McIntosh, who herself worked for the OSS during World War II, has collected the stories of many of these women, from researchers and file clerks to women working undercover.

206. Weatherford, Doris. *American Women and World War II.* New York: Facts on File, 1990.

Weatherford looks at the way the war changed the lives of the women who donned uniforms, those who accepted factory jobs and those who carried on with their lives at home, as housewives and waiting wives and mothers.

207. *"What Did You Do in the War, Grandma?"* An Oral History of Rhode Island Women during World War II by students in the Honors English Program at South Kingston High School, sponsored by the Rhode Island Committee for the Humanities and the Rhode Island Historical Society, 1989.

These oral histories compiled by a class of Rhode Island high school students are valuable first-person accounts of the wide variety of experiences women had during World War II.

B. The Army and Navy Nurse Corps

Army and Navy nurses served around the world during World War II, in general and field hospitals as well as on hospital ships and aircraft. Nurses had plenty of opportunity to demonstrate women's bravery and endurance under fire. Army nurses landed with the troops when Allied forces invaded French North Africa in late 1942. Enemy aircraft bombed Allied hospital ships during the invasion of Sicily in 1943, and the 200 American nurses on Anzio Beachhead suffered repeated bombing between January and February 1944. On January 27, 1944, Lt. Deloris Buckley was wounded in an enemy attack on the beachhead. She later told a reporter that she was putting a post-operative dressing on an abdominal case when she heard the sound of a plane that was quite low. She figured it was friendly craft. Suddenly "there was a mighty roar that sounded as though the heavens had fallen down around my head. My whole body went numb. I remember thinking in a detached way that it was strange for me to be lying on the floor. I somehow managed to get to my feet . . . My feet seemed rooted to the spot. My arms and fingers felt stiff. It seemed strange that I couldn't move, and my eyes moved downwards. They noted without any surprise that my clothing was drenched in blood . . . I saw blood spurting through a pair of holes in my thigh. A piece of shrapnel had entered through one side and gone clear through it. I clamped off the bleeding veins and arteries." Buckley's account can be found in the historian's files of the Women in Military Service for America Memorial Foundation in Arlington, Virginia.

On February 7, 1944, a British plane intercepted a German aircraft attempting to bomb the beachhead. While trying to gain altitude and escape, the German plane jettisoned his antipersonnel bombs over the 95th Evacuation Hospital, killing 3 nurses and 26 male patients and medical personnel. Seven days later, the 33rd Field Hospital was bombed, and three more nurses were killed. Eventually, Army engineers excavated three-and-a-half-foot foundations for the hospital tents and reinforced these protective earthworks with sandbag walls, protecting those inside from flying shrapnel, but not from direct hits. Finally, in June 1944, Allied forces broke out of the beachhead where they had been confined and moved inland.

The story of the Army and Navy nurses who were captured by the Japanese Army in the Far East is among the most compelling of the war. The first to be captured were five Navy nurses assigned to the naval hospital on the island of Guam, which was attacked and overrun by Japanese forces soon after Pearl Harbor. Japanese military officers were shocked to discover American women on the island, and were at first uncertain what to do with them. In the end they were incarcerated in a prison in Japan for seven months and then repatriated along with 624 other American citizens who had been held by the Japanese. The 80 Army and Navy nurses captured in the Philippines were not so lucky. They were held in a civilian prison camp administered by the Japanese military. Late in the war, when the Japanese were losing the empire they had attempted to construct, Japanese officials cut back on the food given to the POWs, including the nurses. By the time the American POWs were rescued by the Army in February 1945, the nurses were on the verge of starvation, having lost an average of more than 40 pounds each.

Flight nurses had extremely risky jobs. Aircraft used to evacuate wounded soldiers from the battle theater doubled as cargo planes, and thus could not display the markings of the Geneva Red Cross to protect them from enemy fire. One type of aircraft used for medical evacuation flights, the C-46, was dubbed the "flying coffin" because heater problems sometimes caused these coffin-shaped planes to explode during flight. Yet the nurses needed to heat the cabin to keep their patients from becoming cold and going into shock.

Navy flight nurses evacuated casualties from the Pacific islands of Guam, Tinian, Kwajelein, Iwo Jima and Okinawa, sometimes while the fighting was still in progress. Navy nurse Irene Freeburger was on an evacuation flight to Okinawa that had to be aborted because rain and mist prevented the pilot from finding the landing strip. Low on fuel, the plane was forced to try for Iwo Jima instead. When the right engine began to falter, Freeburger was given a "Mae West" life jacket in case the pilot had to ditch in the ocean. When the plane limped into Iwo Jima, it was not allowed to land at first because a battle was ongoing. The pilot radioed that he was out of fuel, and the aircraft was finally cleared for landing.

The memoirs and histories below describe some of the multitude of assignments and dangers experienced by Army and Navy nurses during the war.

208. Ahrendson, Frances Wallace. *From Survival to Arrival.* Tacoma, WA: Blue Zoo Books, 1993.

    Ahrendson was an Army nurse injured by a land mine during World War II.

209. Allen, Genevieve Inez "Mickey" O'Reilly. *Chip on My Shoulder.* InstantPublisher.com, 2003.

    Allen served as an Army nurse in Africa and Italy during World War II.

210. Aquilina, LaVada "Rue" Bishop. *Unsung Heroes: Combat Nurses and Army Wives.* El Paso, TX: Trego Hill Publications, 1995.

    Aquilina served as an Army nurse in the southwest Pacific.

211. Archard, Theresa. *G.I. Nightingale: The Story of an Army Nurse.* New York: WW Norton & Co. Inc., 1945.

    Archard was a captain in the Army Nurse Corps and served as the chief nurse of the 48th Surgical Hospital, the first U.S. Army Medical unit to land with the troops in North Africa in 1943. Although Archard's unit landed with combat troops and the nurses were not among the casualties, General Eisenhower later decided that in future operations nurses should be held back until the beachhead was secure. The 48th also saw combat in Sicily.

212. Aynes, Edith. *From Nightingale to Eagle: An Army Nurse's History.* Englewood Cliffs, NJ: Prentice Hall Inc., 1973.

    Major Aynes describes her career in the Army Nurse Corps, which stretched from the 1930s through World War II, during which she served with the 148th General Hospital, and the Korean War where she was assigned to an Army hospital in Japan. Aynes' perspective as a career Army nurse was very different from the young nurses who joined the ANC to serve in World War II and left the Army after the war.

213. Berendsen, Dorothy M. Lt. Col., USAF Ret. *The Way It Was: An Air Force Nurse's Story.*

    Colonel Berendson served as an Army Flight Nurse in the European Theater of war during World War II. This small memoir describes her experiences during the war and also recounts her decision to transfer to the Air Force Nurse Corps on its establishment in 1949.

214. Blassingame, Wyatt. *Combat Nurses of World War II.* New York: Random House, 1967.

Blassingame tells the stories of Army and Navy nurses who served under fire around the world during World War II. Although this book is meant for juveniles, it contains some engaging first-person accounts.

215. Bonine, Gladys. *Reflections of One Army Nurse in World War II.* New York: Vantage Press, 1996.

216. Buchanan, Margaret S. *Reminiscing: An Account of the 300th Army General Hospital during World War II.* Nashville, TN: Williams Printing Co., 1988.

The 300th General Hospital was a Vanderbilt University, Nashville, Tennessee, medical unit shipped overseas to the European Theater early in the war. The 300-patient hospital was located first in Tunisia and later near Naples, Italy.

217. Burrell, Prudence Burns. *Hathaway.* Detroit, MI: Harlo Press, 1997.

This autobiographical account of Burrell's early life includes her years as an Army nurse in World War II.

218. Camp, LaVonne Telshaw. *Lingering Fever: A World War II Nurse's Memoir.* Jefferson, NC: McFarland & Co. Publishers, 1997.

This excellent memoir was written by one of the relatively small number of Army nurses who served in the Far East Theater during the war. Camp spent the entire war in the extremely primitive conditions common to the China–Burma–India Theater.

219. Cooper, Page. *Navy Nurse.* New York: McGraw Hill Book Company, 1946.

This book for young women was written to inspire them to enter nursing and perhaps join the military. It contains some excellent and exciting stories about Navy nurses serving in exotic and unusual locales such as New Guinea and Greenland.

220. Danner, Dorothy Still. *What a Way to Spend a War: Navy Nurse POWs in the Philippines.* Annapolis, MD: Naval Institute Press, 1995.

One of the classic, inspiring World War II nurse POW stories available in print. Danner was one of 11 Navy nurses captured when the Japanese Army seized control of the Philippines. The women endured three years of hardship and malnutrition, but continued working, nursing prisoners of the Japanese throughout their captivity.

221. Dobie, Kathryn S. and Eleanor Lang, eds. *Her War: American Women during World War II.* Lincoln, NE: iUniverse Inc., 2003.

Includes excerpts from out-of-print publications such as Ruth Haskell's *Helmets and Lipstick* (1945), June Wandrey's *Bedpan Commando* (1989), Juanita Redmond's *I Served on Bataan* (1943) and Chief Nurse Jean Truckey's letters, previously published in Alma Lutz's *With Love, Jane* (1945).

222. Fessler, Diane Burke. *No Time for Fear: Voices of American Military Nurses in World War II.* East Lansing, MI: Michigan State University Press, 1996.

Fessler has collected riveting first-person accounts of Army and Navy nurses serving in daunting conditions as POWs and under fire.

223. Gier, Barbara. *In Uniform 1936–1946.* No publication information.

Gier worked as a nurse on the Union Pacific Railroad before joining the U.S. Army Air Corps as a nurse. When she declined parachute training in 1942, she was assigned as an Army nurse. During her initial assignment with the Army, Gier served at Dibble General Hospital in Menlo Park, California, where she worked with wounded combat veterans from the Pacific Theater. In 1944 Gier was sent overseas to the European Theater with the 203rd General Hospital. The 203rd arrived outside of Paris in October 1944. Gier worked with both U.S. and German patients. Her memoir is a compilation of the letters she wrote to friends and family during World War II.

224. Glines, Edna Lee. *Heads in the Sand.* Los Angeles, CA: Authors Unlimited, 1990.

This small book was written by the sister of a Navy nurse stationed aboard the USS *Benevolence* during World War II. The personnel aboard the *Benevolence* witnessed an atom bomb experiment on Bikini Atoll immediately after the war, an experience Glines believes caused the cancer that shortened her sister's life.

225. Haskell, Ruth G. *Helmets and Lipsticks.* New York: G.P. Putnam and Sons, 1944.

A rare, out-of-print, first-person account of an Army nurse who served in the North African and Italian Theaters of war during World War II. Haskell, the mother of a 2-year-old son, left him with his grandparents when she volunteered to serve with the Army Nurse Corps. Haskell was assigned to the 48th Surgical Hospital, the medical unit which landed with the first invasion troops near Arzeu, North Africa, November 8, 1942. Haskell describes assisting during operations on wounded soldiers by flashlight, plagued by a sniper who shot into the operating room whenever he saw a glimmer of light emerging from the blanket-sheltered operating table. Much of this memoir's value lies in its contemporary tone; Haskell's story is unfiltered through time and carries the attitudes, and expectations, of a woman of the 1940s.

226. Jackson, Kathi. *They Called Them Angels: American Military Nurses.* Bison Books, 2006.

Jackson describes the experiences of military nurses by theater, relying on numerous first-person accounts to build interest. She then examines the lives of flight nurses as well as those who served aboard hospital ships.

227. Jopling, Lucy Wilson. *Warrior in White.* San Antonio, TX: Watercress Press, 1990.

This memoir is by an Army nurse selected for evacuation from Corregidor by submarine before that island and other Army nurses serving in the hospital there fell to the Japanese. Jopling later returned to the Pacific Theater as a flight nurse.

228. Kielar, Eugenia M. *Thank You Uncle Sam: Letters of a World War II Army Nurse from North Africa and Italy.* Bryn Mawr, PA: Dorrance and Co. Inc., 1987.

Kielar's diary recounts her experiences as an Army nurse in the European and Italian Theaters of war.

229. Lutz, Alma, ed. *With Love, Jane: Letters from American Women on the War Fronts.* New York: The John Day Company, 1945.

A rare, out-of-print yet exceptional collection of letters of U.S. servicewomen overseas during World War II. These letters demonstrate how close many women were to the fighting and the many hardships they endured. A letter from Army nurse Ruth Haskell (see entry 215) is included in this collection.

230. Mangerich, Agnes. *Albanian Escape: The True Story of U.S. Army Nurses Behind Enemy Lines*, as told to Evelyn Monahan and Rosemary L. Neidel. University Press of Kentucky, 1999.

Mangerich was one of 13 Army nurses on a medical evacuation flight that crashed in the Albanian mountains far behind enemy lines in 1944. They and the plane's crew walked some 800 miles in two months across mountain peaks in blizzard-like conditions to freedom. The Germans were aware of the plane crash and searched constantly for the Americans, even placing "wanted" posters on trees along the route the Germans believed the Americans would take to the coast. Several times during their trek, the Americans hid in ditches and behind bushes from German patrols, and once, German planes patrolling the roads strafed the group. Albanian guides took the group higher up in the mountains to avoid German patrols, and there the party encountered freezing weather and deep snows. The men and women took turns sharing blankets and coats, with the sickest receiving the most food and the warmest clothes. Eventually, a British undercover agent escorted the Americans to a spot on the coast where they were picked up by a boat. This little known episode amply demonstrates women's abilities to survive incredible hardship "behind enemy lines."

231. Matthews, Meredith Miller. *Mother Wore Combat Boots and Chased Troop Trains.* Akron, OH: Grapevine Press, 1998.

232. McCrary, Martha E. Lt. Col. Army Nurse Corps (Ret.) *The Colonel Was a Lady.* D.I. Publications Inc., 1995.

When nurse Martha McCrary joined the Army Nurse Corps during World War II she was a widow with a small child, whom she left in the care of family. Her life experiences gave her a somewhat different outlook on life in the Army than many of her fellow nurses, new graduates from nursing schools. As an officer in charge of other nurses, McCrary's memoir is comparable to those of Peto and Archard.

233. Monahan, Evelyn and Rosemary Neidel-Greenlee. *All this Hell: U.S. Nurses Imprisoned by the Japanese.* Lexington, KY: University Press of Kentucky, 2000.

An outstanding examination of the experiences of the 85 Army and Navy nurses captured by the Japanese on the Philippines during World War II. Monahan and Neidel succeed in bringing these individual women to life through their expert use of interviews, memoirs, and official accounts and testimonies.

234. Monahan, Evelyn and Rosemary Neidel-Greenlee. *And If I Perish: Front line U.S. Army Nurses in World War II.* New York: Alfred A. Knopf, 2003.

Writers Monahan and Neidel reprise their outstanding first book with this exceptional account of Army nurses serving under fire during World War II. Using letters home, memoirs, oral history interviews and other first-hand accounts, the authors bring to life the personalities and experiences of these heroines. Readers of this book will wonder why placing female service members on the front line is still being debated in Congress. Women proved their abilities under fire 60 years ago.

235. Newcomb, Ellsworth. *Brave Nurse: True Stories of Heroism.* New York: D. Appleton-Century Company Inc., 1945.

This interesting compilation of stories includes the Chief Nurse aboard the Navy hospital ship *Solace*, Grace Lally, as well as the Army nurses of Bataan, Army nurses assigned to the grim outpost in Iceland, and those who participated in the invasions of North Africa and Anzio.

236. Norman, Elizabeth. *We Band of Angels: The Untold Story of the American Nurses Trapped on Bataan by the Japanese.* Atria, 2000.

Beautifully written, this very personal and exceptionally dramatic story of the sufferings and eventual triumph of the Army and Navy nurses captured by the Japanese in the Philippines and held as POWs for almost three years may be the best of its genre. Norman personally interviewed several of these exceptional women, and masterfully brought many of their personalities to life.

237. O'Farrell, Elizabeth Kinzer, Lt. USNNC (Ret.) *World War II: A Navy Nurse Remembers.* Talahassee, FL: CyPress Publications, 2007.

Like the majority of World War II Navy nurses, O'Farrell spent the war in a series of stateside Naval hospitals including Great Lakes, IL, St. Albans, NY, and Corona, CA. This excellent memoir describes the challenges inherent in nursing men with devastating wounds who must be prepared to face life as wounded, and in many cases handicapped, veterans.

238. Peto, Marjorie, Lt. Col. ANC. *Women Were Not Expected.* West Englewood, NJ: published by the author, 1947.

Peto was the Chief Nurse of the 2nd General Hospital, assigned early to the European Theater. She dealt with her command's concerns about the newly arrived women in their midst with calm common sense and considerable patience. This memoir is a solid reminder of the sexism World War II era professional women accepted without batting an eye.

239. Redmond, Juanita. *I Served on Bataan.* J.B. Lippincott Co., 1943.

    Redmond was an Army nurse serving in the Philippines when the Japanese invaded the islands in 1941. In this memoir, she describes the horrific conditions suffered by American Army soldiers and nurses as the Americans retreated from the Japanese advance down the Bataan Peninsula. In an especially riveting account, Redmond describes being blown under a desk when Japanese artillery shells hit the open air jungle hospital where she worked.

240. Schorer, Avis D. *A Half Acre of Hell: A Combat Nurse in World War II.* Lakeville, MN: Glade Press, 2000.

    This is a firsthand account of an Army nurse at Anzio Beachhead, where the hospitals were located on a tiny strip of land vulnerable to German shelling. The 200 nurses working at the beachhead hospitals in early 1944 experienced months of enemy bombardment. The problem at Anzio was that the beachhead was so small that hospitals, ammunition and gasoline dumps, airstrips, and antiaircraft batteries were all nestled together within the tiny toehold of territory the Allies had established. German bombers frequently, if inadvertently, hit medical facilities, killing and wounding patients and medical personnel. Patients worried about having to stay in the tented hospitals, believing themselves safer in foxholes on the front lines. The nurses realized they were safer off duty, because they could run to their individual foxholes (everyone dug his or her own) when they heard incoming shells. When they were on duty, however, they would lay on their faces on the floor, unless they were busy with a patient.

241. Schwartz, Doris R. *My Fifty Years in Nursing: Give Us to Go Blithely.* New York: Springer Publishing Company, 1995.

    Although only the second chapter is devoted to Schwartz's World War II experiences as an Army nurse, this single chapter is an excellent resource, dealing as it does with experiences that are not duplicated elsewhere in the literature. Schwartz's first assignment was to the Air Evacuation Center at Mitchel Field, Long Island, as Chief Nurse of the amputee ward that held wounded soldiers from the European Theater. Later Schwartz was assigned to the Army hospital ship *Marigold* in the Pacific Theater, which picked up U.S. POWs from Japanese prison camps. Her third assignment was to Percy Jones General Hospital in Battle Creek, Michigan, where she worked rehabilitating wounded G.I.s.

242. Spangle, Frieda Patterson. *Long Ago and Far Away.* Thomasville, GA: Better Choice, 2003.

    Spangle served in Tongatabu with the 7th Evacuation Hospital and later in the forgotten China–India–Burma Theater.

243. Stoddard, Eleanor. *Fearless Presence: The Story of Lt. Col. Nola Forrest, Who Led the Army Nurses through the Heat, Rain, Mud and Enemy Fire in World War II.* Baltimore, MD: American Literary Press, 2007.

This unusual memoir and tribute is compiled from a series of oral histories. Colonel Forrest joined the Army Nurse Corps in 1924 and served in the southwest Pacific during World War II as the Director of Nurses.

244. Tomblin, Barbara Brooks. *G.I. Nightingales: The Army Nurse Corps in World War II.* Lexington, KY: University Press of Kentucky, 1996.

An excellent scholarly look at the difficult and dangerous assignments undertaken by Army nurses in all theaters.

245. Tayloe, Roberta Love. *Combat Nurse: A Journal of World War II.* Santa Ana, CA: Fifthian Press, 1988.

Letters home from an Army nurse who served in the 9th Evacuation Hospital in North Africa and Italy.

246. Tyrrell, Mary O'Brien, ed. *Reflections on Quiet Adventures and Memoirs of Florence "Flo" Scholljegerdes.* St. Paul, MN: Memories Inc., 2002.

Scholljegerdes served as a Navy nurse during World War II, attended school under the G.I. Bill to gain a four-year degree and was recalled to duty during the Korean War, where she served aboard military sea transport vessels in the Pacific. After the war, Scholljegerdes again used G.I. Bill benefits to obtain a degree in public health, and remained in the Naval Reserve through a career as a public health nurse.

247. Wandrey, June. *Bedpan Commando: The Story of a Combat Nurse during World War II.* Elmore, OH: Elmore Publishing Company, 1989.

Wandrey served with the 10th Field Hospital in the European Theater. While usually several miles behind the front lines, field hospitals were frequently affected by supply shortages and difficult weather conditions. An idealistic young nurse at the start of her service, Wandrey soon learned how to deal with death and hardship and remain cheerful for the wounded soldiers, many of whom were thrilled to see American girls again.

248. Welch, Bob. *American Nightingale: The Story of Frances Slanger, Forgotten Heroine of Normandy.* New York: Atria Books, 2004.

Newspaper reporter and columnist Welch was struck to the heart when he learned the story of World War II Army nurse Frances Slanger, who died from enemy fire at Normandy. Realizing that Slanger had been all but forgotten by history, Welch used his skills as an investigative reporter to track down the details of her story and bring her bravery and commitment to life. Before she died, Slanger had written a letter to the G.I. newsletter *Stars and Stripes* dismissing the hardships she and other nurses dealt with when compared with those faced daily by men on front lines. By the time the paper published her letter, Slanger had been killed.

249. Williams, Denny. *To the Angels.* Denson Press, 1985.

Williams was one of 85 military nurses taken prisoner by the Japanese in the Philippines during World War II. Her book, written in 1985, was the first book written by one of the nurse POWs recounting the difficult years of their imprisonment, and by now is a classic. The nurses spent their time nursing other prisoners, albeit with little or no medicines, food or provisions. The malnutrition, diseases and mental stresses these nurses suffered followed most of them throughout the rest of their lives.

   250. Williams, Winnie. *I Have a Story to Tell.* Self-published.

C. The Women's Army Auxiliary Corps and the Women's Army Corps

The first service to ask Congress for the authority to put non-nursing women into uniform was the U.S. Army. The Women's Army Auxiliary Corps (WAAC) was established on May 15, 1942. Army women, referred to as WAACs, served with the Army rather than in it. They were in uniform and subject to military orders and discipline but they were not technically part of the Army. This legality eventually posed a problem for the Army when WAACs proved to be so essential to the smooth running of the force that the Army decided it wanted to send them overseas. However, if by chance the enemy captured a WAAC, she would not be entitled to the protections of the Geneva Convention because she was not an official member of the Armed Forces. In 1943, the Army returned to Congress and asked to be allowed to dissolve the WAAC and establish in its stead the Women's Army Corps (WAC), which would be part of the Army. Congress agreed and the bill establishing the WAC was passed on July 1, 1943. Before the war was over, more than 150,000 women served in the WAAC/WAC, 20,000 of them overseas in North Africa, Great Britain, France, Germany, Australia, New Guinea, and India. WACs were the only non-nurse military women to receive overseas assignments to non-U.S. territories during the war (WAVES and SPARs went overseas to Hawaii and Alaska late in the war). On their overseas sojourns, WACs were exposed to danger and some were wounded by enemy fire, but in most cases they served far behind the front lines, and no WACs were killed by enemy fire. The ship one group was traveling on was torpedoed and sunk, forcing five WAACs to spend one night on a raft before being rescued. The WACs assigned to London lived and worked under the threat of V-1 and V-2 rocket bombs launched by the Germans. The Army was very lucky that no WACs were killed. One time a bomb landed across the street from the WAC barracks. Another time a bomb demolished the office where many WACs worked during the day—only the bomb hit at night. Four WAC office workers in southern England were wounded by shattered glass when a buzz bomb hit their office building in July 1944. The women were awarded Purple Heart medals.

As time went on, the surprised Army kept finding more and more jobs that women were capable of doing. WACs served as telephone operators, file clerks, secretaries, supply specialists, photo analysts, map makers, translators, mechanics, parachute packers, truck drivers, medical technicians and in many, many other jobs—more than 200 different jobs.

   251. Adkins, Yolanda. *Skirt Patrol: Women's Army Corps, Army of the United States.* New York: Vantage Press Inc., 1993

      A very typical memoir of a young, sheltered idealistic woman inspired to join the Women's Army Corps. In a light-hearted fashion the author describes her training and assignments with the WAC.

252. Bell, Iris. *Los Alamos WAACs/WACs, World War II 1943–1946.* Sarasota, FL: Coastal Printing Inc., 1993.

This small book discusses a group of women often forgotten by history, the Army WACs assigned to the top secret Manhattan Project in the remote mountains of New Mexico. The women worked as clerks and record-keepers. Although the assignment sounds exciting in theory, the women had little idea of the significance of their work, and many suffered from boredom and isolation.

253. Bessey, Carol Hossner. *Battle of the WAC.* Kearney, NE: Morris Publishing Co., 1999.

This WAC memoir describes the military assignments of an average woman in uniform, including the constant struggle WACs had for acceptance from their male counterparts, many of whom assumed they were in the Army only to meet men. In Bessey's case, she did meet the man whom she would eventually marry.

254. Blake, Penelope A. *My Mother's Fort: A Photographic Tribute to Fort Des Moines: First Home of the Women's Army Corps.* Book Surge LLC, 2005.

A photographic history of Fort Des Moines, originally a cavalry post.

255. Bridgers, Jean Johnson. *Stand in for a Soldier.* Eakin Press, 1997.

The author served as a cryptologist at Arlington Hall, Virginia, during the war. After the war, she was assigned to China for a year.

256. Brion, Irene. *Lady G.I.: A Woman's War in the South Pacific.* Presidio Press, 1997.

Brion served as a WAC cryptologist in the southwest Pacific Theater. She and her unit noticed that their clean laundry was coming to them wrapped in pages from a Japanese code book. They obtained the rest of the pages from their Filipino laundress, and were able to decode the pages and contribute to the Allied offensive at the end of the war.

257. Bugbee, Sylvia, ed. *An Officer and a Lady: The World War II Letters of Lt. Col. Betty Bandel, Women's Army Corps.* Lebanon, NH: Women's Military Press and University Press of New England, 2004.

The edited letters of Elizabeth (Betty) Bandel to her mother and friends during her WAAC officer training and assignments in the field and WAC headquarters in Washington, D.C. Bandel had worked as a journalist before training to become a WAC officer, so her letters are well written and engaging. They also shed light on a part of the WAC very few of those 150,000 women knew—the inner workings and personalities of WAC Director Oveta Culp Hobby's office and staff.

258. Dahlgren, Liz Forbes. *We Were First! We Heard the Guns at Wewak.* Brownsville, TX: Springman-King, 1977.

The author was among a select few Army Air WACs who were assigned to teach gunners how to sight their targets.

259. Earley, Charity Adams. *One Woman's Army: A Black Officer Remembers the WAC.* College Station, TX: Texas A&M University Press, 1995.

The 6888th Postal Battalion, commanded by Major (later Lt. Colonel) Charity Adams, was the only unit of African American WACs to be sent overseas. Adams Earley, a former schoolteacher, joined the WAC as one of the first black women officer trainees. Raised by her preacher father and schoolteacher mother to be a lady, Adams Earley had very definite ideas about proper decorum and conduct. For the first couple of years of her Army career she remained at Fort Des Moines training other young women for field assignments. But finally she was selected to head the first unit of black WACs slated for overseas. The battalion was stationed in England in 1945 and eventually moved to Rouen, France, and finally to Paris. The unit was responsible for the redirection of mail to U.S. personnel in the European Theater of Operations. Because military units are rarely stationary and wounded personnel do not stay with their units, forwarding mail to the troops was a monumental task. Working around the clock in eight-hour shifts, the women kept updated data cards on each of 7 million military personnel in the theater. The receipt of mail from home was critical to the morale of the fighting soldier, a fact well known to these WACs, whose persistent efforts quickly cleared the tremendous backlog of misdirected mail.

260. Graydon, Mary Ellen. *Love and War: One WAC Remembers World War II.* 1998.

The author describes her assignment with the Women's Army Corps overseas to England. She and her fellow WACs found themselves serving under fire during the German V-1 and V-2 campaigns over London. Graydon and her colleagues also experienced a "backlash" of feelings about women in uniform (the rumors were that they were sent overseas to service men), which they learned of in letters they received from their friends and families at home.

261. Green, Anne Bosanko. *One Woman's War: Letters Home From the Women's Army Corps 1944–1946.* St. Paul, MN: Minnesota Historical Society Press, 1989.

Green served as a surgical technician during the war.

262. Henderson, Aileen Kilgore. *Stateside Soldier: Life in the Women's Army Corps 1944–1945.* Colombia, SC: University of South Carolina Press, 2001.

The author was one of six female airplane mechanics at Ellington Air Force Base and also worked as a photo technician.

263. Howes, Ruth H. and Caroline L. Herzenberg. *Their Day in the Sun: Women of the Manhattan Project.* Philadelphia, PA: Temple University Press, 1999.

This scholarly look at the women of the Manhattan Project includes some brief sections on the Army WACs assigned to Los Alamos.

264. Loving, Gerry. *Girl in a Pink Skirt.* 1st Books Library, 2003.

"The pink skirt" refers to the term WACs used to describe their often mismatched uniform skirt "pinks," which were really a muted shade of green distinctly different from the olive shade of their jackets. The author recounts her WAC experiences in a cheerful, conversational mode.

265. Meyer, Leisa. *Creating G.I. Jane: The Regulation of Sexuality and Sexual Behavior in the Women's Army Corps during World War II.* New York: Columbia University Press, 1998.

This scholarly examination of the World War II WAC describes how WAC leadership attempted to navigate through World War II America's suspicion of the very idea of women in uniform by insisting that members of the WAC think and act like ladies everywhere they went. Those women who could not or would not conform to this persona were quickly culled from the Corps.

266. Miller, Grace Porter. *Call of Duty: A Montana Girl in World War II.* Baton Rouge, LA: Louisiana State University Press, 1999.

The author served as a cryptologic technician, a very unusual assignment, in the European Theater during the war.

267. Moore, Brenda. *To Serve My Country, To Serve My Race: The Story of the Only African American WACs Stationed Overseas during World War II.* New York University Press, 1996.

The author interviewed enlisted women of 6888th Postal Battalion commanded by Lt. Colonel Charity Adams Earley, whose memoir is described above. Moore's work offers a different perspective of what it was like for African American women who volunteered to serve in the Women's Army Corps during World War II.

268. Moorehouse, Maggie M. *Fighting in the Jim Crow Army: Black Men and Women Remember World War II.* Lanham: Rowman and Littlefield, 2000.

269. Nichols, Pauline E., Major USAF (Ret.). *A Date with Destiny: A WAC in Occupied Japan 1946–1947.*

WAC officer Nichols took the first unit of WACs to occupied Japan after World War II.

270. Pollard, Clarice. *"Hey Lady, Uncle Sam Needs You."* Phoenix, AZ: Clarice Pollard, 1985.

271. Pollard, Clarice. *Laugh, Cry and Remember: The Journal of a G.I. Lady.* Texas Tech University Press, 1991.

272. Roundtree, Dovey Johnson with Kate McCabe. *Justice Older Than the Law: The Life of Dovey Johnson Roundtree.* Jackson, MS: University of Mississippi, 2009.

This outstanding autobiography devotes only one chapter to Roundtree's service in the Women's Army Corps during World War II; these years shaped her entire life. Using the G.I. Bill, Roundtree graduated from law school, and as a practicing lawyer accepted the case of Sarah Louise Keys, a young black woman Army private traveling home to North Carolina on leave who refused to move to the back of a bus.

273. Samford, Doris E. *Ruffles and Drums.* Boulder, CO: Pruett Press, 1966.

    Samford's World War II memoir was one of the earliest to be published. It includes some original artwork by Arminta Neal, and is basically a light-hearted reminiscence. Samford obviously enjoyed her WAC experience.

274. Scott, Vivien. *The Lipstick Explosion.* Deep River, Iowa: Brennan Printing Company, 1988.

275. Shea, Nancy. *The WAACs.* New York: Harper and Brothers Publishers, 1943.

    Shea wrote this for young women who might be considering joining the Women's Army Auxiliary Corps during the war. The book describes the type of training WAACs received and the potential jobs to which they might be assigned.

276. Summersby, Kay, WAC Captain. *Eisenhower Was My Boss.* New York: Dell Publishing Company, 1948.

    An Englishwoman given officer status in the Women's Army Corps because General Eisenhower requested her services as his driver, Summersby's first memoir, written immediately after the war, described her exciting assignment with Eisenhower's close-knit group of aides without alluding to a romantic relationship with her married boss.

277. Summersby, Kay Morgan. *Past Forgetting: My Love Affair with Dwight D. Eisenhower.* New York: Simon and Schuster, 1977.

    Despite rumors about a supposed affair with General Dwight Eisenhower during World War II when the Englishwoman served as the General's driver, Summersby's first memoir, published immediately after the war, described a platonic relationship. Her second book, written just prior to her death, admitted to an affair with Eisenhower. By the time the second book was written, both Eisenhower and his wife were dead, and affairs outside of marriage were more accepted.

278. Thurston, Doris "Joy". *A WAC Looks Back.* Stuart, FL: Norvega Press, 1996.

    Memoirs and poems by Joy Thurston, who looks fondly back on her days in the World War II WAC.

279. Treadwell, Mattie. *The Women's Army Corps: United States Army in World War II Special Studies.* Washington, D.C.: U.S. Army Center of Military History, 1954.

    Treadwell, a former WAC, wrote this classic study of the origins, formation and functioning of the Women's Army Corps during World War II. It is the Army's official history of the World War II WAC. Thoroughly researched and documented, it is the foundation of every other study of this 150,000 woman strong organization.

280. Weirick, Dorothy Millard. *WAC Days of World War II: A Personal Story.* Laguna Niguel, CA: Donald M. and Mary L. Decker, Royal Literary Publications, 1992.

   Dorothy Millard Weirick served as a Signal Corps WAC in the European Theater.

281. Weise, Selene H.C. *The Good Soldier: The Story of a Southwest Pacific Signal Corps WAC.* Shippensburg, PA: White Mane Publishing Company, 1999.

   Weise served as a cryptographic technician during World War II. Her assignment took her to New Guinea, the Philippines and later to occupied Japan. She describes the difficulties she and her fellow WACs had dealing with the uncomfortable climate (unbearable heat, humidity, rain and mud) and extremely limited supplies.

282. Women's Army Corps Veterans Association. *Daughters of Pallas Athene.* Independence, MO: 1983.

   Separate short stories and firsthand accounts of experiences in the early Women's Army Corps.

283. Yellin, Emily. *Our Mothers' War: American Women at Home and at the Front during World War II.* New York: Free Press, 2004.

D. The Navy WAVES

When the Navy approached Congress about establishing a women's component, Navy leaders insisted that they wanted women to serve in the Navy, not with it. Ironically, however, the 81,000 did not serve overseas until the very end of the war, when approximately 4,000 were assigned to Hawaii. After basic training, WAVES served as secretaries, clerks, typists, storekeepers, radiomen, pharmacists' mates, supply specialists, personnel specialists, statisticians, code breakers, and teachers at Naval bases across the country. Although many of the jobs were traditional female jobs performed in the civilian sector, others were not. WAVES were trained to teach aircraft and shore-based gunners the fine points of tracking and targeting enemy aircraft and worked as parachute packers, aircraft control tower operators, link trainers and mechanics. By the end of the war WAVES, like WACs, were performing just about every noncombat job in existence.

284. Alsmeyer, Marie Bennett. *The Way of the WAVES.* Conway, AR: Hamba Books, 1981.

   The personal experiences of a young woman who served in the WAVES during World War II and was trained and served as a pharmacist's mate. The memoir is reconstructed from letters she sent home to her mother.

285. Alsmeyer, Marie Bennett. *Old WAVES Tales.* Printed by Marie Bennett Alsmeyer, 1982.

   A series of humorous short stories of women who served in the WAVES during World War II. Unfortunately the stories do not have attribution.

286. Angel, Joan. *Angel of the Navy: The Story of a WAVE.* New York: Hastings House, 1943.

   A very old-fashioned novel about a young woman inspired to join the WAVES during the war.

287. Bachner, Evan. *Making WAVES: Navy Women of World War II.* Abrams, 2008.

   A photographic history of service in the WAVES during World War II. Photographer Edward Steichen and his team captured women in boot camp and on the job in a wide variety of assignments. Steichen was the director of the Naval Photographic Institute during the war. Bachner's research in the National Archives has enabled him to identify many of the women depicted in the 150 photos in the book.

288. Billings, Charlene. *Grace Hopper: Navy Admiral and Computer Pioneer.* Hillside, NJ: Enslow Publishers, 1989.

   Although written for a juvenile audience, this small biography of Hopper is extremely well done and captures the personality and spirit of this legendary woman.

289. Borsten, Laura Rapaport with Orin Borsten. *Once a WAVE: My Life in the Navy 1942–1946.* Studio City, CA: Amber Publishing Company, 1995.

   An excellent memoir about a professional woman with a job at the National Council of Jewish Women in New York City who decides to join the Navy WAVES, receives officer training at Mt. Holyoke and is assigned to Washington, D.C. Borsten was one of the first women the Navy selected for its WAVES officer training.

290. Collins, Winifred Quick. *More Than a Uniform: A Navy Woman in a Man's World.* Denton, TX: University of North Texas Press, 1997.

   Collins, whose Navy career lasted 20 years, became one of the first female captains in the Navy. She began her career as a Navy WAVE during World War II. Much of Collins' career was in personnel, enabling her to battle military sexism by quietly integrating women into a variety of Navy jobs.

291. Gilbert, Helen. *"Okay, Girls, Man Your Bunks!" Tales from the Life of a World War II Navy WAVE.* Toledo, OH: Pedestrian Press, 2006.

   Former WAVE Helen Gilbert has written a predominantly light-hearted memoir about her experiences as a Navy WAVE and how they colored her life. At 86 years of age, however, Gilbert knows well that not all of life comprises happy memories, and to that end she does tackle subjects such as racism, homosexuality, and alcoholism, as they apply to her personal vision, beliefs and experiences.

292. Gunter, Helen Clifford, Lt. USNR (Ret.). *Navy WAVE Memories of World War II.* Fort Bragg, CA: Cypress House Press, 1992.

   Gunter, a classical archeologist with a PhD from New York University, joined the Navy because she was unable to find work in her male-dominated field. The Navy, perhaps more than the other services, was willing to try to fit professional, highly trained women into the service and utilize them in meaningful ways.

293. Johnson, Louanne. *Making WAVES: A Woman in This Man's Navy.* New York: St. Martin's Press, 1986.

One of the few WAVES memoirs from a non-World War II Navy veteran. Johnson joined the Navy during the 1970s, when its women were still referred to as WAVES. This very honest memoir is a refreshing read.

294. Lander, Grace Skagen. *Wave Goodbye: A Navy WAVE's Memoir.* Edina, MN: Beaver's Pond Press, 2003.

295. Thorpe, Francis Willis. *Navy Blue and Other Colors.* Xlibris Corporation, 2007.

This important memoir is by one of the first two African American women officers in the Navy. The Navy originally hesitated to accept black women, and by the end of the war there were only a handful of African American WAVES. Like Charity Adams Earley in her classic *One Woman's Army*, Willis starts her memoir with her childhood, relating what it was like growing up an African American. Willis then describes her military service but also devotes more time than Earley to her life after the war.

296. Williams, Kathleen Broome. *Grace Hopper: Admiral of the Cyber Sea.* Annapolis, MD: Naval Institute Press, 2004.

The first scholarly biography of Admiral Grace Murray Hopper, who joined the WAVES during World War II and did not leave the Navy for more than 40 years. Hopper had a Ph.D. in mathematics when she joined the WAVES in 1943, and the Navy wisely assigned her to the Bureau of Ordnance Computation Project at Harvard University. After the war, Hopper continued to work in the early computer field, but remained in the Naval Reserve until 1967, when she came back to active duty. She retired from the Navy in 1986 as a Rear Admiral. Williams paints a deft portrait of this brilliant but eccentric woman.

297. Williams, Kathleen Broome. *Improbable Warriors: Women Scientists in the Navy in World War II.* Annapolis, MD: Naval Institute Press, 2000.

Williams discusses the Navy's willingness to employ professional women with particular scientific expertise as Reserve Naval (WAVES) officers during World War II. She focuses on four women: oceanographer Mary Sears, meteorologist Florence van Stratten, computer scientist Grace Hopper, and scientist Mina Spiegel Reese.

298. Wingo, Josette Dermoody. *"Mother Was a Gunner's Mate": World War II in the WAVES.* Annapolis, MD: Naval Institute Press, 1994.

Little did the author know when she took the exciting step of joining the WAVES in World War II that the Navy would train her as an antiaircraft gunner and send her to Treasure Island, California, to teach Navy men how to shoot down enemy aircraft. An excellent memoir by a woman who had an unusual Navy experience.

299. Yaroch, Betty Gougeon. *Cleared for Take Off.* Atlanta, GA: Wings Publishers, 2000.

Yaroch served as a Navy air traffic controller during World War II. Her memoir is upbeat and enjoyable, the story of a young woman eager to enjoy life wherever it led, even to a rather isolated Navy airfield in Florida.

E. The Coast Guard SPARS

The Coast Guard Women's Reserve was established in November 1942. Because the Army and Navy had given their women's components catchy nicknames, the Coast Guard decided to call its women SPARs, derived from the motto Semper Paratus—Always Ready. Before the war was over more than 12,000 women joined the SPARs. Like the WAVES, they did not serve overseas until the very end of the war, when a few SPARs were assigned to the Alaskan Theater. Although many SPARs were assigned desk jobs, others worked as parachute riggers, chaplains' assistants, storekeepers, air tower control operators, radiomen, vehicle drivers, pharmacists' mates and more.

Only one SPAR memoir has appeared in print to date. Robin Thompson's pamphlet on World War II SPARs is an excellent synopsis. For more information about SPARs during World War II, see the chapter on SPARs in the book *In Defense of a Nation: Servicewomen during World War II*, listed under "General Histories" below.

300. Lyne, Mary and Kay Arthur. *Three Years behind the Mast.* Self published in 1946.

301. Thompson, Robin. *The Coast Guard and the Women's Reserve in World War II.* Washington, D.C.: Coast Guard Historian's Office, 1992.

F. Women Marines

The last service to establish a women's component was the Marine Corps. Initially Marine commanders did not believe there was a place for women in what was essentially a combat organization; however, even the Marines needed uniformed personnel to handle paperwork, coordinate budgets and keep communications flowing. As combat in the Pacific took its toll on the number of Marines available for duty, the Corps bowed to the inevitable and asked Congress to authorize the establishment of a women's component. Eventually the Corps trained and assigned 20,000 Women Marines to bases across the country. Usually the first women on a base would have to prove their usefulness to skeptical officers and enlisted men before they were accepted. An oft-repeated quote that made its way around Marine bases was, "First they made us work with monkeys, then dogs—now it's women. We didn't know when we had it good!" Male Marines called the women BAMs—broad-assed Marines. How the women hated that nickname! But the women stuck it out, and most Marines came to appreciate their efficiency at the typewriter and in the scheduling office.

302. Ferris, Inga Fredriksen. *A Few Good Women: Memoirs of a World War II Marine.* Xlibris Corporation, 2002.

Ferris was a 22-year-old defense plant worker when she joined the Women Marines in 1944. Ferris wanted to change her life; her mother was remarrying, her job was being eliminated, and she wanted something different. She joined the Marines and was trained as an aviation machinist mate.

303. Harris, Evelyn Louise Robinson. *Marines? Yes!*

304. Herron, Berneice A. *Dearest Folks: Sister Leatherneck's Letter Excerpts and World War II Experiences.* New York: iUniverse Inc., 2006.

    Two sisters decided to give up their jobs as rural Minnesota schoolteachers and join the Women's Reserve of the Marine Corps. They taught aircraft and ship recognition to fighter pilots at El Toro Marine Base in California.

305. Johnson, Nona J. Hall, USMCWR. *Our Home on the Hill 1943–1946.* Eagle River, AK: Eagle River Type and Graphics, 1996.

306. Yianolos, Theresa Karas. *Woman Marine: A Memoir of a Woman Who Joined the U.S. Marine Corps in World War II to "Free A Marine to Fight".* La Jolla, CA: La Jolla Publishing Co., 1994.

    Yianolos, a defense plant worker, joined the Marine Corps on a whim on a Saturday shopping trip because she was impressed with the sharp uniform worn by the recruiter. The North Tonawanda, New York, native trained at Camp LeJeune, North Carolina, and became a post courier at Quantico Marine Corps Base in Virginia before becoming an inventory clerk at a motor transport garage. This above average memoir does an excellent job of recalling the atmosphere of the 1940s.

307. Soderbergh, Peter. *Women Marines: The World War II Era.* Praeger Publishers, 1992.

    Soderbergh interviewed 146 former Women Marines and uses a wealth of first-person quotes and stories as he explores why women decided to join the Marines, the reactions of friends and family and their experiences in boot camp, training and on the job.

308. Soderbergh, Peter. *Years of Grace, Days of Glory: The Legacy of Germaine Laville.* Baker, LA: Baker Printing Company, 1988.

    The story of one of the few Women Marines to die during World War II, perished in a building fire at the Marine Corps Base in Cherry Point, North Carolina.

309. Women Marines Association. *Women Marine Association Volumes 1–3.* Paducah, KY: Turner Publishing Company, 1992, 1996, 2007.

    A compilation of letters, stories, memoirs and photographs of Women Marines of the World War II era. Contains a wealth of information unavailable elsewhere.

G. Women Airforce Service Pilots

When the United States first entered World War II, many of the country's pilots were siphoned off by the Army and Navy and assigned overseas to combat duty.

A shortage of trained pilots developed on the homefront, and yet somehow the thousands of planes being built in the nation's factories had to be flown to the military bases or posts where they were needed. The Army Air Corps recruited a small group of experienced female pilots to ferry aircraft from factories to military bases in the United States. The success of this group, named the Women's Aircraft Ferrying Squadron (WAFS), inspired the Air Corps to authorize the establishment of the Women Airforce Service Pilots (WASP) to train female pilots for assignment to air bases in the U.S. By the end of 1944 there were approximately 1,100 WASPs ferrying aircraft, testing repaired planes, and towing targets for anti-aircraft artillery students. WASP pilots were not allowed to fly outside of this country, the idea being that male pilots would be assigned the more dangerous overseas work. But homefront flying jobs could also be dangerous. When a combat pilot, for example, noticed something wrong with the way a plane was performing, it was sent back to the States for repair. A WASP would take it up to see what was wrong with it. Another job WASPs did involved training anti-aircraft gunners. They would fly a plane slowly across the horizon, towing a long cloth tail—and student anti-aircraft gunners would be told to shoot at the tail—while avoiding the plane! Unfortunately, the American public wasn't ready to accept female pilots. When plans to militarize the WASPs became public, civilian male pilots, preferring to serve in uniform on the homefront rather than overseas, convinced Congress that the WASP should be disbanded.

310. Bartels, Diane Ruth Armour. *Sharpie: The Life Story of Evelyn Sharp.* Lincoln, NE: Dageford Publishing, 1996.

   A well-written biography of WAF pilot Evelyn Sharp, a Nebraska heroine who died when the P-38 she was delivering lost power on take-off. Bartels succeeds in capturing the vibrant, caring personality of her subject.

311. Carl, Ann B. *A Wasp Among Eagles: A Woman Military Test Pilot in World War II.* Washington, D.C.: Smithsonian Institution Press, 1999.

   An excellent autobiography of one of the few women to serve as a test pilot during World War II. Carl was a WASP, and although some of her colleagues test-flew repaired aircraft, she was the only woman assigned to test-fly experimental aircraft, including jet fighters. Carl describes the difficulties experienced by some of the WASP in gaining acceptance from their male colleagues, aircraft mechanics, and even the American public, many of whom believed women had no business flying airplanes.

312. Cochran, Jackie and MaryAnn Bucknum Brinley. *Jackie Cochran: The Autobiography of the Greatest Woman Pilot in Aviation History.* New York: Bantam Books, 1987.

   Believing Jackie's own autobiography outdated (it was written in 1954 and Cochran passed away in 1980), Brinley put this "autobiography" together after Cochran's death, using Jackie's own writings as well as commentaries from her friends. The result is somewhat laudatory, considering Cochran was well known to be a difficult and controversial woman. For a balanced perspective of Cochran's contributions to aviation and the cause of female pilots in aviation and military aviation, it is best to read both autobiographies as well as the recently published biography by Rich described below.

313. Cochran, Jackie, with Floyd Odlum as Wingman. *The Stars at Noon.* New York: Little Brown and Co., 1954.

This early autobiography devotes some interesting sections to the writer's relationships with other important women of her day, including WAF leader Nancy Love and WAC Director Oveta Culp Hobby. Like many egocentric individuals, Cochran was well aware of the criticisms leveled at her, and she devotes many pages to justifying some of her more controversial actions.

314. Granger, Byrd Howell. *On Final Approach: The Women Airforce Service Pilots of World War II.* Scottsdale, AZ: Falconer Publishing Company, 1991.

A wonderful story of the WASP, chock-full of individual character portraits and reminiscences.

315. Haydu, Bernice "Bee" Falk. *Letters Home 1944–1945.* Topline Printing and Graphics, 2003.

A compilation of letters from WASP pilot Bernice Flak to her parents and siblings at home. Falk describes her training, the jobs to which she and her friends were assigned and some of the difficulties they faced proving their worth and gaining acceptance.

316. Haynsworth, Leslie and David Toomey. *Amelia Earhart's Daughters: The Wild and Glorious Story of American Women Aviators from World War II to the Dawn of the Space Age.* Harper Paperbacks, 2000.

Although the story of the WASP comprises only a portion of this excellent history, it successfully puts the WASP into historical perspective, showing readers what WASPs were allowed to accomplish for their country as well as what the nation would not allow them to do and why.

317. Hodgson, Marion Stegeman. *Winning My Wings: A Woman Airforce Service Pilot in World War II.* Annapolis, MD: Naval Institute Press, 1996.

Hodgson was one of the first women to enter the WASP training program. Here she tells the story of her WASP experiences through a series of letters she wrote to her Marine pilot boyfriend severely injured in a crash.

318. Keil, Sally Van Wagenen. *Those Wonderful Women in Their Flying Machines: The Unknown Heroines of World War II.* Rhinebeck, New York, Four Directions Press 1990.

The niece of a World War II WASP, Keil has caught the spontaneous joy these women felt about being allowed to fly for their country, as well as their heartbreak at the negative attitudes exhibited towards them by their fellow, male pilots and much of the American public, including Congress.

319. Merryman, Molly. *Clipped Wings: The Rise and Fall of the Women Airforce Service Pilots (WASPs) of World War II.* New York: New York University Press, 1998.

A scholarly look at the founding and eventual dissolution of the Women Airforce Service Pilots. Merryman uses a series of primary source documents (newspapers, government reports, Congressional testimony) to explain why public pressure forced the disestablishment of a highly useful and successful wartime organization prior to the end of that war.

320. Noggle, Anne. *For God, Country and the Thrill of It: Women Airforce Service Pilots in World War II.* College Station, TX: Texas A&M University Press, 1990.

This book tells the story of the World War II WASP through a series of outstanding photographs. The author was herself a WASP and later in life a curator of photographs, and in this book her life experiences combine to create magic.

321. Rich, Doris L. *Jackie Cochran: Pilot in the Fastest Lane.* Gainesville, FL: University Press of Florida, 2010.

A long overdue scholarly biography of the flamboyant super-pilot Jackie Cochran. Rich does an excellent job of untangling Cochran's murky early years, much of which Cochran habitually lied about. Although she may not have been a particularly likeable woman, Cochran was a skilled pilot, breaking countless aviation records (of men as well as women) for speed, altitude and distance. Ultimately, Cochran became the first woman to break the sound barrier. In one of her most controversial roles, Cochran, whose relationships with other women pilots were never easy, headed the Women Airforce Service Pilots (WASPs) during World War II.

322. Roberts, Patrick. *"And Still Flying,"... The Life and Times of Elizabeth "Betty" Wall.* Fairbault, MN: Walking Shadow Publications, 2003.

A biography that deals with a woman pilot's life prior to, during and after her World War II WASP experiences. Wall became a typical housewife after the war until she realized that her life was incomplete unless she could fly.

323. Schrader, Helena Page. *Sisters in Arms: British and American Women Pilots during World War II.* Barnsley, UK: Pen and Sword Aviation, 2006.

This book compares the formation, utilization and experiences of the U.S. and British groups of female pilots, both of which flew military aircraft for their respective countries during World War II. The author attempts to discover why the women of the British ATA were universally praised, while those of the WASP were subjected to a nasty and dangerous slander campaign.

324. Strebe, Amy Goodpaster. *Flying for Her Country: The American and Soviet Military Pilots of World War II.* Westport, CT: Praeger Security International, 2007.

The U.S. and Britain were not the only countries forced to utilize female pilots during World War II—the Soviet Union actually sent women pilots into combat. Strebe compares the U.S. WASPs to the Soviet women pilots in this excellent history.

325. Verges, Marianne. *On Silver Wings: The Women Airforce Service Pilots of World War II.* New York: Ballantine Books, 1991.

One of the earlier histories of the WASP, well written and thoughtful.

326. Williams, Vera S. *WASPs: Women Airforce Service Pilots of World War II.* Osceola, FL: Motor Books International Publishers and Wholesalers, 1994.

This book combines photographs with first-person accounts, reminiscences and quotes to provide a dramatic look at the establishment, controversies surrounding and dissolution of the WASPs.

H. Unit Histories

327. *As You Were, the 2629 WAC Battalion, Italy.* Published by the unit, 1945.

328. *History of the WAC Detachment 9th Air Base.* Harrisburg, PA: The Telegraph Press/Military Service Publishing Company, 1946,.

I. Journal Articles

329. Alsmeyer, Marie Bennett. "Those Unseen, Unheard Arkansas Women: WAC, WAVES and Women Marines of World War II." *Minerva: Quarterly Report on Women and the Military* (Summer 1994) 12: 15–33.

Unlike male veterans, women World War II veterans tended to keep quiet about their service for years, feeling that friends and family would not view their service in a positive light. Many of these women were touched by the "scandal campaign" of World War II, when Americans believed that women who joined the service were there primarily to keep servicemen's morale up.

330. Army Times Publishing. "Jacqueline Cochran, Trailblazer, Barrier Breaker." *A Century of Flight: Military Pioneers Who Made Aviation History.* Springfield, VA: Army Times, 2003.

331. Booher, Alice. "American Military Women Prisoners of War." *Minerva: Quarterly Report on Women and the Military* (Spring 1993) 11: 17–22.

332. Campbell, D'Ann. "Women, Combat and the Gender Line." *MHQ: The Quarterly Journal of Military History* (Autumn 1993) 6: 88–97.

Tells the forgotten story of a group of WAACs assigned as an experiment to an anti-aircraft battery in Washington, D.C. The experiment was an undoubted success, much to the surprise of Army leadership. After the experiment the report was buried and the women re-assigned.

333. Campbell, D'Ann. "Women in Combat: The World War II Experience in the United States, Great Britain, Germany and the Soviet Union." *The Journal of Military History* (April 1993) Vol. 57, No. 2: 301–323.

Campbell reminds readers that although the service of women in combat remains controversial, they more than demonstrated their abilities to get the job done under fire 50 years ago.

334. Campbell, D'Ann. "Women in Uniform: The World War II Experiment." *Military Affairs* (July 1987) Vol. 51, No. 3: 137–139.

Campbell discusses the myriad of jobs military women performed during World War II and why their service became so controversial.

335. Night, H. "Christmas Christmas Everywhere! How Army and Navy Nurses Spend Christmas Overseas." *The American Journal of Nursing* (December 1944) Vol. 44, No. 12: 1112–1115.

A light-hearted account of the difficult jobs faced by military nurses overseas during war time.

336. Cornelsen, Kathleen. "Women Airforce Service Pilots of World War II: Exploring Military Aviation, Encountering Discrimination, and Exchanging Traditional Roles in Service to America." *Journal of Women's History* (Winter 2005) Vol. 17, Issue 4: 111–119.

A nice summary of WASPs' backgrounds and experiences during World War II.

337. Darr, Ann. "The Long Flight Home." *U.S. News and World Report* 123 (November 17, 1997): 66–70.

The author recounts her experiences as a WASP during World War II.

338. Fine, Kathryn Berheim. "What's All the Fuss About? My WAFS/WASP Flying Experiences." *American Aviation Historical Society Journal* (Summer 1995) 40: 150–154.

339. "Hi-Ho! Hi-Ho! Back to Nurse I Go!" *The American Journal of Nursing* (Feb. 1944) Vol. 44, No. 2: 139–142.

340. Hock, Cecilia. "Creation of the WAC Image and Perception of Army Women 1942–1944." *Minerva: Quarterly Report on Women and the Military* (Spring 1995) 13: 40–62.

341. *Indians at Work: A News Sheet for Indians and the Indian Service*, U.S. Department of Interior, Office of Indian Affairs, printed between 1940 and 1945.

Vol. XI, No. 2 July/Aug 1943 p. 21 Army Nurse Lt. Ann G. Benton of Bethel Alaska. Vol. XI, No 3 Sept/Oct 1943.

Mentions Mary Jane Arbuckle, WAC, and her husband, both serving in the Army, in an article of the wartime contributions of the Chippewa of the Great Lakes Region, pages 15–18. The same issue contains a photograph and brief write-up of Minnie Spotted Wolf, the first Native American woman to enlist in the Marine Corps Woman's Reserve, pages 32 and 33.

342. Meyer, Lisa D. "Creating G.I. Jane: The Regulation of Sexuality and Sexual Behavior in the Women's Army Corps during World War II." *Feminist Studies* (Autumn 1992) Vol. 18, No. 3: 581–601.

343. Moore, Brenda. "Serving with Dual Mission: African American Women in World War II." *National Journal of Sociology* (Summer 1993) 7: 1–42.

344. "Navy Nurses on the U.S.S. Solace." *The American Journal of Nursing* (October 1941) Vol. 41, No. 10: 1173–1175.

345. "Nurse Draft Bill Passed by the House." *The American Journal of Nursing* (April 1945) Vol. 45, No. 4: 255–256.

346. Pateman, Yvonne C. "Rugged and Right: That's Teresa James." *Aviation Quarterly* (Winter 1989): 63–72.

   James was an airshow and racing pilot before serving as a ferry pilot and WASP during World War II.

347. Petry, Lucile. "U.S. Cadet Nurse Corps: Established Under the Bolton Act." *The American Journal of Nursing* (August 1943) Vol. 43, No. 8: 704–708.

   Lucile Petry was the Director of the Cadet Nurse Corps.

348. Purvis, Emily G. "Nursing Care in Air Ambulances: Navy Nurses Continue to Meet Many Unique Problems in Air Evacuation." *The American Journal of Nursing* (March 1947) Vol. 47, No. 3: 158–160.

349. Spalding, Eugenia K. "The Senior Cadet Nurse." *The American Journal of Nursing* (August 1943) Vol. 43, No. 8: 749–751.

350. Stotz, Evelyn T. "Transport Duty with the U.S. Navy." *The American Journal of Nursing* (September 1946) Vol. 46, No. 9: 610–611.

351. Tomblin, Barbara B. "Beyond Paradise: The U.S. Navy Nurse Corps in the Pacific in World War II Part I." *Minerva: Quarterly Report on Women and the Military* (Spring 1993) 11: 33–53.

352. Tomblin, Barbara B. "Beyond Paradise: The U.S. Navy Nurse Corps in the Pacific in World War II Part II." *Minerva: Quarterly Report on Women and the Military* (Fall 1993) 11: 37–56.

353. Towse, May. "Naval Hospital in San Diego." *The American Journal of Nursing* (March 1943) Vol. 43, No. 3: 268–269.

354. "WAVES, WAACs, SPARs and Nurses." *The American Journal of Nursing* (February 1943) Vol. 43, No. 2: 134–137.

J. Reports and Theses

355. Crockford, Vanessa A. *Oveta Culp Hobby and Her "Lieutenants": Transformational Leadership in Action in the Women's Army Auxiliary Corps of World War II.* Fort Leavenworth, KS: U.S. Army Command and General Staff College, 2003.

356. "Women Pilots with the AAF 1941–1944." Army Air Forces Historical Studies No. 55. AAF Historical Office, Headquarters, Army Air Forces.

VIII

The Korean War: Women Serving Under the Protection of Uncle Sam

Perhaps because the Korean War was fought in the midst of an era better known for Ozzie and Harriet-type families engaged in creating the Baby Boom, histories of military women's contributions to this war are few and far between. However, during this era the federal government took several major steps towards creating our modern-day military and defining women's place in it: the Army-Navy Nurse Act of 1947, the Women's Armed Services Integration Act of 1948, and the establishment of the Defense Advisory Committee on Women in the Service (DACOWITS) in 1951.

During the first years of World War II, Army and Navy nurses were assigned relative ranks, which did not carry the authority and pay of comparable ranks for male officers. In 1944, Army and Navy nurses were granted real commissioned rank, but on a temporary basis for the duration of the war emergency plus six months only. In 1947, with the passage of the Army-Navy Nurse Act, these inequities were finally laid to rest. The act granted military nurses the same commissioned ranks, authority, and compensation as male officers in the Army and Navy.

In 1947 Congress created a new military service, removing the Air Corps from the Army and establishing the United States Air Force. Women who had been serving in the Army Air Corps were suddenly in the Air Force. That service referred to its women as WAF, for Women in the Air Force. In 1949, the Army Nurse Corps transferred 1,200 nurses to the newly established Air Force Nurse Corps.

The World War II non-nursing women's military components had been created for the war emergency only, and the vast majority of servicewomen were demobilized after the war. The military services realized almost immediately, however, that they needed women's administrative skills to function efficiently in times of peace as well as in war, and petitioned Congress to establish permanent women's components in the Army, Navy, Marine Corps, and the newly formed Air Force. This was a fairly controversial request, and not all military men and certainly not all politicians or the public they represented agreed that non-nursing women should serve permanently in the Armed Forces. After two years of testimony and heated debate, Congress finally passed the Women's Armed Services Integration Act of 1948, which established a permanent place for non-nursing women in the regular and Reserves of the Army, Navy, Marine Corps and Air Force. Although the act was viewed as a victory for women, it set forth strict limitations on their service; women could not be commissioned as generals or admirals and could not legally serve aboard combat aircraft or military vessels engaged in a combat mission. The act also limited the number of women in each service to a maximum of 2 percent of the force, and established a set number of senior officer billets in each female component, thus severely constraining women's career ladders. Finally, the act allowed the service secretaries to terminate the commission or enlistment of any woman under circumstances proscribed by the President. In 1951, President Harry Truman used the authority granted to him by the 1948 Act and issued Executive Order 10240, which authorized the services to discharge any woman who, by marriage, birth or adoption, became the parent of a minor child.

Several years earlier, on July 26, 1948, President Truman issued Executive Order 9981, mandating an end to racial segregation and discrimination in the Armed Forces. The process of desegregating the Armed Forces could not, and did not, happen overnight, and was still ongoing during the Korean War. Male and female units in Europe, the U.S. and Japan were integrated during this period, a process described in the memoirs of Brigadier General Clara Adams Ender and Colonel Margaret Bailey, both of which are discussed in the next chapter.

When North Korea invaded South Korea in late June 1950, World War II had been over for only five years, and the American public was not enthusiastic about another war. However, a new enemy, Communism, had emerged to threaten the postwar world. Military and government leaders believed that the Communists were bent on taking over the world, one country at a time. North Korea's attack seemed to prove this theory, and in response the government reinstituted the draft and the Armed Forces began a rapid expansion of manpower.

At least 50,000 women served in the Armed Forces during the Korean War, the vast majority of them assigned far from the battle theater. Although most worked in clerical and communication billets in the United States, WACs and WAF (Air Force women) and small numbers of Navy women and Women Marines served as part of the relatively large U.S. military presence in Europe, where U.S. politicians and military leaders feared that the Soviet Union would attempt to take advantage of the situation in Korea and push into western Europe.

WACs and WAF were also sent to Japan to support the Army and Air Force in the Far East. Most were stationed in Tokyo or Yokohama, where they performed important combat support jobs working as photograph and intelligence analysts, medical technicians, mail processors, telegraph and telephone operators, and typists and file clerks.

Meanwhile, military commanders in the Korean Theater proceeded as if they had very little memory or knowledge of the numerous instances of courage exhibited by servicewomen under fire during the previous war. Although the Army sent medical units, including nurses, into the battle theater within days after the start of the Korean War, field commanders attempted to keep the women as safe as possible. For example, Army nurses assigned to the 8063rd Mobile Army Surgical Hospital (MASH) often did not accompany their hospital when it traveled to a new site. They were held back until the hospital was safely established and then allowed to go forward. War, however, is unpredictable, and the nurses frequently found themselves under fire or close to the front lines when enemy forces appeared unexpectedly or when U.N. forces lost ground during a campaign.

Although the movie and television show *M*A*S*H* introduced the public to the Mobile Army Surgical Hospital in a light-hearted way, few military nurses have felt inclined to publish memoirs of that period of their lives, even those who disagree with the show's characterization of their service. Army nurses in Korea dealt with extremely difficult battlefield conditions similar to those encountered by forward units in every war; a scarcity of clean water and operating equipment, freezing weather, mud, vermin, and overcrowded hospitals. At least one nurse, former ANC Director Brigadier General Anna Mae Hays, has stated that her duty in Korea was much harder and more uncomfortable than her experiences in the China–Burma–India Theater during World War II.

Air Force nurses stationed in Japan crewed aboard medical evacuation flights between Japan and Korea, often landing near the front lines to pick up patients. When the Chinese Communists conducted a surprise attack against U.N. forces in late 1950 and forced them to retreat southwards down the peninsula, hospitals had to pack up and move with the troops. Thousands of patients had to be air evacuated immediately. In several cases, patients were evacuated minutes before enemy troops seized airfields.

Sixteen military nurses died en route to the Korean Theater during the war. The first casualty was Major Genevieve Smith, who died early in July 1950 when the C-47 transporting her from Japan to Korea for her new assignment as Chief of all Army Nurses in Korea crashed into the sea. On August 5, a Navy nurse died when the hospital ship USS *Benevolence*, which had been assigned to the Korean Theater, sank off the coast of California. In mid-September 1950, 11 Navy nurses en route to Yokosuka Navy Hospital in Japan died when their plane crashed on take-off after refueling on Kwajelein Island. Three Air Force nurses perished when the medical evacuation aircraft on which they were working crashed.

Because individual memoirs remain scanty for this period, researchers rely on some very good official and general histories that cover all uniformed women during the Korean War: Major General Jeanne Holm's *Women in the Military: An Unfinished Revolution*; Colonel Bettie Morden's *The Women's Army Corps: 1945–1978*; Jean Ebbert and Mary Beth Hall's *Crossed Currents: Navy Women in a Century of Change*; Susan Godson's *Serving Proudly: A History of Women in the U.S. Navy*; Mary Sarnecky's *The Army Nurse Corps*; and Doris Sterner's *In and Out of Harm's Way: A History of the Navy Nurse Corps*. For complete citations, please see the section under "General Histories."

A. Books

357. Grymwade, Billye. *MATs and Me: WAVES Flight Attendants on Military Aircraft*. Ventura, CA: Puma Press, 2003.

    Grymwade's memoir brings to light a long forgotten group of Navy WAVES who served aboard military aircraft during and after World War II.

358. Horwitz, Dorothy. *We Will Not Be Strangers: Korean War Letters between a MASH Surgeon and His Wife.* University of Illinois Press, 1997.

These wonderfully readable letters of a truly likeable young couple reveal that in 1952, during a lull in the fighting, the Surgeon General's Office decided to try an experiment—a nurse-less MASH. It activated the 8225th MASH and filled it with physicians and medical technicians, who would take the place of nurses. One of these physicians was Mel Horwitz, who explained to his wife that the 8225th would operate far forward of other Army hospitals—close to the front lines. Immediately, however, the hospital began experiencing problems. The doctors complained that the corpsmen consistently made life-threatening mistakes with the patients. It wasn't their fault, really, admitted the doctors—it was impossible to train an individual in two months to take the place of a nurse with three years or more of training and experience. Within months, the Army quietly ended the experiment and brought nurses into the 8225th MASH.

359. Hunter, Gladys Holladay. *Assignment Tokyo.* San Francisco, CA: Nettleton Books, 1980.

Hunter was WAC Master Sergeant who had been stationed in the United States during World War II. When offered an overseas assignment in occupied Japan, she leaped on the opportunity. Her memoir offers a realistic portrait of WAC assignments (mostly clerical) during that time period.

360. Nathan, Amy. *Take a Seat, Make a Stand: A Hero in the Family.* iUniverse Inc., 2006.

Nathan recounts a long forgotten story of a 1950s WAC, Sarah Louise Keys, who refused to move to the back of bus and was arrested. The Keys family hired Washington lawyer Dovey Roundtree, a former WAC, to represent their daughter. The case eventually moved up to the Interstate Commerce Commission and was decided in Key's favor. For another perspective of the Key's case, refer to Dovey Roundtree's memoir in the Women's Army Corps section of the World War II chapter.

361. Nicely, Marian. *The Ladies of First Army.* Ligonier, PA: A Fairfield Street Press Book, 1989.

Nicely combines her own experiences as a member of the Women's Army Corps in the 1950s with an informal history of the WAAC and WAC. Her memoir captures the attitudes and atmosphere of service during the 1950s.

362. Omori, Frances. *Quiet Heroes: Navy Nurses in the Korean War 1950–1953.* Smith House Press, 2001.

Navy officer Frances Omori conducted a series of oral history interviews with women who had served as Navy nurses during the Korean War. The resulting book is filled with compelling, poignant, and inspiring stories. The book fills a large gap in Navy Nurse Corps history. The Navy sent three hospital ships, the *Consolation, Repose,* and *Haven* to Korea. Approximately 30 nurses served aboard each ship during each deployment (each ship returned to the States twice during the war). Although the

Navy nurses' working conditions were far better than those of the Army nurses on shore, shipboard life had its own unique difficulties. The ships were air conditioned, but living and working spaces were confining, and during emergencies, the ships were compelled to take aboard more patients than they had been designed to accommodate. Storms at sea made patient care difficult, and sometimes the vessels rocked so much that no one aboard got any rest. The nurses also dealt with diseases they had never seen before such as smallpox and dengue fever. One of the most emotional sections of the book describes taking aboard Marines who had been trapped at Chosin Reservoir.

363. Soderbergh, Peter. *Women Marines in the Korean War Era.* Westport, CT: Prager, 1994.

Soderbergh should be commended for writing about this "lost generation" of Women Marines. He does an excellent job of recalling the atmosphere of the 1950s and of exploring women's motivations to take the unusual step of joining the Marines. His book is filled with personal accounts and quotes, and is a fun and fascinating read.

364. Witt, Linda et al. *A Defense Weapon Known to be of Value: Servicewomen during the Korean War.* London, NH: University Press of New England, 2005.

This book looks at servicewomen's contributions to the Korean War, examining through oral histories, first-person accounts and official records the experiences of uniformed women in Korea, Europe and the American home front. It then puts these experiences in the context of women's place in American society in the 1950s.

B. Journal Articles

365. Bellafaire, Judith. "Public Service Role Models: The First Women of the Defense Advisory Committee on Women in the Services." *Armed Forces and Society* (April 2006) 424–436.

To help with recruiting women during the Korean War, the Department of Defense created a special commission called the Defense Advisory Committee on Women in the Services (DACOWITS.) This article takes an in-depth look at the cultural reasons behind the creation of DACOWITS, and how society's values shaped the very composition of the committee.

366. Marger, Anne. "Indiana Nurse in Korea." *The American Journal of Nursing* (September 1959) Vol. 59, No. 9: 1194–1198.

367. Roberts, Mary. "The Nurse on the Docks." *The American Journal of Nursing* (July 1954) Vol. 54, No. 7: 854–857.

368. Sherman, Janann. "They Either Need These Women or They do Not: Margaret Chase Smith and the Fight For Regular Status for Women in the Military." *The Journal of Military History* (Jan 1990) Vol. 54, No. 1: 47–78.

The author details the story of the two-year struggle to get the U.S. Congress to pass legislation allowing women to serve in the Regular and Reserve components of the U.S. Armed Forces on a permanent basis.

369. Strickland, Benjamin A. Jr. "The Flight Nurse." *The American Journal of Nursing* (July 1951) Vol. 51, No. 7: 449–450.

Strickland details the exciting experiences of military nurses serving aboard air evacuation flights.

IX

The Vietnam War: The Nurse Heroine and Her Forgotten Sister

The majority of women to serve in-country during the war in Vietnam were military nurses. Navy nurses arrived at the naval hospital in Saigon in 1963, and Army nurses began arriving when the troop levels began increasing in 1965. The approximately 5,000 Army nurses who served in Vietnam during the war had experiences that were dependent on where in the country they served and when they were there. For example, the nurses that were assigned to hospitals in Vietnam relatively early in the war (1965–1966) dealt with supply shortages that made their jobs extremely difficult. Army nurse Sharon Forman Bystran was mobilized with the 85th Evacuation Hospital in July 1965, just as the U.S. was building up its military force in Vietnam. The 85th was located in Qui Nhon, and Bystran's memoir states, "Those early days of establishing a hospital from storage boxes to a functional level were both frustrating and rewarding. In the early months of our arrival, extreme supply and equipment shortages taxed our ability to improvise and still meet the medical/surgical needs of casualties." Another nurse who may have been at Qui Nhon at the same time, Lt. Judy Dennis, remembered receiving hundreds of casualties with limited supplies. "I recall hanging the last bottle of D5W and running out of IV penicillin. We were originally in tents in a valley but due to enemy fire had to move fully operational into the city of Qui Nhon."

Nurses who served during the Tet Offensive of January 1968 worked under frequent enemy fire. Nurse Kathleen Cordova, assigned to the 24th Evacuation Hospital, remembers "shells dropping very very close . . . never knowing when one would fall near you . . . you suppressed the fear and went on with your job . . ." Memoirs of the three above-mentioned nurses are available at the Women's Memorial in Arlington, Virginia.

Air Force nurses arrived in Vietnam in February 1966 when 13 nurses were assigned to the first Air Force hospital in Vietnam, the 12th USAF Hospital at Cam Ranf Bay. At that time nurses were required to wear white uniforms on duty. In September 1967 female flight nurses received aerovac assignments in Vietnam. The Air Force assigned women nurses to Vietnam on a volunteer basis—not so male nurses. But by 1972, the Air Force sent both men and women nurses to Vietnam regardless of whether or not they had volunteered.

Members of the Women's Army Corps (WACs), Air Force women (WAF) and a tiny number of Women Marines also served in Vietnam. The WACs arrived in Vietnam between 1966 and 1967 to work at headquarters in Saigon, Ton San Nhut Air Base, and Long Binh, about 27 miles northeast of Saigon. WAC Director Brigadier General Elizabeth Hoisington insisted that the women in Vietnam appear to be professional at all times, and forbid WACs to wear fatigues, a dictum that irritated the women, who felt that as long they continued to have to "hit the floor or crawl under desks" during episodes of incoming artillery barrages, skirts and hose were impractical. In the end, most elected to wear the fatigues, which the USARV commander authorized for women. They tried to avoid appearing in press photographs dressed in fatigues, however, because the WAC Director disliked seeing her women in them.

Although servicewomen were frequently exposed to enemy fire while in Vietnam, only one military woman, Army nurse Lt. Sharon Lane, was killed in action. Six other Army nurses and one Air Force nurse died in the line of duty in Vietnam.

Most women who served during the Vietnam War were assigned home front billets, however frequently this entailed a different kind of stress. As the war became increasingly unpopular, men and women who wore military uniforms found themselves the recipients of disgusted looks and nasty comments. Remembered Navy hospital corpsman Diane Jacobson, assigned to the Naval Hospital in Oakland, California, "During the day you dealt with wounded soldiers recovering from lost limbs. Once you were off duty and outside the post, you had to deal with the anti-war protesters. Traveling in uniform put you in harm's way, so uniforms were not authorized." Jacobson's memoir is available at the Women's Memorial in Arlington, Virginia.

In 1967 Congress lifted the prohibition against promoting women to general officer rank, and in 1970 the Army promoted the Director of the Army Nurse Corps, Anna Mae Hays, and the Director of the WAC, Elizabeth Hoisington, to brigadier general. One year later the Air Force followed suit, promoting WAF Director Jeanne Holm to brigadier general. Several months later it promoted the Chief of the Air Force Nurse Corps to brigadier general. The 1967 Act also removed the 2 percent cap on the number of women who could serve in the Armed Forces.

The 1967 legislation was a signal that the military was beginning to realize servicewomen's value to the force. Vietnam was an unpopular war, the draft was hated by millions of young men and their families, and women volunteers were seen as essential to the proper functioning of the Armed Forces. In 1973, the war in Vietnam drew to a close, and the All Volunteer Force concept was approved. The AVF became a pivotal event for military women, as the services somewhat hesitantly began to accept larger numbers of women into the ranks and to find more military jobs to which they could be assigned. The following chapter discusses what serving in the U.S. Armed Forces during the 1970s and 1980s was like for military women, and the vast changes in military assignments and policies that took place during that era.

A. Books

370. Adams-Ender, Clara, with Blair S. Walker. *My Rise to the Stars: How a Sharecropper's Daughter Became an Army General.* Lakeridge, VA: Cape Associates, 2001.

An extremely forthright memoir that describes Adams-Ender's early childhood, and her Nurse Corps career. Adams-Ender bluntly discusses the attitudes she dealt with as an African American woman and emphasizes her tactics for overcoming them.

371. Bailey, Margaret E. *The Challenge: Autobiography of Colonel Margaret E. Bailey.* Lisle, IL: Tucker Publications Inc. 1999.

Bailey was the first black nurse promoted to colonel in the Army Nurse Corps. Her memoir recounts her nurse training and career and includes unflinching descriptions of the racism she endured and her methods of dealing with it.

372. Bigler, Philip. *Hostile Fire: The Life and Death of 1st Lieutenant Sharon Lane.* Arlington, VA: Vandamere Press, 1996.

An excellent, poignant, if necessarily short, biography of the life of Army Nurse 1st Lieutenant Sharon Lane, the only U.S. servicewoman to die from hostile fire during the war.

373. Burton, Cora, Lt. Col. U.S. Army and Norman Singer. *If I Don't Laugh, I'll Cry Forever.* Central Plains Book Manufacturing, 2005.

Minority women have begun to speak out about their service during this period, and this book is a good example of the genre. Burton served as an Army nurse in Vietnam between 1969 and 1970. Her memoir is her way of dealing with the twin traumas of the young men she tried to help and the blatant racism she experienced from a supervisor.

374. Gurney, Cynthia. *33 Years of Army Nursing: An Interview with Brigadier General Lillian Dunlap.* Washington, D.C.: U.S. Army Nurse Corps, 2001.

In a series of oral history interviews Dunlap discusses her career as an Army nurse, from World War II through the 1970s. Hers was very much an official outlook; the viewpoint of a chief nurse and headquarters staff nurse as opposed to that of the young lieutenants and captains who served in Vietnam.

375. Hovis, Bobbi, LCRD NC USN. *Station Hospital Saigon: A Navy Nurse in Vietnam 1963–1964.* Annapolis, MD: Naval Institute Press, 1991.

Navy nurse Bobbi Hovis wrote a stirring memoir of the very first months of the war, *Station Hospital Saigon*. Other than these excellent works, historians must rely on official histories and oral histories to gain insight into women's experiences in Vietnam.

376. Norman, Elizabeth. *Women at War: The Story of Fifty Military Nurses Who Served in Vietnam.* University of Pennsylvania Press, 1990.

Elizabeth Norman collected and published 50 oral histories of military nurses who served in Vietnam, and this work remains one of the most informative of the period. Norman talked with Army, Navy and Air Force nurses who served in a variety of locations, including those who served as flight nurses.

377. Powell, Mary Reynolds. *A World of Hurt: Innocence and Arrogance in Vietnam.* Greenleaf Book Group, 2000.

   An Army nurse's memoir of her year in Vietnam 1970–1971.

378. Smith, Winnie. *American Daughter Gone to War: On the Front Lines with an Army Nurse in Vietnam.* New York: William Morrow and Co. Inc., 1992.

   A wrenching description of Smith's assignments in Vietnam as an Army nurse.

379. Sohm, Judith. *Number Ten: A Vietnam Diary.* New York: Vantage Press, 1992.

   Sohm was an Air Force nurse assigned to the hospital at Saigon Airport.

380. Van Devanter, Linda. *Home before Morning: The Story of an Army Nurse in Vietnam.* University of Massachusetts Press, 1991.

   Probably the most famous Vietnam memoir ever written, this incredible, searingly emotional story grabs the reader from the beginning and never lets go. Van Devanter treated soldiers fresh from combat at the 71st Evacuation Hospital near the Cambodian border; but she and her colleagues also treated the civilian casualties of war, Vietnamese children and families.

381. Walker, Keith. *A Piece of My Heart: The Stories of 26 American Women Who Served in Vietnam.* CA: Presidio Press, 1997.

   Walker conducted a series of oral histories with nurses, Red Cross workers, WACs and WAF, and more, all of whose Vietnam experiences marked them for life.

B. Journal Articles

382. Judson, Leona. "Nurse Questions Vietnam War." *The American Journal of Nursing* (May 1966) Vol. 66, No. 5: 1002.

383. Morin, Aline E. "Navy Hospital in Saigon." *The American Journal of Nursing* (September 1966) Vol. 66, No. 9: 1977–1979.

384. Salter, Mary Jo. "Annie, Don't Get Your Gun." *The Atlantic* (June 1980).

   Discusses the issue of women and the draft. Although the All Volunteer Force was less than a decade old, commentators, surprised at the large increase in the numbers of women in the service, began to ask what would happen if the country went to war. Would the services see a decline in the number of volunteers and be forced to return to the draft, and if so, should women be drafted and forced to fight? Another way of asking whether the services should be accepting so many women, since women could not, according to regulation, be assigned to combat billets.

385. Vuic, Kara Dixon. "Officer, Nurse, Woman: Army Nurse Corps Recruitment for the Vietnam War." *Nursing History Review* (2006) Vol. 14.

This article examines the images used by the Army Nurse Corps in its attempt to recruit nurses during a time when an overall nursing shortage plagued the United States.

386. "Women in the Armed Forces." *Newsweek* (February 18, 1980).

    Discusses controversial topics such as women and the draft, women and pregnancy, and women in combat.

C. Official Histories

387. Semi-Annual Histories of the Office of the Surgeon General, Air Force Headquarters, Washington D.C., 1969–1983.

    These reports, compiled twice a year, include submissions from the Chief of the Air Force Nurse Corps.

D. Unpublished Oral Histories and Memoirs

388. Dulinsky, Barbara Jean, Sergeant, USMCWR. Historian's Files, Women in Military Service for America Memorial Foundation Offices, Arlington, Virginia.

    This wonderful account written by one of the few female Marines to serve in Vietnam during the war demonstrates how close the Marine Headquarters was to the action. Dulinsky, who served as a Top Secret Control Officer of Classified Documents at the Military Assistance Command in Vietnam (MACV) Headquarters during the Tet Offensive of 1968, wrote of an "overwhelming light preceded by a horrible screaming noise ended with a devastating explosion." She added "the fear I felt upon this rude awakening I can't put into words. The few seconds I had before the next round landed was spent controlling the panic inside of me. The next round provided the light I needed to stumble towards the inner courtyard windows. A male colleague helped me climb over the window ledge and carrying our boots and weapons, we raced towards our assigned bunker. Another rocket came sailing overhead, and that caused us to bury ourselves in the ground. It took a couple of seconds to see again, then we took off and made it to the bunker. Everyone sat in silence, thinking their own private thoughts. There was no John Wayne movie bravado in the bunker that night."

389. Garrecht, Claire M. December 8, 1982, K239.0512–1710 C.1 and K239.0512–1723 C.2, U.S. Air Force Historical Research Center, Office of Air Force History, Headquarters, U.S.A.F.

    Garrecht describes her career as an Air Force nurse.

390. Hoefly, Ethel A. Brigadier General, U.S. Air Force Nurse Corps, May 13, 1983, K239.0512–1723 C.1, U.S. Air Force Historical Research Center, Office of Air Force History, Headquarters, U.S.A.F.

    Hoefly, who served as a director of the Air Force Nurse Corps, discusses her Air Force career.

E. Unpublished Thesis

391. Rank, Melissa A. Col. USAF. "What Influenced the Development of the Air Force Nurse Corps from 1969–1983?" Air War College, Air University.

    Very little has been published on the history of the Air Force Nurse Corps. Rank's thesis does an excellent job of partially filling this gap for the pivotal period of the 1970s, which included not only the war in Vietnam but the burgeoning women's movement and the establishment of the All Volunteer Force. The thesis contains an excellent bibliography.

X

The All Volunteer Force Through the 1980s: How Many Women Is Too Many Women?

In 1973, the unpopular Vietnam-era draft was abolished and the All Volunteer Force established. The AVF lifted the 2 percent ceiling on the number of servicewomen in the U.S. Armed Forces, which had been imposed in 1948. Rather than accepting all of the physically and mentally qualified males provided by the draft, the armed services selected the most qualified of the volunteers, and in the process found themselves accepting increasing numbers of women and assigning women to a wider variety of military jobs. Before the decade ended, the military services decided that they needed to figure out how many military positions women could fill without weakening deployment and combat capabilities. The 1948 Act, much of which was still in effect, forbid women from serving aboard Navy vessels other than hospital ships and transports, and aircraft engaged in combat missions. These prohibitions left the services significant flexibility, and some important questions, pertaining to the assignment of women. Should women be trained to fly noncombat aircraft, for example? How should the Army assign women to ensure that they would not be exposed to combat, and thus remain within the intent of the bill? The services wrestled with these questions for years, during which time the number of women in the service continued to grow.

By the end of the decade, with the numbers of women volunteers on the rise, service leaders became increasingly uneasy and began to look for reasons to limit the number of women in the Armed Forces. The Navy and Marine Corps insisted that in order to be able to rotate sailors and Marines from shipboard to shore assignments, at least 55–75 percent of enlisted positions had to be filled by males, because legislation prohibited women serving aboard most vessels. The Air Force claimed that because so many bases lacked facilities (restrooms and barracks) for women, the number of positions women could fill was limited. The Army conducted a series of tests and studies that indicated the presence of women in the ranks did not adversely impact readiness and efficiency. The test results surprised the Army, which had been searching for a reason to limit the number of women it was accepting. When the Secretary of Defense saw the test results, he ordered the chagrined Army to double its number of enlisted women by 1983.

With the integration of women into more career fields and units and the dismantling of women's separate career ladders, it became obvious to many in the military that there was no longer any reason to have a separate chain of command for women that administered (trained, assigned, disciplined and promoted) women separately from men—the need for separate women's service components and directors was over. The first service to completely disestablish its women's component was the Navy, a process it began in 1972. The Air Force disestablished the WAF Director's Office in July 1976. The next office to fall was that of the Director of Women Marines, formally abolished in 1977. The Women's Army Corps, unlike the women's networks in the other services, was a bona fide corps in the Army, just like the Quartermaster Corps, Signal Corps, or Medical Corps. As such, it could not be reorganized or phased out but needed to be disestablished by legislation. This did not happen until October 1978.

Two years earlier Congress forced the service academies to accept women. The academies are located at West Point, New York (Army); Annapolis, Maryland (Navy); Colorado Springs, Colorado (Air Force); and Groton, Connecticut (Coast Guard). Although the academies were unhappy with the law, they complied with it. The first year they admitted limited numbers of women, but succeeding years slowly saw greater percentages of women in each class.

The leadership at the academies as well as the alumni and the cadets themselves were concerned that the presence of women cadets would change or dilute the academy experience, where young cadets were hardened into military officers. Superintendent Sidney Berry at West Point publicly opposed women's admission, threatened to resign if they came, and did not resign when they did. His attitude did nothing to help the first 119 women cadets of the class of 1980. They were dispersed throughout the class and treated the same as the male cadets whenever possible. The women cadets themselves tried to be invisible. They wanted to be "cadets" rather than "women cadets." They believed that gathering together would make them stand out, so they avoided doing anything in groups. The cadet officers (upperclassmen) did not allow the women cadets to wear skirts or make-up, although regulations permitted it. By the end of the year, 27 percent of the original 119 freshmen women had resigned, along with 22 percent of the male freshmen. Integration was a long, slow process that was tough on the women involved. Although the first female cadets had no real role models to guide them in the quest to become Army officers, within 15 years the Army was regularly appointing female officers as faculty and company officers, thus exposing young cadets to female authority figures. Even after 15 years of integration, however, more than 70 percent of female cadets stated in a variety of surveys that they were regularly harassed at West Point, the worst record of any of the academies.

At the Naval Academy, 81 women joined 1,212 men to form the class of 1980. Over the following four years, 26 of the women (32 percent) dropped out, as compared with the male rate of 27 percent. Just as at West Point, the avid press attention added to the women cadets' stress and exacerbated the annoyance of their male peers. They also discovered that because Naval Academy rules only limited how much plebes (freshmen) could be harassed, once they got through their first year, there were no limits on the extent of the harassment they could expect. The women were constantly insulted and some were molested. One reason why harassment often peaked during an individual's last two years at the academy is that this was when it became apparent that women would stay in and become officers. Although the worst harassment was not officially condoned, midshipmen who complained or reported abuse were punished for having "ratted" on their peers. Thus many women midshipmen whose harassment levels were officially unacceptable did not report it and attempted to tough it out.

The Air Force Academy leadership approached gender integration somewhat differently than the Army and Navy academies. They selected 157 women for the class of 1980, and deliberately clustered the women together and required them to wear skirts most of the time. The Academy appointed 15 women lieutenants who had received an abbreviated version of academy training to the staff to mentor the incoming female students. The first year, the female attrition rate at the Air Force Academy was the lowest of all the services, even lower than that of the first-year male students. However, the academy was not able to sustain its positive start. Twenty-five years after the entrance of the first women to the academy, several women cadets came forward and accused male cadets of raping them. The subsequent investigation revealed that physical attacks and abuse had been ongoing at the academy for years, but official "blame the victim" type policies and a fear of ostracism for breaking the honor code combined had kept the majority of the victims quiet. The Air Force appointed new leadership to the academy and finally removed the well-known sign at the entryway to academy grounds that proclaimed, "Give Me Men."

At the Coast Guard Academy, more than 10 percent of the first-year students were women and by the end of the fall semester at the academy, a woman was first in academic standing. The school, however, had gender-based problems that were difficult to pinpoint but easier to quantify. The difference between men's and women's attrition rates has remained statistically higher here than at any other military academy; something makes life much tougher for women than for men at the Coast Guard Academy. The academy leadership is now attempting to trace the reasons for this differential so that they can take steps to counteract it.

Other than the admission of women to the service academies, perhaps no other military integration issue caused as much interest in the press and public as the assignment of women as military pilots. The Navy was the first service to accept women into its pilot training program in 1973, and six women graduated from the program in 1974 and became naval aviators. In 1983, female Navy aviators flew supplies to the besieged Marines in Beirut, and, in 1986, Air Force women served as pilots, copilots and boom operators on the KC-135 and KC-10 tankers that refueled FB-111s during the raid on Libya. By 1990, the Navy had 173 women pilots and 80 women NFOs on active duty.

The Army began training women as helicopter pilots in 1974. By 1978, 16 female officers and 25 warrant officers had entered flight training; all but six eventually got their wings. These women understood that, although their positions were officially designated as "combat support," their duties could easily take them into a combat situation. For example, they could be ordered to fly supplies to combat troops or carry troops into combat. Although by law they could not fly combat aircraft (aircraft that actually engaged an enemy in combat), they could still be exposed to enemy fire in the course of performing their duties.

The third service to train women as pilots was the Coast Guard, which began assigning women to flight training in 1975. The Air Force began training women as both pilots and navigators in 1976. The Air Force initially called the training a "test" to see if women were physically and mentally capable of piloting military aircraft. The female trainees proved beyond doubt that women were fully capable, and the Air Force began training women pilots for assignment to noncombat missions such as tanker refueling, weather reconnaissance, and aero medical airlift.

As military women took to the skies for the first time since World War II, the Navy decided to experiment with sending women to sea. In October 1972, the hospital ship *Sanctuary* sailed with a mixed gender crew aboard. Although the experiment was officially a success, proving that "women can perform every shipboard task with equal ease, expertise and dedication as men do," the Navy did not appear to be anxious to integrate any more of its vessels. It would ultimately take a court case to prod the Navy into action (see below). The Coast Guard assigned women to sea duty as crew members aboard the *Morganthau* and the *Gallatin* in 1977. When the crews of both ships performed well and no problems arose, the Coast Guard lifted all restrictions on sea duty assignments for women the following year. In 1979, the Coast Guard made history by placing a woman in command of the cutter *Cape Newagen*.

Although the Army, like the Coast Guard, was not constrained in its combat assignments by the 1948 Integration Act, the Army historically has had the most difficulty with the combat issue. After the disestablishment of the Women's Army Corps, the Army developed its own combat exclusion policy, implemented through the Direct Combat Probability Code (DCPC). The coding system evaluated every position in the Army based on its duties and the unit's mission, tactical doctrine and position on the battlefield. The codes ranged from P1 to P7, with lower P ratings indicating a higher probability of routine engagement in direct combat. Women were prohibited from holding P1 positions.

Operation Urgent Fury, the invasion of Grenada in 1983, was the first test of the Army's combat exclusion policy. Approximately 170 female soldiers deployed during the Operation, most of them members of Army units out of Fort Bragg, North Carolina. Female military police rode armed patrols, stood guard at checkpoints and perimeters, and guarded POW and detainee camps. Other female soldiers worked as members of maintenance and intelligence units or served as interrogators, signal and communications specialists, truck drivers and medical personnel. Twenty-six women were stevedores with a transportation company out of Fort Eustis, who worked loading captured weapons and ammunition onto ships and aircraft. One ordnance captain was responsible for detonating unexploded ammunition. Initially some military policewomen were sent back to Fort Bragg by the commander on the ground in Grenada because of the high risk of exposure to combat. The commanding general of the 82nd Airborne overrode the action and the women were returned to Grenada. The women of other services also participated in the operation. Coast Guard women crewed aboard vessels sent to patrol the waters around the island. An Air Force woman pilot delivered troops to the island, and women were flight engineers and loadmasters on other aircraft involved in the operation.

In 1988, the Department of Defense (DOD) created the Risk Rule, which set a single evaluative standard for all the services to use when classifying specialties and units as male only. Women would be excluded from certain noncombat units and areas on the battlefield if the risks of exposure to direct combat, hostile fire or capture were equal to or greater than the risk experienced by associated combat units in the same theater of operations.

The Risk Rule and its application by DCPC was tested almost immediately when the U.S. invaded Panama during Operation Just Cause in 1989. Approximately

The All Volunteer Force through the 1980s 95

800 servicewomen were involved in the operation. They were either already stationed in Panama or deployed from Fort Ord, California, or Fort Bragg, North Carolina. They made up 4 percent of the 18,400-man invasion force. Army women were MPs, truck drivers, helicopter pilots, or assigned to intelligence or signal corps units. Female helicopter pilots ferried combat soldiers under fire into Panama, and one received the Air Medal. Female truck drivers delivered infantry troops into the downtown area around heavily defended Panamanian Defense Forces Headquarters. A supply officer transported 150 gallons of fuel through the streets of Panama City. Air Force women served as pilots, navigators, flight engineers and loadmasters or were involved in logistics, maintenance and administrative support.

Army Captain Linda Bray, the commander of the 988th MP Company, became the best-known military woman of the invasion. One of the 988th's missions was to seize a Panamanian Defense Force K-9 Corps stronghold, and Bray took part in a firefight, firing at least one shot at enemy attackers. But the Army, the Pentagon and Congress did not want to admit that Bray and the women under her had participated in combat, because that would mean that the Army's assignment policies had failed to protect women from combat. But when newspaper reporters in Panama heard Bray's story and published it, the general public could not understand why the Army claimed Bray had not been in combat. The Army, concerned that its carefully drawn combat exclusion policies would be called into question, tried to prove that the "combat" involved did not occur at the time Bray was there. Congresswoman Patricia Schroeder brought the Army's fears home to roost when she demanded that Congress take a careful look at the Pentagon's combat exclusion policies. She even suggested that the Army open up a combat unit to women for a four-year "trial period." Few other lawmakers were ready to take her suggestion seriously, however, and the controversy eventually died down.

A. Books

392. Anderson, Ruth, Colonel, USAF and "Andy" Anderson, Lt. Col., USAF. *Barbed Wire for Sale: The Hungarian Transition to Democracy 1988–1991.* Graham, WA: Poetic License, 1999.

    Anderson was the first Air Force woman to serve as a Defense Attaché. Although Anderson specifically asked to be assigned to a Warsaw Pact nation, neither she nor the Air Force had any idea that the Hungarian government would break away from the Soviet Union during her tenure. Her perceptive, knowledgeable reports to the Defense Intelligence Agency proved that women could perform attaché duties during times of uncertainty and rapid change.

393. Barkalow, Carol, Capt., U.S. Army with Andrea Raab. *In the Men's House.* New York: Random House, 1992.

    Barkalow was a member of the first West Point class open to women, entering the Academy in 1976 and graduating in 1980. This memoir covers her four years at the Academy, her first assignment as a 2nd Lieutenant to a nuclear missile site in West Germany and her second assignment to a truck company at Fort Lee, Virginia.

394. Binkin, Martin and Shirley J. Bach. *Women and the Military*. Washington, D.C.: The Brookings Institution, 1977.

The authors believed that the services should deliberately seek to increase the numbers of women in the ranks in order to maintain the quality of the force.

395. Cammermeyer, Margarethe with Chris Fisher. *Serving in Silence*. New York: Viking, 1994.

Army National Guard Nurse Colonel Cammermeyer, who had served in Vietnam, was discharged from the Guard in 1989 after she admitted to being a lesbian. Her autobiography describes her military career and her decision to speak out. Cammermeyer began her career in the regular Army, but was forced to leave the service when she had children. She then joined the National Guard. When she was undergoing a review for a Top Secret Clearance (preparatory for nomination to Brigadier General) Cammermeyer admitted to being gay. The National Guard promptly discharged her.

396. Chapman, Anne W. *Mixed-Gender Basic Training: The U.S. Army Experience 1973–2004*. Washington, D.C.: Government Printing Office, 2008.

The establishment of the All Volunteer Force and the end of conscription necessitated the intensified recruitment of women to maintain the desired numbers of personnel on active duty. The Army eliminated the Women's Army Corps in 1978, and began to struggle with the concept of integrated training. Should men and women be trained together and if so at what point should integrated training occur—during basic training or as soldiers trained for specialties? This book charts the Army's efforts to establish a training program that met the goal of military readiness while at the same time provided male and female soldiers with equal treatment and equal opportunity.

397. Disher, Sharon Hanley. *First Class: Women Join the Ranks at the Naval Academy*. Annapolis, MD: Naval Institute Press, 1998.

Disher was one of the 81 women in the first class at the U.S. Naval Academy to admit women. Her book tells the story of two fictional women as they navigate the ignorance of instructors and officials and malice of many of their classmates during their four years at the academy. Although the characters' names are fictional, many of the events recounted are true.

398. Enloe, Cynthia. *Does Khaki Become You? The Militarization of Women's Lives*. Boston: South End Press, 1983.

Enloe sees the military as a patriarchal institution, and believes that the reason why the military attempts to control women's sexuality and the ramifications of this sexuality on men is to maximize military efficiency.

399. Holden, Henry M. *Ladybirds II: The Continuing Story of American Women in Aviation*. Mt. Freedom, NJ: Black Hawk Publishing Co., 1993.

In a sequel to his book *Ladybirds*, which discussed early women aviators, Holden takes his story of women in aviation through World War II and beyond, discussing the WASPs and their successors in military aviation.

400. Janda, Robert Lance. *Stronger Than Custom: West Point and the Admission of Women*. Praeger, 2001.

Janda's work is without doubt the best comprehensive scholarly study of U.S. Military Academy women. He conducted interviews with women members of the first class, male members and faculty, and quotes generously from them, but without identifying them, which allows them the freedom to state what they really think. Janda's recounting of this emotional story is calm and impartial, allowing the reader to draw their own conclusions from the substantive evidence presented.

401. Mitchell, Brian. *Weak Link: The Feminization of the American Military*. Washington, D.C.: Regnery Gateway, 1989.

Mitchell believes that the presence of women in mixed-gender units destroys unit cohesion, encourages fraternization and inhibits command authority. He also insists that women soldiers water down readiness and the overall strength and fitness of the unit to function in the field in combat. These opinions, however, are not backed up with documentary proof. This is not a scholarly study but rather an opinion piece.

402. Pateman, Yvonne, C. Lt. Col. USAF (Ret.). *Women Who Dared: American Female Test Pilots, Flight Test Engineers and Astronauts*. CA: Norstahr Publishing, 1997.

USAF pilot Pateman discusses the WASPs of World War II, describes the 30-year hiatus when women were not allowed to fly for the military and then recounts how and why the military again opened flying positions to women during the 1970s and 1980s.

403. Peterson, Donna. *Dress Gray: A Woman at West Point*. Austin, Texas: Eakin Press, 1990.

Peterson's inspirational autobiography of her experiences at West Point a full decade after Carol Barkalow's sojourn there.

404. Rustad, Michael L. *Women in Khaki: The American Enlisted Woman*. Praeger Special Studies, 1982.

The author looks at the lives and experiences of enlisted women in the U.S. Army in the late 1970s, the early years of the All Volunteer Force. He interviewed over 90 enlisted women and about 140 enlisted men, and draws numerous interesting quotes from his interviews to illustrate his belief that although the Army is willing to enlist women to make up for a dearth of male volunteers, at this juncture (1978) their numbers were so small that they remained "tokens." Rustad believed that his interviewees and Army women in general would suffer significant difficulties attempting to gain acceptance and succeed in the military until their numbers increased.

405. Schneider, Dorothy and Carl J. *Sound Off! American Military Women Speak Out*. New York: E.P. Dutton, 1988.

The authors conducted over 300 oral history interviews with officer and enlisted women in all branches of the service. They describe their motivations for joining up, their experiences during training, and their military jobs. The authors contrast the women they interviewed with what they believed was the prevailing opinion at the time this book was written—that many military women were sluts or lesbians.

406. Schuon, Karl and Lyons Ronald. *Servicewomen and What They Do.* New York: Frankie Watts Inc., 1984.

This book was written for young women considering joining the service, and is organized into sections on Army women, Navy women, Air Force women and Coast Guard women that describe basic training, uniforms and the career fields available to women in each service.

407. Slappey, Mary McGowan, Lt. Commander, US Navy Reserve (Ret.). *Exploring Military Service for Women.* New York: Rosen Publishing Group, 1986.

Navy officer Slappey tells young women what to expect if they elect to join the Armed Forces.

408. Stiehm, Judith Hicks. *Arms and the Enlisted Woman.* Philadelphia, PA: Temple University Press 1989.

Stiehm examines the women of the All Volunteer Force; what they can and cannot do and the problems they face in their military careers; the question of whether or not they should be allowed to serve in combat; the question of whether or not they should be allowed to serve in uniform while pregnant or as sole parents; and the question of whether there should be limits on how many women can serve.

409. Stiehm, Judith Hicks. *Bring Me Men and Women: Mandated Change at the U.S. Air Force Academy.* Berkeley, CA: University of California Press, 1981.

Stiehm tells the story of the initial integration of men and women at the Air Force Academy in the years after Congress mandated opening the military academies to women. The title refers to the legendary quote "Bring Me Men," which for years was etched above the gate to the Air Force Academy. The quote remained there for 30 years after the Academy was integrated, and was only recently removed.

B. Journal Articles

410. Asayesh, Gelareth. "Harassed Female Midshipman Quits." *Baltimore Sun* (May 14, 1990).

411. Bennett, James Gordon. "Shock Waves at the U.S. Naval Academy." *Glamour Magazine* (June 1992).

Discusses sexual harassment problems at the U.S. Naval Academy, focusing on the case of Gwen Dryer.

412. Burke, Carol. "Dames at Sea." *The New Republic* (August 17 and 24, 1992) 16–20.

A discussion of sexual harassment at the Naval Academy, including the use of derogatory cadence calls and nicknames.

413. Clark, Albert P., Lt. Gen. U.S. Air Force. "Women at the Service Academies and Combat Leadership." *Strategic Review* 5 (Fall 1977).

414. DeFleur, Lois et al. "Sex Integration of the U.S. Air Force Academy: Changing Roles for Women." *Armed Forces and Society* 4 (Summer 1978).

An early look at the integration of female cadets into the Air Force Academy.

415. "Female Midshipman Did the Academy a Big Favor." *The Sunday Capital* (May 20, 1990).

Regarding the resignation of Gwen Dryer from the U.S. Naval Academy.

416. "Female Mipshipman Quits Academy After Taunting Incident." *The Washington Post* (May 14, 1990).

417. Gilder, George. "The Case Against Women in Combat." *Parameters* (September 1979): 81–86. (Reprinted from the *New York Times Magazine*, January 28, 1979).

418. Gonzales, Enrique. "2 of 3 Female Midshipmen Cite Harassment at Academy." *The Washington Times* (October 10, 1990).

419. Hooker, Richard D., Jr. "Affirmative Action and Combat Exclusion: Gender Roles in the U.S. Army." *Parameters* (December 1989).

420. Lamar, Jacob V. "Redefining a Woman's Place: The Pentagon Opens up New Posts for Female Soldiers." *Time* (February 15, 1988).

421. Maginnis, Robert L., Col. U.S. Army. "The Future of Women in the Army." *Military Review* (July 1992).

422. "Many at the Academy Believe Women Don't Belong." *Navy Times* (October 22, 1990).

423. McCord, Joel. "Naval Academy is Chided on Sexism." *The Sun* (October 10, 1990).

424. Moore, Molly. "Navy, Congress Open Probes of Harassment at Annapolis." *The Washington Post* (May 18, 1990).

425. Moskos, Charles. "Army Women." *The Atlantic Monthly* (August 1990).

The author discusses Operation Just Cause in Panama and Linda Bray, hailed after the operation as "the first woman to lead men in combat." Moskos includes descriptions of the activities of helicopter pilots Lisa Kutschera and Debra Mann during the same operation. He also discusses controversies such as pregnancy while in uniform and sexual harassment.

426. Rogan, Helen. "Women at Arms." *Life Magazine* (September 1981): 66–78.

427. Sagawa, Shirley and Nancy Duff Campbell. "Sexual Harassment of Women in the Military." Women in the Military Issue Paper, National Women's Law Center, Washington, D.C. (October 1992).

428. Shen, Fern. "Woman to Command Midshipman." *The Washington Post* (April 27, 1991).

About Juliane Gailina, the first female brigade commander at the Naval Academy.

429. Stiehm, Judith Hicks. "The Protected, the Protector, the Defender." *Women's Studies International Forum* (1982) 5: 367–376.

A classic article in which Stiehm describes how the traditional relationship in which men protect women from harm can work against women in uniform. Stiehm believes that until servicewomen are allowed to share equally in the risk of combat participation, their unequal military status will continue to encourage discrimination and harassment and even endanger them.

430. Webb, James. "Women Can't Fight." *Washingtonian* (November 1979).

Webb criticized the admission of women into the service academies, arguing that the traditional role of the service academies was to train combat leaders, and since combat exclusion laws prohibited women from receiving combat-related assignments, women's presence at the service academies was both wasteful and harmful to male cadets, whose training as combat leaders was necessarily watered down due to women's presence.

C. Reports

431. 1990 Navy Women's Study Group. *An Update Report on the Progress of Women in the Navy*. Archives of the Women in Military Service for America Memorial Foundation Inc. Archive # 4539.D. 123.

432. *Department of Defense 1995 Sexual Harassment Survey*. Washington, D.C.: Department of Defense, 1996.

433. U.S. Army Research for the Behavioral and Social Sciences.

Attempted to answer the question, "What percentage of women will it take to degrade unit performance?" by examining the results of an experiment: a three-day field exercise with units ranging from all male to 35 percent female. The results demonstrated that the units performed similarly, with little measurable differences.

D. Oral History

434. Holm, Jeanne, Major General, U.S. Air Force, Ret. with Colonel Donald R. Hargrove and Lt. Colonel Milton R. Little. Available in the archives of Women in Military Service for America Memorial Foundation Inc. Archive # 4539.D. 123.

Major General Holm was the first woman two-star in the U.S. Armed Forces. She is the author of the classic account of the history of women in the U.S. military, *Women in the Military: An Unfinished Revolution*, first published in 1982, with a revised edition in 1992. In this interview, Holm discusses her own military career as well as her feelings about women's place in the Armed Forces.

E. Periodicals Devoted to Women in the Military

435. *Minerva: Quarterly Report on Women in the Military* and *Minerva's Bulletin Board*, published from 1983 through to the present, include scholarly articles and new reports on events, regulations, studies that affect servicewomen. Published by the Minerva Center, a nonprofit educational foundation in Pasadena, MD. For a complete description of the contents of every issue of both the *Quarterly* and the *Bulletin Board*, see the Center's website at http://www.h-net.org/~minerva/toc.html.

436. *Women Military Aviators Incorporated Newsletter*, published from 1991 to the present by the Women Military Aviators Incorporated. The newsletter includes brief articles by and about women aviators from the WASPs of World War II to the present.

F. Archival Collections

437. E. Westcott Mangee Collection, # 1173, Women in Military Service for America Memorial Archives, Arlington, Virginia. Includes the Women's Equity Action League kit on Women and the Military, a study of the status of women in the military throughout the 1980s.

438. Shirley Jolly Minge Collection, #2096. Includes studies, training manuals, briefings and handbooks about women in the Army and women in the military, 1972–1997. Women in Military Service for America Memorial Archives, Arlington, Virginia.

XI

Operations Desert Shield and Desert Storm and the 1990s

A. Women in the Gulf

Operations Desert Shield and Desert Storm proved definitely to the American public (but not necessarily to the leadership of the Armed Forces) what servicewomen were capable of. More than 11 percent of U.S. forces in Saudi Arabia were women, who worked quietly and capably alongside the male members of their units. The U.S. Armed Forces gave the press excellent access to the battle theater throughout the operation and the media covered the war thoroughly. In every newscast, the American public saw deployed servicemen and women working together to accomplish their military missions, and the public came to accept women in uniform and in danger. The press also honed in on another captivating story—military parents—many of them young mothers, leaving their children behind to go to war. Although a few commentators worried about the impact of a mother's absence on the children, most observers seemed to applaud these women's patriotic sacrifice. Operations Desert Shield and Desert Storm led to a general acceptance of servicewomen in the public mind and made the phrases "men and women in uniform" and "servicemen and women" as opposed to "men in uniform" and "servicemen" popular for the first time.

Approximately 31,000 Army women were deployed to the Persian Gulf during Operation Desert Storm. Army women served in combat support and combat service support positions. Combat support units provide direct operational help to combat units and include military police, civil engineering, the transportation of personnel and equipment via truck or helicopter and communications and intelligence support. Combat service support positions provided logistical, technical and administrative services such as personnel, postal, medical and finance to the combat arm. For the United States Navy, Operation Desert Shield became the largest and fastest sealift ever undertaken. More than 240 ships carried more than 9 million tons of supplies and equipment to sustain the gathering military force. Approximately 4,500 Navy women assigned to medical units, support ships, aviation units, construction battalions and cargo handling groups deployed to Saudi Arabia. Navy women served aboard oilers, destroyers, tender and ammunition supply ships and two hospital ships. The 4,250 Air Force women deployed to Saudi Arabia during the war crewed aboard the tanker aircraft that refueled bombers and fighters, served aboard AWACS (airborne warning and control systems) aircraft that controlled air traffic, and serviced, repaired and armed aircraft headed for combat.

Initially, the first Marine Corps units to deploy pulled female Marines and held them back for several days before deploying them. Commanders did not feel comfortable sending women in until sanitary facilities (latrines) could be built. Some of the women were upset by the delay. After the women arrived in the Gulf, they were quartered aboard air-conditioned ships while the males in their units suffered in warehouses on shore. Both men and women were upset by the difference in their treatment and unit cohesion was threatened. Commanders then decided to house units together on shore, and the preferential treatment ended. Women Marines ultimately became part of a support base well forward of most infantry units. Male and female Marines worked together to set up the base from scratch. Approximately 1,200 Marine Corps women were deployed to Saudi Arabia during the war. Because the Coast Guard's official mission entails guarding the shores of the United States, its mission in the Persian Gulf was limited, and as a result only 14 Coast Guard women deployed to the Gulf.

One of the most annoying problems that servicewomen faced while in Saudi Arabia was dealing with the religious and cultural conventions of a country where women were routinely kept out of sight in the home. U.S. servicewomen were expected to conform to the Saudi dress code for women: no skin was supposed to show above a woman's wrists or ankles to prevent men from lusting after them. Servicewomen were granted a dispensation so they did not have to wear face or hair covers, but it was hard trying to keep covered up in daily temperatures of 120 degrees. Male soldiers wore tee shirts and shorts, but servicewomen were expected to wear long sleeved shirts and pants. Servicewomen dealt with other restrictions as well; they couldn't drive military vehicles or accompany men into restaurants. While servicewomen who worked in urban areas had to conform, those assigned to U.S. bases in the desert did not experience as many problems. They were able to dress like their male colleagues and only experienced strictures when they had to travel into town.

Servicewomen noticed that the military's acquiescence to the Saudi culture made it easier for the men who believed that women didn't belong in the military. "They make constant jokes about how we could learn something about subservience from the Saudi women," said one Air Force lieutenant. "We don't think it's very funny." Unbelievably, in some areas of the country, the U.S. military required servicewomen to wear abayas, a head to toe dark garment that covered them completely. When the women complained, they were told that they were guests of the Saudi government and should follow the rules. Many women thought privately that had Saudi Arabia followed apartheid rules, it is doubtful the military would have agreed to place limitations on minority soldiers.

The U.S. Armed Forces learned that combat exclusion and combat probability coding policies could not keep servicewomen safe from harm during war; six servicewomen died during the operations, several others died in the days immediately after the ceasefire. Two Army women, one officer and one enlisted, were captured by the Iraqi Army and held as POWs. Of course, not all servicewomen deployed to the Gulf during the war; thousands remained in their assigned jobs in the United States and thousands more were deployed to other regions, many to "back fill" for units that had deployed to Saudi Arabia.

If Operation Desert Storm was "the test" of the All Volunteer Force and its unprecedented reliance on volunteers, women and reservists, it passed with flying colors. The American public saw women doing their jobs without complaint on television every night and accepted the roles servicewomen were playing. When servicewomen gave their lives for their country, there were few outcries from the public. After the war Congress, reflecting public opinion, expanded the roles women could perform in combat by rescinding the statutes that barred women from serving aboard combat aircraft and vessels. The history of women's military service to the nation entered another era.

A1. Books

439. Binkin, Martin and Shirley Bach. *Who Will Fight the Next War? The Changing Face of the American Military.* Washington, D.C.: The Brookings Institution, 1993.

    The authors examine women soldiers' performance during Operations Desert Shield and Desert Storm and predict that the numbers of women in the All Volunteer Force will continue to grow.

440. Cornum, Rhonda as told to Peter Copeland. *She Went to War: The Rhonda Cornum Story.* Novato, CA: Presidio Press, 1992.

    Cornum's excellent memoir describes her early life and decisions to become a physician and to join the Army and become a flight surgeon as well as her deployment, the mission that led to her capture and her experiences under captivity. The book is honest and forthright and well worth reading. Note: Cornum was an Army major at the time of her capture. She is now a brigadier general in the U.S. Army.

441. Figueroa, Denise. *The Most Qualified: A Nurse Reservist's Experiences in the Persian Gulf War.* New York: Vantage Press, 2002.

    The author served as an Army Reserve nurse in the 312th Evacuation Hospital during the Persian Gulf War. The 312th treated U.S. and British personnel as well as Iraqi prisoners of war. Figueroa's memoir of that time period describes the difficulties she encountered prior to deployment (training) in addition to her experiences in the Gulf and her feelings on returning home.

442. Francke, Linda Bird. *Ground Zero: The Gender Wars in the Military.* New York: Simon & Schuster, 1997.

    Journalist Franke describes attending the funeral of Army helicopter pilot Marie Rossi. After talking with Rossi's family about their daughter, Franke became interested in the institutional problems faced by many patriotic servicewomen who are simply trying to do their jobs to the best of their ability. Inspired by Rossi's story, Franke traced the gender integration of women in the military from Operation Just Cause through Operations Desert Shield and Desert Storm, focusing on the stories of

Army Captain Linda Bray in Panama and flight surgeon Rhonda Cornum and truck driver Melissa Rathbun Nealy during the Gulf War.

443. Gann, Sheila, 2nd Lt. U.S. Army Nurse Corps Reserve. *Operation Desert Storm: Diary of an Army Nurse*. Talala, OK: R. & J Publishing, 1991.

Gann describes her service in the Gulf War as an Army nurse. Gann was one of many Army Reservists who were somewhat taken aback about being deployed (for years Reservists could count on regular stateside assignments). However, Gann deployed with her unit and served in an Army hospital in the desert. She describes the hardships she and her colleagues faced in the harsh desert environment and her relief on making it home.

444. Hasan, Heather. *American Women of the Gulf War*. New York: Rosen Publishing Group, 2004.

Hasan profiles servicewomen engaged in a wide variety of military jobs in the Gulf, including mechanics, truck drivers, pilots, communications specialists, medics, and guards. She includes a section on how U.S. servicewomen had to adapt to Saudi Arabian culture while in the Gulf.

445. Kassner, Elizabeth. *Desert Storm Journal: A Nurse's Story*. Lincoln Center, MA: The Cottage Press, 1993.

Army 2nd Lieutenant Kassner was a relatively new, inexperienced nurse when she deployed to the Persian Gulf with her unit in 1991. In her diary, Kassner describes dealing with the brutally hot and dry desert environment as well as her personal fears when the war started, fears which she was able to put aside when she needed to focus on doing her job as a surgical intensive care nurse.

446. Kwiatkowski, Dianah. *When Duty Called: Even Grandma Had to Go*. Unionville, NY: Silk Label Books, 2003.

Kwiatkowski joined the Army Reserves hoping to further her nursing education and never dreaming that she would be called upon to deploy. Her memoir describes her experiences in Iraq, from pre-deployment training through her unit's assignment in southwest Asia and finally to the return trip home.

447. Shubert, Frank N. and Theresa L. Kraus, eds. *The Whirlwind War: The United States Army in Operations Desert Shield and Desert Storm*. Washington, D.C.: U.S. Army Center of Military History, 1995.

In Chapter 9, "Profile of the New Army," historian Judith Bellafaire describes how the personnel policies of the All Volunteer Force worked to create an older, more highly educated Army with larger numbers of women and minorities and looks at this "new" Army's performance in the Gulf War.

448. Stabe, Mary E. *Diary from the Desert*. Bedford, IN: Jo Na Books, 2003.

Stabe was a newly wed intelligence specialist when she was deployed to the Gulf in 1991. Her book is a compendium of letters she wrote to her family in Iowa from the Persian Gulf.

A2. Journal Articles

449. Aspy, Catherine. "Should Women Go Into Combat?" *Reader's Digest* (February 1999).

450. Barkalow, Carol. "Women Have What It Takes: An Army Captain Tells Why Females Should Fight." *Newsweek* (August 5, 1991).

451. Beck, Melinda et al. "Our Women in the Desert: Sharing the Duty (and Danger) in a 'Mom's War.'" *Newsweek* (September 10, 1990).

  Looks at a number of servicewomen deployed to the Gulf with children at home and examines the ways in which they cope with their split responsibilities.

452. Chavez, Linda. "What of the Women Who Want No Combat Role? Supporters Are Not Always the Ones Who Would Fight." *Minneapolis Star Tribune* (July 30, 1993).

  Chavez points out that while many female officers believe that gaining a combat command would help their military careers, many of the enlisted women who would be on the front lines prefer not to be assigned combat missions.

453. D'Amico, Francine. "Feminist Perspectives on Women Warriors." *Peace Review* 8 (Sept. 1996): 379–384.

  D'Amico disagrees with the idea that servicewomen's performance in the Gulf War proved their abilities to serve in combat and hostile and challenging environments.

454. Dunivin, Karen, Lt. Col. U.S. Air Force. "Military Culture: A Paradigm Shift?" *Maxwell Paper No. 10*, Air War College, Maxwell Air Force Base, AL: 1997.

455. Gutman, Stephanie. "Sex and the Soldier." *The New Republic* (February 24, 1997).

  Gutman believes that a gender-integrated military is by definition a weaker military, with less challenging training and requirements.

456. Hackworth, David, Colonel U.S. Army (Ret.). "War and the Second Sex: Women Are Smart and Capable. But Would Battlefield Equality Hurt Combat Readiness?" *Newsweek* (August 5, 1991).

  Hackworth fears that assigning female soldiers combat roles would weaken the effectiveness of these units.

457. Jordan, Bryant. "'We've Come a Long Way': NCO's Career Shows Women's Progress." *Air Force Times* (February 12, 1996).

  This article focuses on Chief Master Sergeant Patricia Hoffman, who in January 1996 retired as the most senior master sergeant in the Air Force.

458. Kantrowitz, Barbara with Eleanor Clift and John Barry. "The Right to Fight: The Taboo on Women in Combat May Finally Crumble as

Congress Debates a Bill to Allow Women to Fly Warplanes." *Newsweek* (August 5, 1991).

Military women's exemplary performance during Desert Storm caused Congress to examine the Combat Exclusion Laws.

459. McNeil, Donald G., Jr. "Should Women Be Sent Into Combat?" *The New York Times* (July 21, 1991).

McNeil discusses both sides of the combat issue.

460. Milko, James D. "Comment: Beyond the Persian Gulf Crisis: Expanding the Role of Servicewomen in the United States Military." *The American University Law Review* (Summer 1992).

Examines the arguments for and against limiting servicewomen's combat role in lieu of their performance in the Persian Gulf and comes to the conclusion that combat assignments should be opened to servicewomen on a volunteer basis.

461. Moskos, Charles. "Army Women." *The Atlantic Monthly* (August 1990).

The author discusses Operation Just Cause in Panama and Linda Bray, Lisa Kutschera, Debra Mann, the women in combat controversy and the issues of pregnancy and sexual harassment.

462. Muradian, Vago. "Embattled N.Y. Fliers Face New Era." *Air Force Times* (January 15, 1996).

The article is referring to the case of N.Y. Air Guard Major and pilot Jacquelyn Parker, who accused the Guard of sexual harassment and discrimination.

463. Nantais, Cynthia and Martha E. Lee. "Women in the United States Military: Protectors or Protected? The Case of Prisoner of War Melissa Rathbun-Nealy." *Journal of Gender Studies* (July 1999) Vol 8, No 2: 181–191.

Applies Judith Hicks Stiehm's framework of the protector (traditionally male) and the protected (traditionally female) to an examination of military and public reaction to the capture of female POW Melissa Rathbun-Nealy. The authors conclude that after the postwar return to "normalcy" the gendered image of women as citizens needing protection returned to public consciousness, a theory public reaction to the capture of POW Jessica Lynch during the second Gulf War proved to be correct.

464. Pexton, Patrick. "63 Women Get Carrier Orders." *Navy Times* (March 21, 1994).

Regarding the assignment of women on the USS *Eisenhower*, the first gender-integrated combat vessel.

465. Revkin, Andrew C. "2 Air National Guard Officers Relieved of Command in Sex Discrimination Case: A Report Says that a Female Fighter Pilot Was Denied Missions that Men were Given." *The New York Times* (October 22, 1995).

Revkin discusses the Parker case on sexual discrimination in the N.Y. Air National Guard.

466. Ralston, Jeanne. "Women's Work." *Life Magazine* (May 1991).

 Looks at the types of jobs servicewomen performed in the Saudi Arabian desert during Operations Desert Shield and Desert Storm. During these operations the media consistently presented a positive story on servicewomen's performance in the desert, leading the American public to view military women in a positive light.

467. Sadler, Georgia, Captain, U.S. Navy (Ret.). "From Women's Services to Servicewomen," in Francine D'Amico and Laurie Weinstein, eds., *Gender Camouflage: Women and the U.S. Military.* New York: New York University Press, 1999.

 Sadler traces the expanding numbers, presence, and missions of women in the Army, Air Force, Navy and Marines. Operations Desert Shield and Desert Storm, she says, served to spotlight how integral women have become to the Armed Forces' ability to perform their missions.

468. Schultz, Vicki. "Reconceptualizing Sexual Harassment." *Yale Law Review* 107 (April 1998).

 Discusses sexual harassment in a hostile work environment and how complaints have been handled in the courts.

A3. Government Reports

469. Aspin, Les, Secretary of Defense. "Subject: Policy on the Assignment of Women in the Armed Forces." Memorandum for Secretaries of the Military Departments, Washington, D.C., April 28, 1993.

470. "Conduct of the Persian Gulf War: Final Report to Congress, Pursuant to Title V of the Persian Gulf Conflict Supplemental Authorization and Personnel Benefits Act of 1991 (Public Law 102–25), April 1992.

471. U.S. General Accounting Office. *Women in the Military: Deployment in the Persian Gulf War: Report to the Secretary of Defense.* Washington, D.C.: General Accounting Office, 1993.

472. U.S. Presidential Commission on the Assignment of Women in the Armed Forces. *Women in Combat: Report to the President.* Washington, D.C.: Brassey's, 1993.

B. Dismantling Combat Exclusion Regulations and 1990s Military Operations

Although most Americans appeared to have approved of servicewomen's performance in the Persian Gulf War, Congress remained uncertain whether the public and the services themselves were ready to see military women undertake expanded combat roles. Throughout 1991 and well into 1992, the debate over whether to allow servicewomen to fly combat aircraft and serve aboard military vessels with combat missions simmered in Congressional hearing rooms, Pentagon offices, newspaper columns and radio talk shows.

The battle began when supporters of servicewomen in the House of Representatives inserted a provision into the 1992 Defense Authorization Bill repealing the section of the 1948 Women's Armed Services Integration Act that prohibited women flying combat aircraft in the Air Force, Navy and Marine Corps. Conservatives were taken unaware, and the bill passed the House by a voice vote and moved to the Senate. Initially, with servicewomen's performance in the Gulf still being applauded, few lawmakers were inclined to object to the provision. The Secretary of Defense, Richard Cheney, appeared to accept the bill and several influential senators, including John McCain, Republican from New Mexico, John Warner, Republican from Virginia, and William Roth, Republican from Delaware, spoke in favor of it. Only Lt. General Gordon Sullivan, President Bush's nominee to become the Army's new chief of staff, mentioned any reservations. Sullivan said that he didn't think it was the right time for the Army to allow women to fly combat aircraft. Since the Army was not included in the legislation, however, reaction to Sullivan's comment was muted.

Within weeks it became apparent that other senators just as powerful and influential as McCain, Warner and Roth had deep reservations about lifting the combat aircraft ban. John Glenn, a Democrat from Ohio, and Sam Nunn, a Democrat from Georgia, announced they disagreed with the idea. Nunn was the Chairman of the Senate Armed Services Committee. Nunn's great uncle, Georgia Representative Carl Vinson, was one of the original architects of the Navy's combat exclusion section in the 1948 Women's Armed Services Integration Act. Then, once it became apparent how controversial such a measure was to the senior military leadership, Senators McCain and Warner began backing away from the idea. Only Senator Edward Kennedy, Democrat from Massachusetts, and Senator Roth remained unabashed supporters of the bill.

The main reason the service chiefs didn't like the idea of allowing women to fly combat aircraft, it appeared, was that they saw this as the beginning of the dismantling of all combat exclusionary policies. They, and many other conservatives, believed that the military was standing on the edge of a "slippery slope," and this step, once taken, would be the beginning of a slide that would eventually lead to military women participating in all combat jobs, even perhaps hand-to-hand ground combat. Because of this, testimonies and arguments during Congressional hearings on the bill rarely focused on the issue of whether women could capably fly combat aircraft. Instead, those testifying spoke of the horrors of combat in general. Marine Commandant General Robert Barrow explained, "Exposure to danger is not combat. Being shot at, even being killed, is not combat. Combat is finding . . . closing with . . . and killing or capturing the enemy. It is killing and it is done in an environment that is often as difficult as you can possibly imagine. Extremes of climate. Brutality. Death. Dying. It's . . . uncivilized! And women can't do it! Nor should they even be thought of as doing it. The requirements of strength and endurance render them unfit to do it. And I may be old fashioned but I think the very nature of women disqualifies them from doing it. Women give life. Sustain life. Nurture life. They don't TAKE it."

Such rhetoric totally obscured the actual purpose of the hearings, to discuss whether women should be allowed to fly combat aircraft. Ironically, no law on the books actually prohibited women from participating in ground combat as practiced by the Army and the Marine Corps. The combat exclusion policies as delineated in the 1948 Women's Armed Services Integration Act specifically barred women from flying combat aircraft and crewing aboard all Navy vessels other than hospital and transport ships. The Army and Marine Corps were simply expected to follow the "intent of Congress" when establishing their assignment policies.

At the end of the testimonies and debates, the Senate Armed Services Committee's version of the Defense Authorization Bill emerged with no provision pertaining to women in combat aircraft. Instead, the Senate recommended that the President appoint a 15-member committee to study the issue. The committee was to report to the President with its recommendations by November 15, 1992.

By this time the Presidential Commission on Women in Combat issued its official report in late 1992, national elections had been held and a new, Democratic administration was scheduled to assume power. Considering the make-up of the Commission, its report surprised few observers. The Commission voted by a margin of one to recommend the reinstatement of the combat exclusion law against women pilots. Although the commissioners realized that women were capable of flying combat aircraft, they "distinguished between the questions of can and should," and decided that the risk of women aircrew being captured by enemy forces warranted their continued exclusion. Unexpectedly, the Commission voted by a margin of one to allow women to serve aboard combat vessels, although the five conservatives demanded that they be allowed to append a section in the report entitled "Alternative Views: The Case Against Women in Combat." Finally, the Commission recommended that Congress enact a new combat exclusion law for Army and Marine Corps women to protect them from ground combat.

The Clinton administration ignored the Presidential Commission's recommendations on combat in April 1993, when Secretary of Defense Les Aspin opened combat aviation to women and expanded the assignments women could hold on noncombatant ships. He also removed the DOD's Risk Rule, saying that it was "no longer appropriate." He defined direct ground combat as the basis for closing positions to women, and established a new assignment rule for women under which women could not be assigned to units below the brigade level whose primary mission is direct ground combat, or to units required to physically collocate and remain with direct combat units. This meant that in the Army, women could work in combat brigade headquarters but they remained excluded from smaller combat battalions, companies and platoons.

In 1993, the 1994 Defense Authorization Act repealed the law prohibiting women from permanent assignment aboard combatant vessels. This opened all jobs in the Navy except those on submarines and as special operations SEALS to women. The Marine Corps opened pilot positions to women, which meant that approximately 62 percent of jobs in the Marine Corps were open to women. Nearly all Air Force and Coast Guard jobs were already open to women. By 1998, 22 percent of the Navy's women were at sea as opposed to 55 percent of its men, and 57 of the Navy's 117 combatant ships had male and female officers and enlisted crewmembers.

Servicewomen participated in a series of military and humanitarian operations conducted by the United States and its United Nations allies during the 1990s, including Operation Restore Hope (Somalia 1992), Operation Uphold Democracy (Haiti 1994), and a series of North Atlantic Treaty Organization sponsored operations in the former Yugoslavia. During these operations, commanders sometimes found themselves skirting around combat exclusion policies with great care; and at other times discretely ignoring them. When the Army needed military intelligence officers in order to help infantry and armor units confiscate weapons and identify trouble spots in Bosnia, commanders sent in three women officers, even though Army policy banned women from working alongside combat troops. When officers needed medics to travel with combat engineer companies, they temporarily "attached" rather than assigned three female medics, because combat exclusion policies forbid the assignment of women to such companies. Commanders explained that sometimes they were forced to choose between adhering to the policy and protecting their troops, and they chose the safety of the troops every time. "Necessity is driving the chain," one officer explained. "If someone is needed to bring clean water to troops—and that person is a woman, commanders on the ground don't have time to worry whether she will be going into a combat area or not."

B1. Books

473. Fenner, Lorry and Marie De Young. *Women in Combat: Civic Duty or Military Liability.* Washington, D.C.: Georgetown University Press, 2001.

    An excellent look at this controversial issue. Both Fenner and De Young are former military officers whose personal experiences have led them to opposite points of view of this very controversial issue.

474. Harrell, Margaret et al. *Assessing the Assignment Policy of Army Women.* Washington, D.C.: Rand, 2007.

    The Army's assignment policy dates from 1992, while DOD's policy dates from 1994, and the two policies differ enough to make the assignment issue confusing and frustrating for commanders. The Army's policy forbids routine direct combat; however, the DOD does not want women assigned anywhere the primary mission is direct combat. Harrell also discusses the definition of such terms as primary mission.

475. Mitchell, Brian. *Women in the Military: Flirting with Disaster.* Washington, D.C.: Regnery Publishing Inc., 1998.

    Mitchell believes that sexual chemistry and attraction between men and women erodes military discipline and camaraderie and weakens unit cohesion as well as fighting and command abilities.

476. Gutmann, Stephanie. *The Kinder, Gentler Military: How Political Correctness Affects Our Ability to Win Wars.* New York: Scribner, 2000.

    Gutmann believes that from basic training forward, the military services have changed and/or weakened strength and skill-related criteria to accommodate the needs of the weaker sex, and that as a result the military itself is now a physically weaker organization.

477. Kerber, Linda K. *No Constitutional Right to Be Ladies: Women and the Obligations of Citizenship.* New York: Hill and Wang, 1998.

    Kerber's analysis of the legal "rights" and obligations of women under the U.S. Constitution challenges us to think of citizenship in a different way— as women have come to enjoy greater rights and obligations of citizenship, should they now be expected to be subject to military duties (obligations) such as the draft and combat assignments?

478. Simon, Rita James, ed. *Women in the Military.* Rutgers, NJ: Transaction Publishers, 2001.

   A group of well-known scholars including sociologists Brenda Moore and Mady W. and David R. Segal, and historians Jean Bethke Elshtain and Lorry Fenner examine the issues of gender integration and women in combat.

479. Skaine, Rosemarie. *Women at War: Gender Issues of Americans in Combat.* Jefferson, NC: McFarland and Co. Inc., 1999.

   Discusses the issue of women in combat by analyzing their performance in the Gulf War, the public's acceptance of women's presence near the front lines and the impact of regulations on women's service.

480. Stiehm, Judith Hicks, ed. *It's Our Military Too: Women and the U.S. Military.* Philadelphia, PA: Temple University Press, 1996.

   Women's place in the military is examined, including the phenomenal integration achieved in the 20 years between 1976, when women were first admitted into the military service academies, and 1996, when the book was written. These years included the Persian Gulf War and the resulting Congressional decisions to allow women to serve aboard combat aircraft and Navy combat vessels.

481. Weinstein, Laurie Lee. *Wives and Warriors: Women in the Military in the United States and Canada.* Westport, CT: Bergin and Garvey, 1997.

   Analyses the issue of servicewomen and combat.

B2. Journal Articles

482. Armor, David J. "Race and Gender in the U.S. Military." *Armed Forces and Society* (Fall 1996) Vol. 23, No 1: 7–27.

483. Baldwin, Sherman. "Creating the Ultimate Meritocracy." *U.S. Naval Institute Proceedings* (June 1993) 119: 33–36.

484. Berens, Robert J. "Is It Combat or 'Combat?'" *Marine Corps Gazette* (November 1997) 81: 71–72.

   Berens argues that just because servicewomen are assigned to the combat theater, it does not mean they necessarily participate in actual combat.

485. Buckley, James J. "The Unit Cohesion Factor." *Marine Corps Gazette* (Nov. 1997) 81: 66–70.

486. Cadenhead, Julia T. "Pregnancy on Active Duty: Making the Tough Decisions." *Proceedings: U.S. Naval Institute* (April 1995) 121: 52–53.

487. Fletcher, Jean W., Joyce S. McMahon and Aline Quester. "Tradition, Technology, and the Changing Roles of Women in the Navy." *Minerva: Quarterly Report on Women and the Military* (Fall 1993) 11: 57–85.

488. Geraci, Karen Sellers. "Women in Combat?" *Minerva: Quarterly Report on Women in the Military* (Spring 1995) 13: 1–14.

489. Griffin, Rodman D. "Women in the Military: What Role Should Women Play in the Shrinking Military?" *The CQ Researcher*, published by the Congressional Quarterly Inc. in conjunction with EBSCO publishing (September 25, 1992), Vol. 2, No. 36.

490. Harris, Beverly C. and Others. "Why Promotable Female Officers Leave the Army." *Minerva: Quarterly Report on Women and the Military* (Fall 1994) 12: 1–23.

491. King, Raymond E. and Suzanne E. McGlohn. "Female United States Airforce Pilot Personality: The Right Stuff." *Military Medicine* (October 1997) 162: 695–697.

492. Korb, Lawrence and Robert McGinnis. "Should Men and Women Train and Go Into Combat Together?" *Retired Officer* (October 1997) 53: 40–45.

The authors present pros and cons on the issues of gender-integrated training and women in combat.

493. Mariner, Rosemary. "A Soldier is a Soldier." *Joint Forces Quarterly* (Winter 1993) 3: 54–61.

494. Peach, Lucinda. "Women at War: The Ethics of Women in Combat." *Minerva: Quarterly Report on Women in the Military* (Winter 1994) 12: 1–64.

495. Pfluke, Lillian A. "Question: Will Combat Roles for Women Downgrade Military Readiness? No: Women Have Proved They Can Do the Job." *Insight on the News* (May 8, 1995) 11.

496. Raynor, Richard. "The Warrior Besieged." *New York Times Magazine* (June 22, 1997): 24–29.

497. Rogers, Phillipe D., Captain, U.S. Marine Corps. "John Has to Do It, Because Jane Can't." *U.S. Naval Institute Proceedings* (September 1996): 122–146.

Rogers explains that although Marine combat aircraft units have been gender integrated, because women are still not allowed to serve in combat specialty aviation occupations, male members of these units can't help but resent women. He believes that these fields should either be completely open to women or completely closed.

498. Rosen, Leora N. "Cohesion and Readiness in Gender-Integrated Combat Service Support Units: The Impact of the Acceptance of Women and Gender Ratio." *Armed Forces & Society* (Summer 1996) 22: 537–553.

499. Sadler, Georgia C. and Patricia J. Thomas. "Rock the Cradle, Rock the Boat?" *Proceedings: U.S. Naval Institute* (April 1995) 121: 51–56.

500. Stoddard, Ellwyn R. "Married Female Officers in a Combat Branch: Occupation Family Stress and Future Career Choices." *Minerva: Quarterly Report on Women in the Military* (Summer 1994) 12: 1–14.

501. Watkins, Gayle L. and Mary C. Bourg. "The Effects of Gender on Cadet Selection for Leadership Positions at the United States Military Academy."

Minerva: Quarterly Report on Women and the Military (Fall Winter 1997) 15: 63–81.

502. Wingrove-Haugland, Erik. "How Can Male Leaders Promote Sexual Equality in Military Academies?" *Minerva: Quarterly Report on Women and the Military* (Fall Winter 1997) 15: 47–62.

B3. Theses

503. Adams, Darrell E., Major, U.S. Air Force. *Mentoring Women and Minority Officers in the U.S. Military.* Maxwell Air Force Base, AL: Air Command and Staff College, 1997.

504. Adams, Kerry G. *Dual Army Couples and Their Impact on Readiness.* Military Studies Program Paper, Carlisle Barracks, U.S. Army War College, 1990.

505. Alderman, Marc. *Women in Direct Combat: What is the Price for Equality?* Fort Leavenworth, KS: U.S. Army Command and General Staff College, December 1992.

506. Baxter, Dwayne F. *Women and Nontraditional Occupations in the Navy: A Study Over Time.* Monterey, CA: Naval Postgraduate School, September 1993.

507. Bell, Nicole S. et al. *High Injury Rates among Female Army Trainees: A Function of Gender?* Natick, MA: Army Research Institute of Environmental Medicine, 1994.

508. Brown, Nancy, Commander, U.S. Navy. *Women in Combat in Tomorrow's Navy.* Carlisle Barracks, PA: U.S. Army War College, April 1993.

509. Butcher, Meredith A. *The Impact of Pregnancy on U.S. Army Readiness.* Research Report, Maxwell Air Force Base, AL: Air University, Air Command and Staff College, 1999.

510. Fitzgerald, Cheryl L., Captain, U.S. Marine Corps. *Analysis of Female Attrition from Marine Corps Officer Candidate School.* Monterey, CA: Naval Post Graduate School, 1996.

511. Gibson, Owen. *Breaking the Mold: Issue Redefinition and Policy Change Concerning Women in Combat.* Auburn, Alabama: Auburn University, 1996.

512. Holt, James R., Jr. *Ladies Fix Bayonets: Impossible Policy Decision.* Maxwell Air Force Base, AL: Air War College, 1996.

513. Lossius, Robert. *Women in Combat Arms: A Combat Multiplier?* Fort McNair, Washington, D.C.: Industrial College of the Armed Forces, April 1992.

514. McTamney, Carol M. *Opportunities for Women in the Air National Guard.* Maxwell Air Force Base, AL: Air Command and Staff College, 1997.

515. Mosher, Mary A. *Army Women in Combat: An Examination of Roles, Opportunities, Administration and Social Acceptability.* University of Alabama, 1993.

516. Obenauer, Diana. *Female Vs. Male Differences in Communication: Obstacles and Solutions to Future Leadership Potential Within the U.S. Military.* Carlisle Barracks: Senior Service College Fellowship Paper, U.S. Army War College, 1994.

517. Rigotti, Marie Y., Major, U.S. Air Force. *Mentoring of Women in the United States Air Force.* Maxwell Air Force Base, AL: U.S. Air Command and Staff College, 1997.

518. Rowe, Elizabeth A. *Enlisted Women at Sea: A Quantitative Analysis.* Newport, RI: Naval War College, March 1994.

519. Sowell, Maureen R. *Women: Their Fight to Fight.* Thesis, California State University, Dominquez Hill, 1996.

B4. Government Reports

520. Army Policy for the Assignment of Female Soldiers, Army Regulation 600–13, Headquarters, Department of the Army, Washington, D.C., March 27, 1992.

521. Brennan, Thomas F.X. and Stephen Del Giacco. "Mismanagement and Missed Opportunities: The F-18 Training of Major Jacquelyn S. Parker at the New York Air National Guard's 174th Fighter Wing," released by the State of New York, Office of the Inspector General, December 1997.

522. Congressional Commission on Military Training and Gender-Related Issues: Final Report: Transcripts and Legal Consultants Reports. Vol. 2, July 1991.

523. Congressional Quarterly Researcher. "Women in the Military: What Role Should Women Play in the Shrinking Military?" Vol. 2, No. 36, September 25, 1992.

524. Defense Equal Opportunity Council. *Report of the Task Force on Discrimination and Sexual Harassment, Vols 1 and 2.* 1995.

525. Defense Equal Opportunity Management Institute, Research Division, Patrick Air Force Base, Florida, February 1991.

526. Deleon, Rudy. *Report on the Responses of the Armed Services to the Federal Advisory Committee on Gender-Integrated Training and Related Issues and Additional Direction by the Secretary of Defense.* Washington, D.C.: Undersecretary of Defense, 1998.

527. Donnelly, Elaine. "Politics and the Pentagon: The Role of Women in the Military." May 5, 1991.

528. Harrell, Margaret and Laura Miller. "New Opportunities for Military Women: Effects upon Readiness, Cohesion and Morale." Draft report, prepared for the Office of the Secretary of Defense by RAND National Defense Research Institute, July 1997.

529. Klapka, Miriam A. and Others. "Women on Ships: An Historical Look at Unplanned Losses." Alexandria, VA: Center for Naval Analyses, 1995.

Examines statistics to determine whether there are gender differences in personal losses aboard deployed naval vessels and whether pregnancy plays a role in female losses.

530. Navy Women's Study Group. "An Update Report on the Progress of Women in the Navy." 1990.

Examines such issues as the retention of women in the officer corps and among enlisted occupations deemed "nontraditional" as well as shipboard losses.

531. "New Military Culture." *Congressional Quarterly Researcher* 6 (April 1996).

An entire issue devoted to women, minorities and homosexuals in the military.

532. Office of the Inspector General, Department of Defense. *The Tailhook Report.* New York: St. Martin's Press, 1993.

533. Office of the Under Secretary of Defense for Personnel and Readiness. *Career Progression of Minority and Women Officers* (August 1999).

534. Presidential Commission on the Assignment of Women in the Armed Forces. *Report to the President* (November 15, 1992).

535. RAND. *Military Readiness: Women Are Not A Problem.* Washington, D.C.: 1997

Determines that gender integration in military units had a relatively small effect on readiness, cohesion and morale and that unit leadership and training were the key factors affecting these characteristics.

536. Roper Organization, Inc. *Attitudes Regarding the Assignment of Women in the Armed Forces: The Military Perspective.* Conducted for the Commission on the Assignment of Women in the Armed Forces, September 1992.

537. *Special Inspection on Initial Entry Training Equal Opportunity Sexual Harassment Policies and Procedures, December 1996–April 1997.* Washington, D.C.: U.S. Department of the Army, Office of the Inspector General, 1997.

538. Thomas, Patricia J. and Zannette A. Uriell. *Pregnancy and Single Parenthood in the Navy: Results of a 1997 Survey.* San Diego: Navy Personnel Research and Development Center, 1998.

539. U.S. Army Training and Doctrine Command. *Family Readiness: Techniques and Procedures on Family Support Initiatives.* Fort Leavenworth, Kansas: Center for Army Lessons Learned, 2001.

540. United States Congress, House Committee on Armed Services, Military Forces and Personnel Subcommittee. *Assignment of Army and Marine Corps Women under the New Definition of Ground Support.* 102nd Congress, 2nd Session. Washington, D.C.: Hearing held October 6, 1994.

541. United States Congress, House Committee on Armed Services, Military Forces and Personnel Subcommittee. *Women in Combat.* 103rd Congress, 1st Session. Washington, D.C.: May 12, 1993.

542. U.S. Department of the Army. *Army Policy for the Assignment of Female Soldiers.* Army Regulation 600–13. Washington, D.C.: U.S. Department of the Army, 1992.

543. U.S. Department of Defense. *Career Progression of Minority and Women Officers.* Washington, D.C.: Office of the Under Secretary of Defense Personnel and Readiness, 1999.

544. U.S. General Accounting Office. *Gender Issues: Information on DOD's Assignment Policy and Direct Ground Combat Definition: Report to the Ranking Minority member, Subcommittee on Readiness, Committee on Armed Services, U.S. Senate.* Washington, D.C.: 1998.

545. U.S. Presidential Commission on the Assignment of Women in the Armed Forces. *Women in Combat: Report to the President, November 15, 1992.* Washington, D.C.: Brassey's, 1993.

546. "Women in the Navy: The Past, Present and Future." Alexandria, VA: Center for Naval Analysis, March 1994.

C. Gender Discrimination and Sexual Harassment

The years following the successful operations in southwest Asia saw a series of incidents in the U.S. Armed Services that indicated that the integration of women into the ranks was not proceeding smoothly at the grassroots level, or even up the chain of command. During these years numerous female service members, both enlisted and officer, encountered blatant and covert, deliberate and subconscious, institutionalized and individually driven sexual harassment. Although many of these cases went unreported when women chose to deal with the harassment on their own, those incidents that did become public knowledge shocked the nation and forced the services to take more concrete steps to eradicate institutionalized gender bias and put in place regulations for reporting harassment complaints up the chain of command. These fixes have succeeded in reducing but not eliminating the ongoing problem of gender discrimination in the U.S. Armed Forces.

Three major incidents that underscored the difficulties the military services were still having with gender equality included the sexual harassment and abuses suffered by uniformed and civilian women at the September 1991 Tailhook Association Convention; the 1996 Aberdeen Proving Ground rape and harassment scandal; and the harassment accusations made against Sergeant Major of the Army Eugene McKinney.

The 35th annual Tailhook Association Convention was held at the Las Vegas Hilton Hotel in Nevada in September of 1991, when the euphoria over the Gulf War victory was still high. Over the course of the convention, "high spirits" and subliminal concern over the advances of women into one of the last bastions of masculinity, the cockpit, coalesced into coarse banter, unwanted touching and groping and blatant sexual assault in the hospitality suites and corridors of the Hilton. Before it was over more than 100 Navy and Marine Corps aviation officers had sexually assaulted more than 80 women officers and civilians attending the convention. When an initial Navy investigation concluded only that some young officers had acted inappropriately, a second investigation was conducted by the Inspector General of the Department of Defense at insistence of Assistant

Secretary of the Navy. The second investigation revealed the seriousness of the so-called "indiscretions." Ultimately 14 admirals and 300 Navy pilots felt the impact of those findings on their careers.

Five years later, the Army was forced to face the fact that its gender relations also needed considerable work. A group of approximately one dozen drill sergeants at the Army Ordnance Center and School at Aberdeen Proving Ground in Maryland were accused by female recruits serving under them of regularly pressuring women to have sexual relations with them. The shocked Army immediately investigated, and set up a telephone "Hot Line," allowing soldiers who experienced sexual harassment to report incidents without having to go through their chain of command. Four of the accused drill sergeants were eventually sent to prison for their crimes. Eight of their colleagues were either discharged or punished administratively, and letters of reprimand were sent to Aberdeen's commanding general and three of its highest ranking officers.

The final casualty of the Aberdeen scandal was Sergeant Major of the Army Eugene McKinney, the well-liked first black Sergeant Major of the Army, who was appointed to his post in 1995. In 1996, McKinney was asked to serve as a member of a task force established to advise Secretary of the Army Togo West on how to respond to Aberdeen Proving Ground sexual assault scandal. In early 1997 McKinney himself was accused of sexual misconduct by a former female subordinate. The Army suspended him during the ensuing investigation, during which five other female soldiers came forward accusing him of improprieties. McKinney was eventually acquitted of all sexual harassment charges but was convicted of one count of obstruction of justice and reduced in rank from an E-10 to an E-8.

C1. Books

547. Addis, Elizabetta and Valeria E. Russo and Lorenza Sebesta. *Women Soldiers: Images and Realities.* New York: St. Martin's Press, 1994.

    A compilation including an article by Cynthia Enloe on "The Politics of Constructing the Woman Soldier."

548. Burke, Carol. *All American, Hanoi Jane, and the High and Tight: Gender, Folklore and the Changing Military Culture.* Boston, MA: Beacon Press, 2004.

    Burke looks at military culture from basic training forward and finds strong strands of misogynist thought throughout; she also examines the variety of methods military women use in their attempt to fit into military culture. Her analysis of the Tailhook scandal makes perfect sense.

549. Cummings, Missy. *Hornet's Nest: The Experiences of One of the Navy's First Female Fighter Pilots,* Lincoln, NE: iUniverse.com Inc., 1999.

    The author relates her experiences as one of the first female naval pilots assigned to a Hornet fighter pilot squadron after 1993, when Congress modified the combat exclusion policy and allowed women to serve aboard combat aircraft. Unfortunately, the majority of the male pilots in Cummings' new squadron were unhappy with her presence, and made life as difficult for her as possible, eventually forcing her to resign from the Navy.

550. D'Amico, Francine and Laurie Weinstein, eds. *Gender Camouflage: Women and the U.S. Military.* New York: New York University Press, 1999.

A series of essays addressing women's place in the U.S. military services from historical, social, psychological and feminist perspectives. The essays are an excellent mix of scholarly articles and first-person accounts.

551. DeYoung, Marie. *This Woman's Army: The Dynamics of Sex and Violence in the Military.* Central Point, OR: Hellgate Press, 1999.

Marie DeYoung served as a chaplain in the U.S. Army, and her experiences and those of the women she counseled have convinced her that gender integration is bad for the military and damaging to the women who serve.

552. Dickerson, Debra. *An American Story.* New York: Pantheon Books, 2000.

The autobiography describes Dickerson's American success story and the personal toll it took upon her. Born on the wrong side of St. Louis, Dickerson's desire to get out drove her into the Air Force, where she became an Intelligence Officer and experienced both sexual harassment and rape. Dickerson allowed none of this to stop her, however, and ended up with a Harvard degree and a coveted position as a respected journalist.

553. Diekman, Diane J. *Navy Greenshirt: A Leader Made Not Born.* Clear Lake, SD: Altruria Publishing Co., 2001.

Diekman's memoir of her military experiences should be read as a counterpart to some of the more negative views of the military described in this section. Diekman became an aviation maintenance officer in the Navy in 1978, which made her one of the first women in this field. She had to prove herself without the benefit of female mentors—in effect this quiet, unassuming woman became a path breaker for women following her, ending up a Navy captain, without sacrificing her sense of self as a woman.

554. Flinn, Kelly. *Proud to Be: My Life, the Air Force, the Controversy.* New York: Random House, 1997.

Flinn, a graduate of the U.S. Air Force Academy, class of 1993, and the first woman to pilot the B-52 bomber, saw her Air Force career shatter when she fell in love with "the wrong man," the spouse of an enlisted woman at Offutt Air Force Base. Flinn was threatened with court martial because she lied to her commander about the relationship and disobeyed a direct order to stay away from the man. She elected to leave the service instead.

555. Herbert, Melissa. *Camouflage Isn't Only for Combat: Gender, Sexuality and Women in the Military.* New York: New York University Press, 1998.

Herbert describes the various methods gay and straight women use to "get along" in the often misogynistic, male-dominated military.

556. Hirschman, Loree Draude and Dave Hirschman. *She's Just Another Navy Pilot: An Aviator's Sea Journal.* Annapolis, MD: Naval Institute Press, 2000.

Hirschman served as a carrier pilot on the USS *Abraham Lincoln* in 1995 as the only female member of an S-3B Viking anti-submarine warfare unit. She was one of 18 women aviators assigned to the *Lincoln*. During pre-deployment exercises, F-14 Tomcat pilot Kara Hultgreen had crashed while attempting to land on the carrier, putting enormous pressure on the other female pilots assigned aboard the carrier. The author exemplifies the attitude of many successful military women today—they do not want to be seen as a "woman pilot" or a "woman engineer" or a "woman officer," they simply want to be seen as military pilots, engineers and officers.

557. Katzenstein, Mary Fainsod. *Faithful and Fearless: Moving Feminist Protest Inside the Church and Military*. Princeton, NJ: Princeton University Press, 1998.

Traces the efforts of military women to challenge hidebound military assumptions and regulations that discriminate against female soldiers.

558. Katzenstein, Mary Fainsod and Judith Reppy, eds. *Beyond Zero Tolerance: Discrimination in Military Culture*. Lanham, MD: Rowman and Littlefield, 1999.

The authors examine the institutional culture of the U.S. Armed Forces in an attempt to explain continued sexual and racial discrimination that occurs in the service: ie the scandals at the Tailhook convention and at Aberdeen Proving Grounds. Putting zero tolerance rules in place, they warn, may not be enough to fix the problem. They recommend changing the core values of military culture.

559. Kennedy, Claudia. *Generally Speaking: A Memoir by the First Woman Promoted to Three Star General in the United States Army*. New York: Warner Books, 2001.

Kennedy joined the service when the Women's Army Corps was still a separate entity and most members were restricted to clerical duties. As Kennedy learned, many young WACs assigned to work as a commander's secretary were often chosen on the basis of appearance—the prettier the secretary, the more clout the commander was assumed to have. Kennedy successfully negotiated her way around dead-end assignments by choosing intelligence as her specialty. At the end of her career, however, when she was the Deputy Chief of Staff of Intelligence, she accused a two-star general of sexually harassing her (via an unwanted kiss), deliberately derailing his career only because it looked as if he would be promoted to a position responsible for overseeing sexual harassment charges, a position he was obviously unfit for.

560. McMichael, William H. *The Mother of All Hooks: The Story of the U.S. Navy's Tailhook Scandal*. New Brunswick, NJ: Transaction Publishers, 1997.

The author tells the story of the infamous Tailhook scandal, examines its significance and the ultimate impact it had on the U.S. Navy. The foreword is written by the well-known policy analyst Charles Moskos.

561. Nelson, T.S. *For the Love of Country: Confronting Rape and Sexual Harassment in the U.S. Military*. New York: The Haworth Maltreatment and Trauma Press, 2002.

An in-depth look at rape and sexual harassment in today's Armed Services, the ways in which the services attempt to handle the problem, and the damages inflicted on individual service personnel as well as on the services themselves. The author interviewed numerous victims and recounts their stories with perspective and compassion. His examination of the McKinney case is particularly important because this unfortunate episode in military history is not often discussed in scholarly literature.

562. Spears, Sally. *Call Sign Revlon: The Life and Death of Navy Fighter Pilot Kara Hultgreen.* Annapolis, MD: Naval Institute Press, 1998.

In October 1994, Navy aviator and fighter pilot Lt. Kara Spears Hultgreen was killed when she attempted to land her F-14 Tomcat on an aircraft carrier off the coast of southern California. Hultgreen was the first female pilot to qualify to fly the F-14. She had logged more than 217 hours in F-14s, had made 50 carrier landings, and had completed thousands of hours in other aircraft. An investigation into the crash determined that the left engine of her F-14A stalled, and she was unable to correct the plane's pitch in the seconds before hitting the water. The Hultgreen crash was not unique; the Tomcat was a notoriously difficult plane to fly, and several pilots (up to that time male) died in crashes each year. A whispering campaign, however, hinted that Hultgreen crashed because she was actually unqualified to fly the F-14 and was only allowed to fly because the Navy was attempting to be "politically correct." Author Sally Spears was Kara Hultgreen's mother. Incensed by the way opponents of women flying combat aircraft attempted to use her daughter's training record to bolster their claims that women were inherently incapable of flying combat aircraft but were receiving special treatment by the military for political correctness, Spears wrote this memoir to defend her daughter's record and preserve her memory. The book details Hultgreen's pilot training records, which showed that her flying grades were average and that she was third in her gender-integrated class of seven.

563. Stremlow, Mary V., Colonel, U.S. Marine Corps Reserve. *Coping with Sexism in the Military.* New York: Rosen Publishing Group Inc., 1990.

Colonel Stremlow's book, albeit somewhat outdated, describes for readers the officially sanctioned steps servicewomen should take dealing with a variety of difficult situations they may encounter during their military service. Most of Stremlow's advice is geared to situations that might impact career advancement rather than violent harassment, which she assumes would never be condoned.

564. Vistica, Gregory. *Fall from Glory: The Men Who Sank the U.S. Navy.* New York: Simon & Schuster, 1995.

Ultimately, Pentagon investigators referred 119 Navy officers and 21 Marine Corps officers for possible disciplinary actions related to their activities at the 1991 Tailhook convention. These individuals were cited for incidents of indecent assault, indecent exposure, conduct unbecoming an officer, or failing to act properly in a leadership capacity. Investigators also accused 51 individuals of making false statements during the investigation as they attempted to protect fellow officers by stonewalling the investigation. In the end, half of the 140 cases were dropped for lack of evidence and the remaining officers sustained punishments such as fines and letters of reprimand. As Vistica makes clear, however, it was the publicity surrounding the Tailhook "incident," and the Defense Department's subsequent investigation, and not the Navy's, that ultimately damaged the careers of 14 admirals and almost 300 naval aviators. In the end, a Navy wide policy was implemented in which any officer who came up for promotion had to sign a paper asking if he or anyone in his command had been at Tailhook 91. If the answer was "yes" the candidate's promotion was set aside for special evaluation. As for subsequent Tailhook conventions, they became smaller, quieter affairs that were significantly less prestigious.

565. Zimerman, Jean. *Tailspin: Women at War in the Wake of Tailhook.* New York: Doubleday, 1995.

    Zimmerman looks at the Tailhook scandal and what that episode as well as the resulting military and congressional inquiries meant for servicewomen and the U.S. Armed Forces. The author points out that the 1991 convention directly followed the decisive Gulf War victory and many Navy pilots were in a celebratory mood. The convention also occurred six weeks after the Senate voted to open combat flying to women. Some male pilots disagreed with that decision. They valued their lifestyle, and feared the presence of women in their units would change it. Subconsciously, they may have felt that if women wanted to become combat pilots, they should be made to accept the consequences and accept raucous and rowdy behavior. It was notable, said the author, that those women who fought back when groped and molested were treated more roughly than those who simply walked away.

C2. Journal Articles

566. Capaccio, Tony. "Pilot Errors." *American Journalism Review* (October 1997) 19: 18–27.

    Examines the media's coverage of the Kelly Flinn case.

567. Dunivin, Karen O. "Military Culture: Change and Continuity." *Armed Forces and Society* (1994) 20: 531–547.

568. Morris, Madeline. "By Force of Arms: Rape, War and Military Culture." *Duke Law Journal* (February 1996) 45: 651–781.

569. Palmer, Laura. "Her Own Private Tailhook." *New York Times Magazine* (May 28, 1995).

    The article describes Cadet Elizabeth's Saun's experiences while participating in a mandatory survival course. Trainers attempted to demonstrate the sexual degradation that might possibly be used on a captured female.

570. "Resistance and Escape Training Dropped by Air Force Academy." *The New York Times* Section 1 (April 30, 1995): 32.

The simulated sexual assault and harassment training delivered to female cadets was deemed to be in and of itself a form of harassment, causing the Academy to drop the training.

C3. Unpublished Conference Papers

571. Hanson, Christopher. "A Story That Keeps Exploding: Kelly Flinn, the Defense Department and the Power of the Double Standard Narrative."

572. Hanson, Christopher. "G.I. Jane Trapped in Stereotype: How Television Magazine Shows Bolster Gender Bias While Purporting to Fight it in Their Coverage of Military Women."

C4. Theses

573. Daniels, Kathleen, Lt. U.S. Navy. *The Social Construction of Race and Gender: Black Woman Officers in the U.S. Navy.* Monterey, CA: Naval Postgraduate School, 1994.

574. Ernst, Robert W. and Robert J. Gilbeau. *Gender Bias in the Navy.* Monterey, CA: Naval Postgraduate School Thesis, June 1993.

    A discussion of sexual harassment and gender bias in the Navy from a male perspective. The issue of women in combat is also discussed.

575. Margosian, Mary Ann B., LCDR, U.S. Navy and Judith M. Vendrzyk, LT U.S. Navy. *Policies, Practices and the Effect of Gender Discrimination on the Integration of Women Officers in the Department of the Navy.* Monterey, CA: Naval Postgraduate School, 1994.

576. Miller, Scott Andrew, Commander, U.S. Navy. *Perceptions of Racial and Gender Bias in Naval Aviation Flight Training.* Monterey, CA: Naval Post Graduate School, December 1994.

577. Westwood, John and Hughes Turner. *Marriage and Children as Impediments to Career Progression of Active Duty Career Women Army Officers.* Carlisle Barracks, PA: Army War College, May 1996.

C5. Government Reports

578. Booth-Kewley, Stephanie. "Factors Affecting the Reporting of Sexual Harassment in the Navy." San Diego, CA: Navy Personnel Research and Development Center, September 1995.

579. Mauskopf, Roslynn R., State Inspector General. "Management and Missed Opportunities: The F-16 Training of Major Jacqueline S. Parker and the New York Air National Guard's 174th Fighter Wing." Albany, NY: State of New York, Office of the Inspector General, Executive Chamber State Capitol, 1997.

580. United States Congress, House Committee on Armed Services, Military Forces and Personnel Subcommittee. *Gender Discrimination in the*

Military. 102nd Congress, 2nd Session. Washington, D.C.: GPO, July 29–30, 1992.

D. Gender and Military Academies

During the 1990s two famous military schools, South Carolina's Citadel and the Virginia Military Institute, were forced by the Supreme Court to accept women students. Although the United States Congress had compelled the service academies to begin accepting women in 1976, this ruling had not affected private academies that provided a military-type college education to young men. During the 1990s, two such colleges, the Virginia Military Institute and the Citadel in South Carolina, were sued in court to force them to accept women. The basis of these suits was that both VMI and the Citadel received funding from their state governments; thus taxpayers were supporting these schools, which were denying admittance to 50 percent of the taxpaying public. The first school to lose in court was the Citadel, which in 1995 was forced to admit the young woman who had sued them, Shannon Faulkner. Faulkner, the sole woman in the student body, was hazed and tormented so unmercifully that she dropped out of the school after only one week, citing stress and heat-induced illness as the reasons. Male students cheered, but the Citadel could not hold back time. In 1996, four women were admitted. Two women were unable to handle the rough hazing they were subjected to and dropped out after only one semester. In their eagerness to push the women out, Citadel upperclassmen went over the line, even setting the women on fire by dousing their uniforms with nail polish remover and setting them afire with a lighter. When the story came out, the Citadel clamped down on excessive hazing and the remaining two women made it through and graduated from the school.

That same year, the United States Supreme Court ordered the Virginia Military Institute to open its doors to women or lose state funding. The vote was 7 to 1. VMI admitted 30 women and 394 men in the fall of 1997. Haircuts and uniforms were the same for male and female students. Although the service academies had decided not to shave women students' heads, VMI administrators, alumni and students were determined that the presence of women would have no impact of the revered traditions of the school. The women's heads were shaved. Interestingly, VMI had begun shaving students' heads only in the early 1980s, so this particular "tradition" was less than 15 years old. The school was also determined that the physical fitness test not be watered down for women students, nor would they establish separate standards for men and women. The women cadets agreed with this philosophy. They were there because they wanted to prove they could do everything their male peers could do, and most of them (23 out of 30) succeeded.

D1. Books

581. Brodie, Laura Fairchild. *Breaking Out: VMI and the Coming of Women.* New York: Pantheon Books, 2000.

    Brodie, a part-time English professor at the Institute, observed the changes VMI made in its facilities and rules in order to accommodate female cadets, and then watched the women arrive and the Institute's transition into a coed community. Brodie does an excellent job of explaining the VMI culture and the numerous large and small changes the arrival of women forced on the sometimes resentful VMI community.

582. Dwyer, Gail O'Sullivan. *Tough As Nails: One Woman's Journey Through West Point*. Ashland, Oregon: L&R Publishing, 2009.

   The author was a member of the West Point Class of 1981, the second class of academy graduates to contain women. This book begins as a memoir of her years at the Academy, and continues through her life as an Army officer and wife of another West Point graduate, and finally as the mother of two West Point cadets. Dwyer views the Academy from a variety of valuable perspectives, and willingly shares her wisdom and experiences with her readers.

583. Mace, Nancy with Mary Jane Ross. *In the Company of Men: A Woman at the Citadel.* New York: Simon and Schuster, 2001.

   A riveting first-person account of the first woman to graduate from the Citadel.

584. Manegold, Catherine S. *In Glory's Shadow: The Citadel, Shannon Faulkner and a Changing America.* New York: Vintage Books, 1999.

   Beautifully written and illuminating, Manegold's book connects the history of a small, quintessentially Southern town and its populace to the Citadel, and explains atmosphere and attitudes that have created that unique school's essence.

585. McAleer, Donna. *Porcelain on Steel: Women of West Point's Long Gray Line*. Fortis Publishing, 2010.

   McAleer profiles selected women graduates of West Point, who describe in their own words their experiences at the Academy, the lessons they learned there, and how those years have shaped their lives and careers. These women, many who have achieved stellar careers in and out of the service, believe that the Academy changed their lives for the better and gave them the leadership skills and character to lead lives they can be proud of. These women serve as role models for all of us.

586. Strum, Philippa. *Women in the Barracks: The VMI Case and Equal Rights.* University Press of Kansas, 2004.

   An outstanding, thoughtful look at the debate surrounding the entrance of women into the Virginia Military Academy from a legal perspective.

D2. Journal Article

587. Campbell, D'Ann. "Servicewomen and the Academies: The Football Cordon and Pep Rally as a Case Study of the Status of Female Cadets at the U.S. Military Academy." *Minerva: Quarterly Report on Women in the Military* (Spring 1995) 13: 1–14.

D3. Government Reports

588. *DoD Service Academies: Further Efforts Needed to Eradicate Sexual Harassment.* Washington, D.C.: United States General Accounting Office, February 1994.

589. *DoD Service Academies: More Actions Needed to Eradicate Sexual Harassment.* Washington, D.C.: United States General Accounting Office, January 1994.

590. *Military Academy: Gender and Racial Disparities.* Washington, D.C.: United States General Accounting Office, March, 1994.

591. *Naval Academy: Gender and Racial Disparities.* Washington, D.C.: United States General Accounting Office, April 1993.

592. United States Congress, House Committee on Armed Services. *Honor Systems and Sexual Harassment at the Service Academies.* Washington, D.C: GPO, 103rd Congress, 2nd Session, February 3, 1994.

XII

The All Volunteer Force and the War on Terror

By the end of the twentieth century the All Volunteer Force had been tested on all fronts and proven to be strong and capable. The Armed Forces had conducted a large and successful deployment in the Persian Gulf during which active duty and Reserve members of the AVF had performed skillfully and efficiently. Over the next decade the nation sent elements of the AVF around the world in a series of smaller contingency deployments. Just as importantly, the AVF was also tried and tested through a series of scandals that affected all the services at every level from trainees through general officers. In response to these challenges, the services strengthened their equal opportunity programs and the policies, which discouraged discrimination and harassment based on gender and race. Although far from perfect, the Armed Forces could reasonably claim to be one of the top performance-based institutions in the country by 2000, providing more opportunities for promotion to greater numbers of women and minorities than many corporations. The proportion of women and minorities in the services continued to climb, with 15 percent of the active duty force and 18 percent of the Reserves female. Minority women accounted for 48 percent of active duty women and 42 percent of women Reservists. One of the mantras of the AVF was that in diversity lies strength, through expanded knowledge, greater sophistication and a wider range of abilities. Months into the new century the U.S. Armed Services were called upon to face what may be their greatest challenge yet—the war against worldwide terrorism.

On October 12, 2000, the Navy vessel USS *Cole*, a four-year-old, $1 billion guided missile destroyer, stopped at the port of Aden in Yemen for refueling. The *Cole* carried some of the most sophisticated military technology in the world, including surface-to-air missiles and advanced radar equipment. The refueling started at 10:30 am. Less than an hour later, a small craft approached the port side of the vessel, and an explosion occurred that put an 80-foot-wide hole in the ship's side, tearing apart an engine room and a mess room. Seventeen sailors were killed instantly, and 37 others were injured. Two of those killed were women.

Male and female members performed heroically after the explosion, reacting in the way they had been trained. After the crew returned home, the ship's executive officer was asked how women crewmembers had performed during the emergency. He explained that immediately after the explosion, without stopping to think twice, he ordered one of his best marksmen, a woman, to man a .50 caliber machine gun on the flight deck. He explained, "It didn't cross my mind that the first person I ordered to such an exposed position was a woman. And by the speed by which she raced to man that dangerous post, it obviously didn't cross her mind either. We had fighting sailors aboard the ship that day, not men or women."

On September 11, 2001, four commercial U.S. airplanes were hijacked by terrorists. Two planes were deliberately flown into the World Trade Center Towers in New York City, while another was flown into the Pentagon outside of Washington, D.C. The fourth plane crashed in a field in Pennsylvania because its passengers fought back and prevented the hijackers from crashing it into whatever target they had planned—possibly the White House.

When American Airlines Flight 77 crashed into the Pentagon, the 64 people aboard and 125 Pentagon employees died. Ten active duty, reserve and retired servicewomen were among the casualties, but women were among the hundreds of heroes as well, as their military training took over and they and their male colleagues led people out of the burning building and took care of the burned, wounded and shell-shocked.

As a result of the terrorist attacks on the USS *Cole* and the Pentagon, the U.S. embarked on a "War on Terror" in Afghanistan and Iraq. The following books, studies and articles examine the servicewomen fighting these current wars, their expanding roles and missions as well as the way they feel about their deployments, missions and service careers.

A. Books

593. Benedict, Helen. *The Lonely Soldier: The Private War of Women Serving in Iraq.* Beacon Press, 2009.

    Written by a journalist who interviewed officer and enlisted women of the Army, Air Force, Navy and Marine Corps who served in Iraq. The stories some of these interviewees recount will make readers wonder whether the military has made any progress at all in dealing with gender bias, sexual harassment and even rape. Obviously, not every servicewoman sent to Iraq encounters these horrific conditions, however, the fact that even some do should not be tolerated.

594. Dansby, Mickey R., James B. Stewart and Schuyler C. Webb, eds. *Managing Diversity in the Military: Research Perspectives from the Defense Equal Opportunity Management Institute.* New Brunswick, NJ: Transaction, 2001.

    See especially the article written by Brenda Moore, "Women Assigned to Combat Units: Perceptions of the Military Equal Opportunity Climate."

595. Enloe, Cynthia. *Maneuvers: The International Politics of Militarizing Women's Lives.* Berkeley, CA: University of California Press, 2000.

    Enloe sees the military as a male-centrist organization inherently hostile to women, whether these women are soldiers, the wives of soldiers, or women whose lives have been impacted by the military. She believes that many women connected to the military are too prone to accept masculine values and are often sidelined and damaged as a result.

596. Frese, Pamela R. and Margaret C. Harrell, eds. *Anthropology and the United States Military: Coming of Age in the Twenty-First Century.* New York: Palgrave MacMillan, 2003.

A series of essays written by the editors and other authors that looks at such diverse themes as "Medical Risks and the Volunteer Army," "Gender and Class Based Role Expectations," and "Weight Control and Physical Readiness Among Navy Personnel."

597. Germain, Deanna, Lt. Colonel U.S. Army Reserve, Ret. with Connie Lounsbury. *Reaching Past the Wire: A Nurse at Abu Ghraib.* MN: Borealis Books, 2007.

Germain's account of her 18 months as a Reserve Lt. Colonel and nurse assigned to Abu Ghraib, Iraq. Germain treated Iraqi prisoners as well as U.S. soldiers and Marines, dealing with relentless heat, supply shortages, and substandard quarters and facilities.

598. Goldstein, Joshua S. *War and Gender: How Gender Shapes the War System and Vice Versa.* Cambridge University Press, 2001.

See especially the article "Bodies: The Biology of Individual Gender."

599. Holmstedt, Kirstin. *Band of Sisters: American Women at War in Iraq.* Stackpole Books, 2007.

Describes the experiences of women soldiers in Iraq as medics, convoy drivers and guards, military police, and a wide variety of other assignments. Although they serve under fire and can return fire if fired upon, female soldiers are not officially assigned to serve in front line jobs with a combat mission. Holmstedt emphasizes how well female soldiers perform in challenging positions. While upbeat, the book doesn't shirk at telling the stories of women who were wounded in the line of duty, and emphasizes their positive attitudes and plans for the future.

600. Holmstedt, Kirstin. *The Girls Come Marching Home.* Stackpole Books, 2009.

In her second book, Holmstedt tells the stories of over a dozen female veterans of the war in Iraq as they transitioned back into their lives at home. Many experienced post-traumatic stress syndrome and had difficulties readjusting, and all admit that their days in Iraq will live in their memories forever.

601. Karpinsky, Janis, Brigadier General, U.S. Army Reserve. *One Woman's Army: The Commanding General of Abu Ghraib Tells Her Story.* Miramax, 2005.

Karpinsky describes her military career, including her deployment in the first Gulf War, up through her assignment in Iraq as the commander of military police at the infamous prison. She believes she was resented as the commander at Abu Ghraib, both because she was a reservist and because she was a female. She discusses the old boys' network in the Army and explains that there was no clear chain of command at the prison or even in Iraq.

602. Kraft, Heidi Squier. *Rule Number Two: Lessons I Learned While in a Combat Hospital in Iraq.* New York: Little Brown and Company, 2007.

A clinical psychologist deployed to Iraq when her twins were 15 months old describes her experiences while deployed.

603. Lynch, Jessica and Rick Bragg. *I Am a Soldier, Too.* New York: Vintage Books, 2003.

Lynch's autobiography describes her early life in West Virginia, her decision to join the Army and the experiences that led to her capture in the Iraqi desert during the second Gulf War.

604. Manning, Lory. *Women in the Military: Where They Stand.* 5th edition. Washington, D.C.: Women's Research and Education Institute, 2005.

A brief snapshot of women in the U.S. Armed Forces via statistical charts and graphs and helpful definitions of such terms as combat, combat support and combat service support.

605. Murray, Gene. *Covering Sex, Race and Gender in the American Military Services.* Mellen Studies in Journalism, Volume 6. Lewiston, NY: Edwin Mellen Press, 2003.

The author examines the media's coverage of equal opportunity cases in the U.S. military during the 1990s, including sexual harassment and gender-integrated training.

606. Olson, Kim, Colonel USAF Ret. *Iraq and Back.* Annapolis, MD: Naval Institute Press, 2006.

Olson describes the enormously frustrating experiences she had during her assignment immediately after Operation Iraqi Freedom, the attempts of herself and others to help the Iraqi people rebuild their nation and the variety of problems that stood in the way of Coalition hopes.

607. Ruff, Cheryl Lynn, Cdr. USN (Ret.) and Cdr. Sue K. Roper USN (Ret.). *Ruff's War: A Navy Nurse of the Front line in Iraq.* Annapolis, MD: Naval Institute Press, 2005.

An excellent memoir that sets the scene for the author's experiences in Iraq by describing her Navy Nurse Corps career, including a number of shipboard assignments, so that the reader can understand the strengths, training and experiences Commander Ruff, a CRNA (Certified Registered Nurse Anesthetist) brought with her into the Desert field hospital where she found herself in 2003.

608. Sheldon, Sara. *The Few, the Proud, Women Marines in Harm's Way.* Westport, CT: Praeger Security International, 2008.

The author interviewed women Marines serving in Operation Iraqi Freedom. They describe their jobs and how they handle the everyday dangers of their lives in a combat theater.

609. Solaro, Erin. *Women in the Line of Fire: What You Should Know about Women in the Military.* Emeryville, CA: Seal Press, 2006.

Solaro, a journalist, was embedded with combat units in Iraq and Afghanistan. As she watched female soldiers go about their assignments under fire in wars with no front lines, she came to believe that all remaining restrictions on women in combat should be officially removed.

610. Williams, Kayla and Michael E. Staub. *Love My Rifle More than You: Young and Female in the U.S. Army.* W.W. Norton and Company, 2006.

This important book provides readers with an enlisted woman's perspective on military service. Williams describes her military training and career, which appear to have been fairly standard, until she was sent to Iraq, where she faced the typical age-old male soldier's belief that all servicewomen were either whores or lesbians. Assigned to rough isolated duty in the field with minimal comforts for weeks on end with a small group of men, Williams' Iraq experiences may have been tougher than normal. She appears to believe, however, that the attitudes she was forced to deal with are not unique, and may possibly be correct in her assessment.

611. Wise, James E. and Scott Baron. *Women at War: Iraq, Afghanistan and Other Conflicts.* Annapolis, MD: U.S. Naval Institute Press, 2006.

The authors profile 30 military women, demonstrating the diverse duties undertaken by uniformed women in Iraq and Afghanistan. Some of the assignments described include patting down Iraqi women at checkpoints, guarding convoys of supply trucks and piloting aircraft. The authors emphasize that soldiers in Iraq and Afghanistan face insurgent enemies who do not limit their attacks to the battlefield. In these areas, soldiers can be killed while performing clerical duties or eating in mess halls. Although military women have been killed while performing non-combat related duties in previous eras (one thinks of the Army nurses at Anzio Beachhead during World War II) these episodes were out of the norm, whereas in Iraq and Afghanistan "fronts" don't exist; the entire country is a battlefield. This makes the combat distinction irrelevant.

612. Van Creveld, Martin. *Men, Women and War.* London: Cassell, 2001.

Van Creveld believes men and women should train separately and serve in separate military units.

613. Zeigler, Sara L. and Gregory R. Gunderson. *Moving Beyond G.I. Jane: Women and the U.S. Military.* University Press of America, 2005.

Examines the major social issues facing the U.S. Armed Forces as they attempt to further integrate women into the military services and proposes possible answers.

B. Theses and Academic Papers

614. Calahan, Philip D. *The Code of the Warrior: The Kinder, Gentler Military and Marksmanship: Changing a Culture.* Strategy Research Project. Carlisle Barracks: U.S. Army War College, 2002.

The "Kinder, Gentler Military" referred to above refers to Stephanie Gutman's controversial book, *The Kinder, Gentler Military.*

615. Culler, Kristen W. *The Decision to Allow Military Women into Combat Positions: A Study in Policy and Politics.* Monterey, CA: Naval Postgraduate School, 2000.

616. DiSilverio, Laura A.H. *Winning the Retention Wars: The Air Force, Women Officers and the Need for Transformation.* Maxwell Air Force Base, AL: Air University Press, 2003.

617. Evertson, Adrienne and Amy Nesbitt. *The Glass Ceiling Effect and Its Impact on Mid-Level Female Officer Career Progression in the United States Marine Corps and Air Force.* Monterey, CA: Naval Postgraduate School, 2004.

    The author examines the reasons why so many female officers opt out of the military after 10 years of service.

618. Fulton, Christopher T. *Field Artillery (Wo)men: Time for a Relook?* Strategy Research Project. Carlisle Barracks: U.S. Army War College, 2003.

619. Golding, Susan J. *Women: Ready for the Challenges of the Future U.S. Armed Forces.* Strategy Research Project. Carlisle Barracks: U.S. Army War College, 2002.

620. Henkel, Louis O. *The Impact of Army Transformation on the Integration of Enlisted Women.* Strategy Research Project. Carlisle Barracks: U.S. Army War College, 2002.

621. King, Charles A. *The Trivialization of Gender and Its Impact on Combat Effectiveness.* Strategy Research Project. Carlisle Barracks: U.S. Army War College, 2000.

    King believes it would be a mistake to integrate combat units.

622. Myers, Susan R. *Preparing Women for Strategic Leadership Roles in the Army.* Strategy Research Project. Carlisle Barracks: U.S. Army War College, 2003.

623. Porter, Laurie M. and Rick V. Adside. *Women in Combat: Attitudes and Experiences of U.S. Military Officers and Enlisted Personnel.* Monterey Naval Postgraduate School, December 2001.

    The authors explore the different viewpoints of officer and enlisted personnel on the women in combat issue.

C. Journal Articles

624. Alvarez, Lizette. "G.I. Jane Breaks the Combat Barrier." *The New York Times* (August 16, 2009).

    Part of the special series, "Women at Arms." In this article, the author points out that in the war against terror being fought in Iraq and Afghanistan, there are no front lines, and that female soldiers holding noncombat billets often find themselves in combat situations.

625. Alvarez, Lizette. "Wartime Soldier, Conflicted Mom." *The New York Times* (September 27, 2009).

Part of the special series, "Women at Arms." This article examines the pressures soldier mothers experience during deployment, as well as the effect the deployment has on the children involved. Often, the deployment irrevocably changes the relationship between mother and child, and many soldier mothers elect to leave the service rather than continually subject their children to these stressors.

626. Baldauf, Scott. "In Taliban Territory, GI Janes Give Afghans a Different View." *Christian Science Monitor* (November 4, 2003): 1.

627. Bogle, Lori Lyn. "Women at Sea: 'It's All about Leadership.'" *Proceedings: U.S. Naval Institute.* (March 2004) 130: 93–96.

Points out that gender-related problems such as sexual harassment are mitigated on vessels led by strong captains who adhere to the same rules they set for their crew.

628. "Breaking Through the Glass Ceiling: General Ann E. Dunwoody Becomes the First Woman Four-Star in the U.S. Military." *Soldiers Magazine* (March 2009).

629. Brower, J. Michael. "A Case for Women Warfighters." *Military Review* (November December 2002) 82: 61–66.

630. Brower, J. Michael. "Viewpoint: De Facto Women Warriors: End Combat Exclusions." *Armed Forces Journal* (August 2003) 141.

The author of the above articles believes that female soldiers who can qualify physically for combat billets should be allowed serve on the front lines.

631. Buller, Jerome and Todd Albright, Alan Gehrich and Johnnie Wright, Jr. "Pregnancy during Operation Iraqi Freedom/Enduring Freedom." *Military Medicine* (May 2007) Vol. 172, Issue 5: 511–515.

632. Cave, Damien. "A Combat Role, and Anguish Too." *The New York Times* (November 1, 2009).

Part of the special series, "Women at Arms." Examines the effects of post-traumatic stress syndrome on women veterans.

633. Coppola, Nicholas and Kevin G. LaFrance. "The Female Infantryman: A Possibility?" *Military Review* (November–December 2002) 82.

634. DiSilverio, Laura, Lt. Col. U.S. Air Force. "Winning the Retention Wars: The Air Force, Women Officers and the Need for Transformation." *Fairchild Paper.* Air University Press, Maxwell Air Force Base, 2003.

635. Dominus, Susan. "On September 11, an Aimless, Gun-Fearing Bath and Body Works Clerk Decided to Sign Her Life Away to the Army." *Glamour Magazine* (March 2002): 218.

Profiles a young woman who found a new purpose in life after September 11, 2001.

636. Field, Kim and John Nagl. "Combat Roles for Women: A Modest Proposal." *Parameters* (Summer 2001) 31: 74–88.

637. Holland, S. "The Dangers of Playing Dress Up: Popular Representations of Jessica Lynch and the Controversy Regarding Women in Combat." *Quarterly Journal of Speech* (2006) Vol. 92, No. 1: 27–50.

638. Howard, John W. III and Laura C. Prividera. "The Fallen Woman Archetype: Media Representations of Lynndie England, Gender, and the (Ab)uses of U.S. Female Soldiers." *Women's Studies in Communication* (Fall 2008) Vol. 31, No. 3.

639. Howard, John W. III and Laura C. Prividera. "Gendered Nationalism: A Critical Analysis of Militarism, Patriarchy and the Ideal Soldier." *Texas Speech Communication Journal* (2006) Vol. 30, No. 2: 34–45.

640. Howard, John W. III and Laura C. Prividera. "Rescuing Patriarchy or Saving Jessica Lynch: The Rhetorical Construction of the American Woman Soldier." *Women and Language* (2004) Vol. 27, No. 2: 89–97.

641. Jeffreys, S. "Double Jeopardy: Women, the U.S. Military and the War in Iraq." *Women's Studies International Forum* (2007) 30: 16–25.

642. Jonsson, Patrick. "A New Commander to Train US Drill Sergeants? Yes, Ma'am!" *Christian Science Monitor* (July 13, 2009).

643. Kier, Elizabeth. "Uniform Justice: Assessing Women in Combat." *Perspectives on Politics* (2003) 1: 343–347.

644. Kimmel, Gerhard. "When Boy Meets Girl: The 'Feminization' of the Military: An Introduction Also to be Read as a Postscript." *Current Sociology* (2002) 50: 615–639.

645. Lawless, J. "Women, War and Winning Elections: Gender Stereotyping in the Post September 11 Era." *Political Research Quarterly* (2004) Vol. 75, No. 3: 479–490.

646. Mann, Howard, "Vernice Armour: The First African American Woman Combat Pilot." *Black Collegian* (February 2008) Vol. 38, Issue 2.

Mann interviews Marine pilot Vernice Armour, who flew the Super Cobra attack helicopter for two tours in Iraq between 2003 and 2004.

647. McSally, Martha. "Women in Combat: Is the Current Policy Obsolete?" *Duke Journal of Gender Law and Policy* (May 2007).

McSally points out that current combat exclusion policies, designed to keep women away from the front lines, cannot work in a combat theater where front lines do not exist. McSally, an Air Force colonel, has significant experience challenging the status quo. In December 2001, Air Force Lt. Colonel Martha McSally sued Defense Secretary Donald Rumsfeld over a policy that forced U.S. military women in Saudi Arabia to wear Muslim religious garb whenever they went off base. She argued that the practice was offensive to her as a Christian, and that it was unnecessary because other women working in that Middle Eastern nation, such as government contractors and U.S. embassy staffers, were not forced to wear the long, black cloaks known as abayas.

To McSally and many other military women assigned to the Middle East, the abaya represented women's place in that society, which was totally subservient to men. Donning the garment placed servicewomen in a theoretically inferior position to the men with whom they worked. The abaya, argued McSally, was a badge of inferiority. Ultimately, Congress agreed and passed a resolution prohibiting DOD from requiring or formally urging servicewomen to wear the abaya. Shortly after McSally filed suit, the Air Force started giving her negative job evaluations. After years of stellar reviews and fast-tracked promotions, she was suddenly labeled unfit for a leadership post. She vowed to keep up her fight until the Air Force fixed her personnel file and restored her career prospects. In mid-2004 McSally was given a plum assignment as a fighter squadron commander, making her the first woman to command a fighter squadron. She serves as an example of how it can be possible to challenge gender discrimination without ruining one's military career.

648. Myers, Steven Lee. "Another Peril in War Zones: Sexual Abuse by Fellow G.I.s." *The New York Times* (December 28, 2009).

Part of the special series, "Women at Arms." Discusses the problems servicewomen experience with sexual harassment in war zones and the military's flawed system of handling sexual harassment complaints. Many women, fearing that lodging a complaint will negatively impact their own career, elect to try to handle the situation on their own.

649. Myers, Steven Lee. "Living and Fighting Alongside Men, and Fitting In." *The New York Times.* (August 17, 2009).

Part of the special series, "Women at Arms." Examines the various ways women acclimate to a masculine environment. Some women strive to be one of the boys, others find private ways to connect with their feminine side.

650. Pershing, J. "Why Women Don't Report Sexual Harassment: A Case Study of an Elite Military Institution." *Gender Issues* (2003) Vol. 2, No. 4: 3–30.

Military women believe that reporting harassment can harm their careers. They hesitate to draw attention to themselves, to cause problems for leadership or to be viewed as whiners, complainers and troublemakers.

651. Pershing, Jana L. "Gender Disparities in Enforcing the Honor Concept at the U.S. Naval Academy." *Armed Forces & Society* (Spring 2001) 27: 419–442.

652. Prividera, Laura and John Howard. "Masculinity, Whiteness and the Warrior Hero: Perpetuating the Strategic Rhetoric of U.S. Nationalism and the Marginalization of Women." *Women and Language* (2006) Vol. 29, No. 2: 29–37.

653. Quindlen, Anna. "Not Semi-Soldiers; It's No Longer a Question of Whether Women Should Be in Combat, It's a Matter of the Regulations Catching Up with Reality." *Newsweek* (November 12, 2007) Vol. 150, Issue 20.

The author points out that women are already serving in combat, and suggests that military regulations be changed to accept that fact.

654. Scarborough, Sheila A. "When Mom Wears Steel-Toed Boots." *Proceedings: U.S. Naval Institute* (February 2002) 128: 36–40.

655. Schafer, Susanne M. "1st Woman Takes Charge of Army's Drill Sergeants." *Salon* (September 18, 2009).

656. Segal, Mady Wechsler. "Women's Military Roles Cross Nationally: Past, Present and Future." *Gender and Society* Vol. 9, No. 6: 757–775.

Segal examines how other nations have handled the women in combat question.

657. Simons, Anna. "Women in Combat Units: It's Still a Bad Idea." *Parameters* (Summer 2001) 31: 89–100.

Simons explains why she believes women do not belong in combat units.

658. Silva, Jennifer M. "A New Generation of Women? How Female ROTC Cadets Negotiate the Tension between Masculine Military Culture and Traditional Femininity." *Social Forces* (December 2008) Vol. 87, Issue 2.

Silva interviewed 38 female cadets to learn how they handled being female in a traditionally male environment.

659. Snyder, R. Claire. "The Citizen Soldier Tradition and Gender Integration of the U.S. Military." *Armed Forces & Society* (Winter 2003) 29: 185–204.

660. Stern, Seth. "Who Would Fight: A Diverse Military: Changes in the Army Since the Gulf War Include More Latinos, Muslims and Women." *Christian Science Monitor* (March 2003)18.

661. Titunik, Regina F. "The Myth of the Macho Military." *Polity* (April 2008) Vol. 40, No. 2: 137–163.

The author tackles the military's reputation as being a male-dominated culture inimical to women. The military's emphasis on teamwork, camaraderie and "can-do," she maintains, fosters an environment where a great many women succeed and excel.

662. U.S. Federal News Service. "Back from Combat, Women Struggle for Acceptance." Washington, D.C.: December 15, 2009.

663. U.S. Federal News Service. "Women Take Command in Combat." September 15, 2008.

Air Force Colonel Patricia Searcy, Lt. Col. Dawn Keasley, Lt. Col. Helen Brasher and Colonel Carol Timmons, all group commanders or deputy commanders serving with the Air Force in Afghanistan, are interviewed.

664. Valpoline, Paolo et al. "Gender and War." *Jane's Defense Weekly* (June 1999) 31.

665. Van Creveld, Martin. "Less Than We Can Be: Men, Women and the Modern Military." *Journal of Strategic Studies* (December 2000) 23: 1–20.

The author believes that men and women should train and serve in separate units, because women's presence in integrated units degrades unit integrity.

666. Wojack, Adam N., Captain, U.S. Army. "Integrating Women into the Infantry." *Military Review* (November–December 2002) Vol. 82, No. 6.

Wojack favors integrating women into the combat arms.

667. "Women Warriors." *The New York Times* (April 30, 1993).

   Regarding the opening of combat aircraft to women.

668. Yeager, Holly. "Soldiering Ahead." *The Wilson Quarterly* (Summer 2007) Vol. 31, No. 3: 54–63.

   Examines the slow growth of servicewomen's integration into greater percentages of military jobs. The author speaks to female military leaders and scholars who believe that the expansion will continue, but will stop short of full integration into direct combat positions.

D. Official Reports and Policies

669. Air Force Inspector General. *Summary Report Concerning the Handling of Sexual Assault Cases at the United States Air Force Academy*. Washington, D.C.: Air Force Inspector General's Office, September 2004.

670. Center for Military Readiness. *Issues: Co-Ed Basic Training: CMR Compiles Definitive Summary of Findings on Co-Ed Basic Training*. Washington, D.C.: September, 2003.

   Points out that training male and female recruits together can result in increased physical injuries to women. However, when trainers water down the physical requirements, male enlistees are not physically challenged.

671. Center for Military Readiness. *Issues: Recruiting/The Draft Court Dismisses Lawsuit to Include Women in Draft Registration*. Washington, D.C.: September, 2003.

672. Center for Military Readiness. *Issues: Women in Combat: Bush Administration Upholds Law and Regulations Exempting Women from Land Combat*. Washington, D.C.: May 2002.

673. Center for Military Readiness. *Issues: Women in Combat: Enlisted Women Opposed to Combat Assignments*. Washington, D.C.: September 2003.

   Explains that many enlisted women are against the idea of assigning women to combat positions because they understand the hardship and danger entailed in serving on the front lines.

674. Center for Military Readiness. *Issues: Women in Combat: Jessica Lynch Reality Shatters Amazon Myth*. Washington, D.C.: December 2004.

675. *Evaluation of Sexual Assault, Reprisal and Related Leadership Challenges at the United States Air Force Academy*. Washington, D.C.: Office of the Inspector General of the Department of Defense, December 2004.

   Following the sexual assault scandal at the U.S. Air Force Academy in Colorado, the DOD Inspector General examined the Academy's institutional culture and assault-reporting practices, regulations and procedures.

676. RAND Corporation. Washington, D.C.: 2001.

   Examines the reasons for the gap in retention rates between male and female officers and concludes that female officers face greater conflicts between career and family demands than men. Female officers are more likely than men to be married to another military officer, making career-related moves far more difficult.

677. RAND Corporation. Washington, D.C.: 2007.

This study determines that although the U.S. Army is currently following DOD policy barring the assignment of women to units whose mission is primarily direct combat, the policies are difficult to understand and there is no consensus among senior defense officials about the objectives of the policies.

678. *Report Concerning the Assessment of USAF Sexual Assault Prevention and Response.* Washington, D.C.: Office of the Assistant Secretary of the Air Force Manpower and Reserve Affairs, August 2004.

679. *Report of the Panel to Review Sexual Misconduct Allegations at the U.S. Air Force Academy* (also known as the Fowler Report). Arlington, Virginia: September 2003.

680. *Report of the Working Group Concerning the Deterrence and Response to Incidents of Sexual Assault at the U.S. Air Force Academy.* Washington, D.C.: Headquarters, U.S. Air Force, June 2003.

681. U.S. Department of Defense. *Report on the Status of Female Members of the Armed Forces: Report to Congress.* Washington, D.C.: Office of the Undersecretary of Defense, Personnel and Readiness, 2004.

Conclusion

Although servicewomen are still not assigned direct combat duties, the wars in Iraq and Afghanistan are proving that in modern warfare, the front lines are too fluid to keep servicewomen safe. So necessary have servicewomen become to the Armed Forces' ability to function that commanders have repeatedly requested the authority to be able to assign their troops where they were most needed without having to hold back over 15–25 percent of the unit because the members in question were female. Historians of women's military service have frequently stated that women's service has often been in direct proportion to the need for their services. When women's services are needed, whether to fill in during a manpower shortage or to provide specific female-dominated skills such as nursing or serving as telephone operators, the nation's political and military leaders somehow contrive methods by which women can be utilized. This phenomenon continues even today; in Afghanistan, male soldiers are culturally prohibited from communicating with half of the native population. In response, the Marine Corps now sends specially trained female Marines into dangerous Taliban-controlled territories to meet and engage with Afghan women and help the U.S. Armed Services win "the hearts and minds" of the Afghan people.

As America's War on Terror continues, its Armed Forces will need increasing numbers of committed young men and women volunteers. Over time, the gender of these young volunteers has slowly become less and less important. Today's military urgently needs to fill an increasingly wide variety of highly skilled, genderless, technical jobs. The roster of positions women can't fill shrinks every few years; for example, this year the Navy announced that it will begin assigning women to positions in submarines. Whether or not women will ever officially break the combat barrier remains to be seen but, if history is any indicator, that time may not be as far away as we think.

Index

All Volunteer Force, 91–101
  archival collections
    E. Westcott Mangee Collection, 101
    Shirley Jolly Minge Collection, 101
  books, 95–98
    Arms and the Enlisted Woman, 98
    Barbed Wire for Sale: The Hungarian Transition to Democracy 1988–1991, 95
    Bring Me Men and Women: Mandated Change at the U.S. Air Force Academy, 98
    Does Khaki Become You? The Militarization of Women's Lives, 96
    Dress Gray: A Woman at West Point, 97
    Exploring Military Service for Women, 98
    First Class: Women Join the Ranks at the Naval Academy, 96
    In the Men's House, 95
    Ladybirds II: The Continuing Story of American Women in Aviation, 96
    Mixed-Gender Basic Training: The U.S. Army Experience 1973–2004, 96
    Servicewomen and What They Do, 98
    Serving in Silence, 96
    Sound Off! American Military Women Speak Out, 97–98
    Stronger Than Custom: West Point and the Admission of Women, 97
    Weak Link: The Feminization of the American Military, 97
    Women and the Military, 96
    Women in Khaki: The American Enlisted Woman, 97
    Women Who Dared: American Female Test Pilots, Flight Test Engineers and Astronauts, 97
  journal articles, 98–100
    2 of 3 Female Midshipmen Cite Harassment at Academy, 99
    Affirmative Action and Combat Exclusion: Gender Roles in the U.S. Army, 99
    Army Women, 99
    Dames at Sea, 98
    Female Midshipman Did the Academy a Big Favor, 99
    Female Mipshipman Quits Academy After Taunting Incident, 99
    Harassed Female Midshipman Quits, 98
    Many at the Academy Believe Women Don't Belong, 99
    Naval Academy is Chided on Sexism, 99
    Navy, Congress Open Probes of Harassment at Annapolis, 99
    Redefining a Woman's Place: The Pentagon Opens up New Posts for Female Soldiers, 99
    Sex Integration of the U.S. Air Force Academy: Changing Roles for Women, 99
    Sexual Harassment of Women in the Military, 99
    Shock Waves at the U.S. Naval Academy, 98
    The Case Against Women in Combat, 99
    The Future of Women in the Army, 99
    The Protected, the Protector, the Defender, 100
    Woman to Command Midshipman, 99–100
    Women at Arms, 99
    Women at the Service Academies and Combat Leadership, 99
    Women Can't Fight, 100
  oral history
    Women in the Military: An Unfinished Revolution, 100
  periodicals devoted to women in military
    Minerva: Quarterly Report on Women in the Military and *Minerva's Bulletin Board*, 101
    Women Military Aviators Incorporated Newsletter, 101
  reports
    An Update Report on the Progress of Women in the Navy, 100
    Department of Defense 1995 Sexual Harassment Survey, 100
    U.S. Army Research for the Behavioral and Social Sciences, 100
War on Terror, 127–38
  books, 128–31
  journal articles, 132–37
  official reports and policies, 137–38
  theses and academic papers, 131–32
American Civil War
  Arlington National Cemetery website, 34
  journal articles, 33–34
    Battle Time: Gender, Modernity, and Confederate Hospitals, 34
    Captain Sally Tompkins: Angel of the Confederacy, 33
    Commissioned by God: Mother Bickerdyke during the Civil War, 33
    In Search of Women of African Descent Who Served in the Civil War Navy, 33
    Kady Brownell, a Rhode Island Legend, 33
    Little Women: Alcott's Civil War, 33
    The Inhospitable Hospital: Gender and Professionalism in Civil War Medicine, 34
  memoirs and biographies, 25–33
    A Black Woman's Civil War Memoirs: Reminiscences of My Life in Camp with the 33rd U.S. Colored Troops, Late 1st South Carolina Volunteers, 32

Index

A Lost Heroine of the Confederacy: The Diaries and Letters of Belle Edmondson, 28
A Woman Doctor's Civil War: Esther Hill Hawk's Diary, 31–32
A Woman of Honor: Dr. Mary E. Walker and the Civil War, 28–29
A Yankee Spy in Richmond: The Civil War Diary of "Crazy Bet" Van Lew, 31
An Uncommon Soldier: The Civil War Letters of Sarah Rosetta Wakeman Alias Private Lyons Wakeman, 26
Angels of Mercy: An Eyewitness Account: A Primary Source by Sister Ignatius Sumner of the Civil War and Yellow Fever, 30
Belle Boyd in Camp and Prison, 26
Belle Boyd: Confederate Spy, 32
Bound for the Promised Land: Harriet Tubman: Portrait of an American Hero, 30
Cathy Williams: From Slave to Female Buffalo Soldier, 32
Civil War Hospital Sketches, 25
Civil War Nurse Mary Ann Bickerdyke, 28
Civil War Nurse: The Diary and Letters of Hannah Ropes, 31
Cyclone in Calico, 25
Exile to Sweet Dixie: The Story of Euphemia Goldsborough: Confederate Nurse and Smuggler, 27
Harriet Tubman: The Life and Life Stories, 30
Harriet Tubman: The Road to Freedom, 27
Hospital Days: Reminiscence of a Civil War Nurse, 33
Kate: The Journal of a Confederate Nurse, 28
Letters of a Civil War Nurse, 29
Memoirs of a Soldier, Nurse and Spy in the Union Army: A Woman's Adventures in the Union Army, 28
Memories, 25
My Heart toward Home: Letters of a Family during the Civil War, 29
My Story of the War: The Civil War Memoirs of the Famous Nurse, Relief Organizer and Suffragette, 30
Neither Heroine nor Fool: Anna Ella Carroll of Maryland, 27
Our Army Nurses: Stories from Women in the Civil War, 29–30
Pauline Cushman: Spy of the Cumberland, 26–27
Southern Lady, Yankee Spy: The True Story of Elizabeth Van Lew, A Union Agent at the Heart of the Confederacy, 32
The Colors of Courage: Gettysburg's Forgotten History: Immigrants, Women and African Americans in the Civil War's Defining Battle, 27–28
The Confederate Nurse: The Diary of Ada W. Bacot 1860–1863, 25–26
The Lady Nurse of Ward E, 32
The Woman in Battle: The Civil War Narrative of Loreta Janeta Velazquez, Cuban Woman and Confederate Soldier, 33
Turn Backward, O Time: Civil War Diary of Amanda Shelton, 29
Wild Rose: Rose O'Neale Greenhow, Civil War Spy, A True Story, 26
With Courage and Delicacy: Civil War on the Peninsula: Women and the U.S. Sanitary Commission, 28
Woman of Valor: Clara Barton and the Civil War, 30–31
military women, 19–34
scholarly monographs, 20–25
  All the Daring of the Soldier: Women of the Civil War Armies, 22–23
  Battle Scars: Gender and Sexuality in the American Civil War, 21
  Civil War Sisterhood: The U.S. Sanitary Commission and Women's Politics in Transition, 21–22
  Confederate Heroines: 120 Southern Women Convicted by Union Military Justice, 23
  Confederate Women, 25
  Daughters of the Union: Northern Women Fight the Civil War, 24
  Divided Houses: Gender and the Civil War, 24
  Lincoln's Daughters of Mercy, 22
  Patriotic Toil: Northern Women and the American Civil War, 20
  Patriots in Disguise: Women Warriors of the Civil War, 22
  She Went to the Field: Women Soldiers of the Civil War, 24
  Southern Women, the Civil War and the Confederate Legacy, 21
  The Bonnet Brigade: American Women and the Civil War, 23
  The Women and the Crisis: The Women of the North and the Civil War, 24
  They Fought Like Demons: Women Soldiers in the American Civil War, 20–21
  To Bind Up the Wounds: Catholic Sister Nurses in the U.S. Civil War, 23
  Women and the American Civil War: An Annotated Bibliography, 23
  Women at the Front: Hospital Workers in Civil War America, 24
  Women at War: Civil War Heroines, 21
  Women during the Civil War: An Encyclopedia, 22
  Women in the American Civil War, 21
  Women in the Civil War: Extraordinary Stories of Soldiers, Spies, Nurses, Doctors, Crusaders and Others, 21
  Women of the South in War Times, 20
  Women of the War, 24
  Women on the Civil War Battlefront, 22
  Women Who Spied for the Blue and Gray, 22
American Revolution, 1
archival records, 17–18
books, 13–16

A Journal of the March of a Party of Provincials from Carlisle to Boston and from Thence to Quebec, Begun the 13th of July and Ended the 31st of December 1775, 14–15
America's First Woman Warrior: The Courage of Deborah Sampson, 14
Belonging to the Army: Camp Follower and Community during the American Revolution, 15
Founding Mothers: The Women Who Raised Our Nation, 15–16
Liberty's Daughters: The Revolutionary Experience of American Women 1750–1800, 15
Masquerade: The Life and Times of Deborah Sampson, Continental Soldier, 16
Noble Deeds of American Women: With Biographical Sketches of Some of the Most Prominent, 13
Revolutionary Mothers: Women in the Struggle for America's Independence, 13
The Female Marine and Related Works: Narratives of Cross-Dressing and Urban Vice in America's Early Republic, 13–14
The Female Review, 15
The Revolution Remembered: Eyewitness Accounts of the War for Independence, 14
The Women of the American Revolution, 14
To be Useful to the World: Women in Revolutionary America 1740–1790, 14
Women of the Republic: Intellect and Ideology in Revolutionary America, 15
Women Patriots of the American Revolution, 13
journal articles
  As Private Robert Shurtliff, Deborah Sampson Served 18 Months in the Continental Army, 16
  Revolutionary Women, 16
  Standing Tall with Sarah Bowman: The Amazon of the Border, 16
  Women of the American Revolution, 16
military women, 12–18
official records, 16–17
  Colonel Records of Pennsylvania, Volume 15, 17
  Documents of the Assembly of the State of New York, Vol. 18, 16–17
Arendt, Helena Maria Gottschalk, 39
Armed Forces, 139
Army Nurse Corps, 2, 9
Army-Navy Nurse Act of 1947, 79

Bray, Linda, 95
Bystran, Sharon Forman, 85

Cam Ranf Bay, 85
Chase, Ann, 18
Citadel, 124
Civil War, 1
Coast Guard Women's Reserve, 71
Cole, Mary Ann, 17
Combat Exclusion Laws, 4

combat exclusion regulations and military operations, 108–17
books, 111–12
  Assessing the Assignment Policy of Army Women, 111
  It's Our Military Too: Women and the U.S. Military, 112
  No Constitutional Right to Be Ladies: Women and the Obligations of Citizenship, 111
  The Kinder, Gentler Military: How Political Correctness Affects Our Ability to Win Wars, 111
  Wives and Warriors: Women in the Military in the United States and Canada, 112
  Women at War: Gender Issues of Americans in Combat, 112
  Women in Combat: Civic Duty or Military Liability, 111
  Women in the Military, 112
  Women in the Military: Flirting with Disaster, 111
government reports, 115–17
  An Update Report on the Progress of Women in the Navy, 116
  Army Policy for the Assignment of Female Soldiers, 115, 117
  Assignment of Army and Marine Corps Women under the New Definition of Ground Support, 116
  Attitudes Regarding the Assignment of Women in the Armed Forces: The Military Perspective, 116
  Career Progression of Minority and Women Officers, 116, 117
  Congressional Commission on Military Training and Gender-Related Issues: Final Report: Transcripts and Legal Consultants Reports, 115
  Congressional Quarterly Researcher 6, 116
  Defense Equal Opportunity Management Institute, 115
  Family Readiness: Techniques and Procedures on Family Support Initiatives, 116
  Gender Issues: Information on DOD's Assignment Policy and Direct Ground Combat Definition: Report to the Ranking Minority member, Subcommittee on Readiness, Committee on Armed Services, U.S. Senate, 117
  Military Readiness: Women Are Not A Problem, 116
  Mismanagement and Missed Opportunities: The F-18 Training of Major Jacquelyn S. Parker at the New York Air National Guard's 174th Fighter Wing, 115
  New Opportunities for Military Women: Effects upon Readiness, Cohesion and Morale, 115
  Politics and the Pentagon: The Role of Women in the Military, 115
  Pregnancy and Single Parenthood in the Navy: Results of a 1997 Survey, 116

Index

Report of the Task Force on Discrimination and Sexual Harassment, 115
Report on the Responses of the Armed Services to the Federal Advisory Committee on Gender-Integrated Training and Related Issues and Additional Direction by the Secretary of Defense, 115
Report to the President, 116
Special Inspection on Initial Entry Training Equal Opportunity Sexual Harassment Policies and Procedures, 116
The Tailhook Report, 116
Women in Combat, 116
Women in Combat: Report to the President, November 15, 1992, 117
Women in the Military: What Role Should Women Play in the Shrinking Military?, 115
Women in the Navy: The Past, Present and Future, 117
Women on Ships: An Historical Look at Unplanned Losses, 115
journal articles, 112–14
A Soldier is a Soldier, 113
Cohesion and Readiness in Gender-Integrated Combat Service Support Units: The Impact of the Acceptance of Women and Gender Ratio, 113
Creating the Ultimate Meritocracy, 112
Female United States Airforce Pilot Personality: The Right Stuff, 113
How Can Male Leaders Promote Sexual Equality in Military Academies?, 114
Is It Combat or 'Combat'?, 112
John Has to Do It, Because Jane Can't, 113
Married Female Officers in a Combat Branch: Occupation Family Stress and Future Career Choices, 113
Pregnancy on Active Duty: Making the Tough Decisions, 112
Question: Will Combat Roles for Women Downgrade Military Readiness? No: Women Have Proved They Can Do the Job, 113
Race and Gender in the U.S. Military, 112
Rock the Cradle, Rock the Boat?, 113
Should Men and Women Train and Go Into Combat Together?, 113
The Effects of Gender on Cadet Selection for Leadership Positions at the United States Military Academy, 113–14
The Unit Cohesion Factor, 11
The Warrior Besieged, 113
Tradition, Technology, and the Changing Roles of Women in the Navy, 112
Why Promotable Female Officers Leave the Army, 113
Women at War: The Ethics of Women in Combat, 113
Women In Combat?, 112
Women in the Military: What Role Should Women Play in the Shrinking Military?, 113
theses, 115–16

Analysis of Female Attrition from Marine Corps Officer Candidate School, 114
Army Women in Combat: An Examination of Roles, Opportunities, Administration and Social Acceptability, 114
Breaking the Mold: Issue Redefinition and Policy Change Concerning Women in Combat, 114
Dual Army Couples and Their Impact on Readiness, 114
Enlisted Women at Sea: A Quantitative Analysis, 115
Female Vs. Male Differences in Communication: Obstacles and Solutions to Future Leadership Potential Within the U.S. Military, 115
High Injury Rates among Female Army Trainees: A Function of Gender?, 114
Ladies Fix Bayonets: Impossible Policy Decision, 114
Mentoring of Women in the United States Air Force, 114
Mentoring Women and Minority Officers in the U.S. Military, 114
Opportunities for Women in the Air National Guard, 114
The Impact of Pregnancy on U.S. Army Readiness, 114
Women and Nontraditional Occupations in the Navy: A Study Over Time, 114
Women in Combat Arms: A Combat Multiplier?, 114
Women in Combat in Tomorrow's Navy, 114
Women in Direct Combat: What is the Price for Equality?, 114
Women: Their Fight to Fight, 115
communism, 80
Corbin, Margaret, 17
Cummings, Missy, 118

Darragh, Lydia, 12–13
Defense Advisory Committee on Women in the Service (DACOWITS), 2, 79
Defense Authorization Act (1994), 110
Defense Authorization Bill (1992), 109
Dennis, Judy, 85
Diekman, Diane J., 119
Direct Combat Probability Code (DCPC), 94
Dix, Dorothea, 19

Executive Order 10240 (1951), 2, 80
Executive Order 9981, 80

gender and military academies, 124–26
  books, 124
    Breaking Out: VMI and the Coming of Women, 124–25
    In Glory's Shadow: The Citadel, Shannon Faulkner and a Changing America, 125
    In the Company of Men: A Woman at the Citadel, 125

Porcelain on Steel: Women of West Point's Long Gray Line, 125
Tough As Nails: One Woman's Journey Through West Point, 125
Women in the Barracks: The VMI Case and Equal Rights, 125
  government reports, 126
    DoD Service Academies: Further Efforts Needed to Eradicate Sexual Harassment, 126
    DoD Service Academies: More Actions Needed to Eradicate Sexual Harassment, 126
    Honor Systems and Sexual Harassment at the Service Academies, 126
    Military Academy: Gender and Racial Disparities, 126
    Naval Academy: Gender and Racial Disparities, 126
  journal article, 125
    Servicewomen and the Academies: The Football Cordon and Pep Rally as a Case Study of the Status of Female Cadets at the U.S. Military Academy, 124
gender discrimination and sexual harassment, 117–24
  books, 118–22
    All American, Hanoi Jane, and the High and Tight: Gender, Folklore and the Changing Military Culture, 118
    An American Story, 118
    Beyond Zero Tolerance: Discrimination in Military Culture, 120
    Call Sign Revlon: The Life and Death of Navy Fighter Pilot Kara Hultgreen, 121
    Camouflage Isn't Only for Combat: Gender, Sexuality and Women in the Military, 119
    Coping with Sexism in the Military, 121
    Faithful and Fearless: Moving Feminist Protest Inside the Church and Military, 120
    Fall from Glory: The Men Who Sank the U.S. Navy, 121–22
    For the Love of Country: Confronting Rape and Sexual Harassment in the U.S. Military, 120–21
    Gender Camouflage: Women and the U.S. Military, 118
    Generally Speaking: A Memoir by the First Woman Promoted to Three Star General in the United States Army, 120
    Hornet's Nest: The Experiences of One of the Navy's First Female Fighter Pilots, 118
    Navy Greenshirt: A Leader Made Not Born, 118
    Proud to Be: My Life, the Air Force, the Controversy, 119
    She's Just Another Navy Pilot: An Aviator's Sea Journal, 119–20
    Tailspin: Women at War in the Wake of Tailhook, 122
    The Mother of All Hooks: The Story of the U.S. Navy's Tailhook Scandal, 120
    This Woman's Army: The Dynamics of Sex and Violence in the Military, 118
    Women Soldiers: Images and Realities, 118
  government reports
    Factors Affecting the Reporting of Sexual Harassment in the Navy, 123
    Gender Discrimination in the Military, 123–24
    Management and Missed Opportunities: The F-16 Training of Major Jacqueline S. Parker and the New York Air National Guard's 174th Fighter Wing, 123
  journal articles
    By Force of Arms: Rape, War and Military Culture, 122
    Her Own Private Tailhook, 122
    Military Culture: Change and Continuity, 122
    Pilot Errors, 122
    Resistance and Escape Training Dropped by Air Force Academy, 122–23
  theses, 123
    Gender Bias in the Navy, 123
    Marriage and Children as Impediments to Career Progression of Active Duty Career Women Army Officers, 123
    Perceptions of Racial and Gender Bias in Naval Aviation Flight Training, 123
    Policies, Practices and the Effect of Gender Discrimination on the Integration of Women Officers in the Department of the Navy, 123
    The Social Construction of Race and Gender: Black Woman Officers in the U.S. Navy, 123
  unpublished conference papers
    A Story That Keeps Exploding: Kelly Flinn, the Defense Department and the Power of the Double Standard Narrative, 123
    G.I. Jane Trapped in Stereotype: How Television Magazine Shows Bolster Gender Bias While Purporting to Fight it in Their Coverage of Military Women, 123
Ginsburg, Ruth Bader, 3

Heavren, Rose, 38–39
Hello Girls, 43
Hodgers, Jennie, 20–21
Hultgreen, Kara Spears, 120, 121

Integration Act (1948), 94

Jacobson, Diane, 86

Korean War, 2
  books, 81–3
    A Defense Weapon Known to be of Value: Servicewomen during the Korean War, 83
    Assignment Tokyo, 82
    MATs and Me: WAVES Flight Attendants on Military Aircraft, 81
    Quiet Heroes: Navy Nurses in the Korean War 1950–1953, 82–83

Index

Take a Seat, Make a Stand: A Hero in the Family, 82
The Ladies of First Army, 82
We Will Not Be Strangers: Korean War Letters between a MASH Surgeon and His Wife, 81–82
Women Marines in the Korean War Era, 83
journal articles, 83–84
Indiana Nurse in Korea, 83
Public Service Role Models: The First Women of the Defense Advisory Committee on Women in the Services, 83
The Flight Nurse, 84
The Nurse on the Docks, 83
They Either Need These Women or They do Not: Margaret Chase Smith and the Fight For Regular Status for Women in the Military, 83
women serving under the protection of Uncle Sam, 79–84

McGee, Anita Newcomb, 38, 40
McSally, Martha, 134–35
Mexican American War of 1846–1848, 1
military women
All Volunteer Force, 91–101
archival collections, 101
books, 95–98
journal articles, 98–100
oral history, 100
periodicals devoted to women in military, 101
reports, 100
American Civil War, 19–34
Arlington National Cemetery website, 34
journal articles, 33–34
memoirs and biographies, 25–33
scholarly monographs, 20–25
American Revolution, 12–18
archival records, 17–18
books, 13–16
journal articles, 16
official records, 16–17
defense of the nation across the centuries, 5–10
encyclopedias, 10–11
Amazons to Fighter Pilots: A Biographical Dictionary of Military Women. 2 Volumes, 10–11
The Encyclopedia of Amazons: Women Warriors from Antiquity to the Modern Era, 11
Women and the Military: An Encyclopedia, 11
Women and the Military: Over 100 Notable Contributors, Historic to Contemporary, 10
Women and War: A Historical Encyclopedia from Antiquity to the Present, 10
general histories, 5–7
Battle Cries and Lullabies: Women in War from Prehistory to the Present, 5
Dressed for Duty: America's Women in Uniform Volumes 1 and 2, 7

Hell Hath No Fury: True Stories of Women at War from Antiquity to Iraq, 6–7
Salute to Freedom: 100 Years of Women in Military Service, 7
Side by Side: A Photographic History of American Women in War, 6
War and American Women: Heroism, Deeds and Controversy, 5
War and Gender: How Gender Shapes the War System and Vice Versa, 6
Women at Risk: We Also Served, 5–6
Women in the Military: An Unfinished Revolution, 6
Women Warriors: A History, 6
guides to sources, 10
American Women and the U.S. Armed Forces: A Guide to the Records of Military Agencies in the National Archives Relating to American Women, 10
Women in the United States Military, 1901–1996, 10
journal articles
The Face of Courage on the Battlefield, 11
True Confessions of an Ex-Chauvinist: Fodder for Your Professional Reading on Women and the Military, 11
Korean war, 79–84
books, 81–83
journal articles, 83–84
Operations Desert Shield and Desert Storm, 102–26
dismantling combat exclusion regulations and 1990s military operations, 108–17
gender and military academies, 124–26
gender discrimination and sexual harassment, 117–24
women in the Gulf, 102–8
Spanish American War nurses, 38–41
books, 40
journal articles, 40
website, 41
thematic and service-specific histories, 7–10
A History of Women Marines 1946–1977, 9–10
Answering the Call: Nurses of Post 122, 7
Crossed Currents: Navy Women in a Century of Change, 8
Fifty Years of Air Force Dietetics 1949–1999, 8
History of the American Dietetic Association 1917–1959, 8
History of the Army Nurse Corps, 9
In and Out of Harm's Way: A History of the Navy Nurse Corps, 9
On the Field of Mercy: Women Medical Volunteers from the Civil War to the First World War, 8–9
Serving Proudly: A History of Women in the U.S. Navy, 8
The Army Medical Specialist Corps, 8
The Women's Army Corps: 1945–1978, 9
We Are Marines: World War I to the Present, 9
Women Doctors at War, 8

War on Terror and All Volunteer Force, 127–38
  books, 128–31
  journal articles, 132–37
  official reports and policies, 137–38
  theses and academic papers, 131–32
Western frontier, 35–37
  books, 35–37
World War II
  bedpans, typewriters and lipstick, 51–78
Mobile Army Surgical Hospital, 80–81

Navy Nurse Corps, 2
navy nurses, 41
Newcom, Elizabeth, 17–18

Operation Desert Shield, 4
Operation Desert Storm, 4
Operation Just Cause, 3–4
Operation Urgent Fury, 3–4, 94
Operations Desert Shield and Desert Storm, 102–26
  dismantling combat exclusion regulations and 1990s military operations, 108–17
    books, 111–12
    government reports, 115–17
    journal articles, 112–14
    theses, 114–15
  gender and military academies, 124–26
    books, 124–25
    government reports, 126
    journal article, 125
  gender discrimination and sexual harassment, 117–24
    books, 118–22
    government reports, 123–24
    journal articles, 122–23
    theses, 123
    unpublished conference papers, 123
  women in the Gulf, 102–8
    books, 104–5
    government reports, 108
    journal articles, 106–8
Osborn, Sarah, 14

Pentagon attack, 128
Pickersgill, Mary, 17

Redman, Alice, 12
Risk Rule, 94, 110

Sampson, Deborah, 12, 14, 15
Semper Paratus, 71
Spanish American War, 2
  books, 40
    History of the Army Nurse Corps, 39
    Marvels of Charity: History of American Sisters and Nuns, 40
  journal articles
    Band of Angels: Sister Nurses in the Spanish American War, 40
    The Navy Nurse Corps, 40
    Women Nurses in the Spanish American War, 40
    Women Physicians in the Spanish American War, 40
  military women nurses, 38–40
  website, 41
SPARS, 71

Tailhook scandal, 118, 119, 120, 121
Tet Offensive, 86

United States Air Force, 79
USS *Benevolence,* 81
USS *Cole,* 127–28

Vietnam War, 2
  books, 86–88
    33 Years of Army Nursing: An Interview with Brigadier General Lillian Dunlap, 87
    A Piece of My Heart: The Stories of 26 American Women Who Served in Vietnam, 88
    A World of Hurt: Innocence and Arrogance in Vietnam, 88
    American Daughter Gone to War: On the Front Lines with an Army Nurse in Vietnam, 88
    Home before Morning: The Story of an Army Nurse in Vietnam, 88
    Hostile Fire: The Life and Death of 1st Lieutenant Sharon Lane, 87
    If I Don't Laugh, I'll Cry Forever, 87
    My Rise to the Stars: How a Sharecropper's Daughter Became an Army General, 86–87
    Number Ten: A Vietnam Diary, 88
    Station Hospital Saigon: A Navy Nurse in Vietnam 1963–1964, 87
    The Challenge: Autobiography of Colonel Margaret E. Bailey, 87
    Women at War: The Story of Fifty Military Nurses Who Served in Vietnam, 87
  journal articles, 88–89
    Annie, Don't Get Your Gun, 88
    Navy Hospital in Saigon, 88
    Nurse Questions Vietnam War, 88
    Officer, Nurse, Woman: Army Nurse Corps Recruitment for the Vietnam War, 88–89
    Women in the Armed Forces, 89
  official histories, 89
    Semi-Annual Histories of the Office of the Surgeon General, 89
  unpublished oral histories and memoirs, 89
  unpublished thesis, 90
    What Influenced the Development of the Air Force Nurse Corps from 1969–1983?, 90
Virginia Military Institute, 124

Wakeman, Sara Rosetta, 1–2
War of 1812, 1
War on Terror, 4, 139
  All Volunteer Force, 127–38
  books, 128–31
    Anthropology and the United States Military: Coming of Age in the Twenty-First Century, 129

Index

Band of Sisters: American Women at War in Iraq, 129
Covering Sex, Race and Gender in the American Military Services, 130
I Am a Soldier, Too, 130
Iraq and Back, 130
Love My Rifle More than You: Young and Female in the U.S. Army, 131
Managing Diversity in the Military: Research Perspectives from the Defense Equal Opportunity Management Institute, 128
Maneuvers: The International Politics of Militarizing Women's Lives, 128–29
Men, Women and War, 129
Moving Beyond G.I. Jane: Women and the U.S. Military, 131
One Woman's Army: The Commanding General of Abu Ghraib Tells Her Story, 129–30
Reaching Past the Wire: A Nurse at Abu Ghraib, 129
Ruff's War: A Navy Nurse of the Front line in Iraq, 130
Rule Number Two: Lessons I Learned While in a Combat Hospital in Iraq, 130
The Few, the Proud, Women Marines in Harm's Way, 130
The Girls Come Marching Home, 129
The Lonely Soldier: The Private War of Women Serving in Iraq, 128
War and Gender: How Gender Shapes the War System and Vice Versa, 129
Women at War: Iraq, Afghanistan and Other Conflicts, 131
Women in the Line of Fire: What You Should Know about Women in the Military, 131
Women in the Military: Where They Stand. 5th edition, 130
journal articles, 132–37
1st Woman Takes Charge of Army's Drill Sergeants, 136
A Case for Women Warfighters, 133
A Combat Role, and Anguish Too, 133
A New Commander to Train US Drill Sergeants? Yes, Ma'am!, 134
A New Generation of Women? How Female ROTC Cadets Negotiate the Tension between Masculine Military Culture and Traditional Femininity, 136
Another Peril in War Zones: Sexual Abuse by Fellow G.I.s, 135
Back from Combat, Women Struggle for Acceptance, 136
Breaking Through the Glass Ceiling: General Ann E. Dunwoody Becomes the First Woman Four-Star in the U.S. Military, 133
Combat Roles for Women: A Modest Proposal, 133
Double Jeopardy: Women, the U.S. Military and the War in Iraq, 134
G.I. Jane Breaks the Combat Barrier, 132
Gender and War, 136

Gender Disparities in Enforcing the Honor Concept at the U.S. Naval Academy, 135
Gendered Nationalism: A Critical Analysis of Militarism, Patriarchy and the Ideal Soldier, 134
In Taliban Territory, GI Janes Give Afghans a Different View, 133
Integrating Women into the Infantry, 136
Less Than We Can Be: Men, Women and the Modern Military, 136
Living and Fighting Alongside Men, and Fitting In, 135
Masculinity, Whiteness and the Warrior Hero: Perpetuating the Strategic Rhetoric of U.S. Nationalism and the Marginalization of Women, 135
Not Semi-Soldiers; It's No Longer a Question of Whether Women Should Be in Combat, It's a Matter of the Regulations Catching Up with Reality, 135
On September 11, an Aimless, Gun-Fearing Bath and Body Works Clerk Decided to Sign Her Life Away to the Army, 133
Pregnancy during Operation Iraqi Freedom/ Enduring Freedom, 133
Rescuing Patriarchy or Saving Jessica Lynch: The Rhetorical Construction of the American Woman Soldier, 134
Soldiering Ahead, 137
The Citizen Soldier Tradition and Gender Integration of the U.S. Military, 136
The Dangers of Playing Dress Up: Popular Representations of Jessica Lynch and the Controversy Regarding Women in Combat, 134
The Fallen Woman Archetype: Media Representations of Lynndie England, Gender, and the (Ab)uses of U.S. Female Soldiers, 134
The Female Infantryman: A Possibility?, 133
The Myth of the Macho Military, 136
Uniform Justice: Assessing Women in Combat, 134
Vernice Armour: The First African American Woman Combat Pilot, 134
Viewpoint: De Facto Women Warriors: End Combat Exclusions, 133 Wartime Soldier, Conflicted Mom, 132–33
When Boy Meets Girl: The 'Feminization' of the Military: An Introduction Also to be Read as a Postscript, 134
When Mom Wears Steel-Toed Boots, 135
Who Would Fight: A Diverse Military: Changes in the Army Since the Gulf War Include More Latinos, Muslims and Women, 136
Why Women Don't Report Sexual Harassment: A Case Study of an Elite Military Institution, 135
Winning the Retention Wars: The Air Force, Women Officers and the Need for Transformation, 133

Women at Sea: 'It's All about Leadership, 133
Women in Combat: Is the Current Policy Obsolete?, 134–35
Women in Combat Units: It's Still a Bad Idea, 136
Women Take Command in Combat, 136
Women, War and Winning Elections: Gender Stereotyping in the Post September 11 Era, 134
Women Warriors, 137
Women's Military Roles Cross Nationally: Past, Present and Future, 136
official reports and policies, 137–38
Evaluation of Sexual Assault, Reprisal and Related Leadership Challenges at the United States Air Force Academy, 137
Issues: Co-Ed Basic Training: CMR Compiles Definitive Summary of Findings on Co-Ed Basic Training, 137
Issues: Recruiting/The Draft Court Dismisses Lawsuit to Include Women in Draft Registration, 137
Issues: Women in Combat: Bush Administration Upholds Law and Regulations Exempting Women from Land Combat, 137
Issues: Women in Combat: Enlisted Women Opposed to Combat Assignments, 137
Issues: Women in Combat: Jessica Lynch Reality Shatters Amazon Myth, 137
RAND Corporation, 137, 138
Report Concerning the Assessment of USAF Sexual Assault Prevention and Response, 138
Report of the Panel to Review Sexual Misconduct Allegations at the U.S. Air Force Academy, 138
Report of the Working Group Concerning the Deterrence and Response to Incidents of Sexual Assault at the U.S. Air Force Academy, 138
Report on the Status of Female Members of the Armed Forces: Report to Congress, 138
Summary Report Concerning the Handling of Sexual Assault Cases at the United States Air Force Academy, 137
theses and academic papers, 131–32
Field Artillery (Wo)men: Time for a Relook?, 132
Preparing Women for Strategic Leadership Roles in the Army, 132
The Code of the Warrior: The Kinder, Gentler Military and Marksmanship: Changing a Culture, 131
The Decision to Allow Military Women into Combat Positions: A Study in Policy and Politics, 132
The Glass Ceiling Effect and Its Impact on Mid-Level Female Officer Career Progression in the United States Marine Corps and Air Force, 132

The Impact of Army Transformation on the Integration of Enlisted Women, 132
The Trivialization of Gender and Its Impact on Combat Effectiveness, 132
Winning the Retention Wars; The Air Force, Women Officers and the Need for Transformation, 132
Women in Combat: Attitudes and Experiences of U.S. Military Officers and Enlisted Personnel, 132
Women: Ready for the Challenges of the Future U.S. Armed Forces, 132
Western frontier
books, 35–37
Army Wives on the American Frontier: Living by the Bugles, 36
Boots and Saddles, or Life in Dakota with General Custer, 35
Elizabeth Bacon Custer and the Making of a Myth, 36
Following the Guidon, 35–36
Members of the Regiment: Army Officers' Wives on the Western Frontier, 37
Reminiscences of a Soldier's Wife, 35
She Wore a Yellow Ribbon: Women Soldiers and Patriots of the Western Frontier, 35
Tenting on the Plains or General Custer in Kansas and Texas, 36
The Colonel's Lady on the Western Frontier: The Correspondence of Alice Kirk Grierson, 36
Vanished Arizona: Recollections of the Army Life of a New England Woman, 37
Women of the Frontier Army, 35
Women of the New Mexico Frontier 1846–1912, 36
women in the Gulf, 102–8
books, 104–6
American Women of the Gulf War, 105
Desert Storm Journal: A Nurse's Story, 105
Diary from the Desert, 106
Ground Zero: The Gender Wars in the Military, 104–5
Operation Desert Storm: Diary of an Army Nurse, 105
She Went to War: The Rhonda Cornum Story, 104
The Most Qualified: A Nurse Reservist's Experiences in the Persian Gulf War, 104
The Whirlwind War: The United States Army in Operations Desert Shield and Desert Storm, 105–6
When Duty Called: Even Grandma Had to Go, 105
Who Will Fight the Next War? The Changing Face of the American Military, 104
Women in the Military: An Unfinished Revolution, 105
government reports
Conduct of the Persian Gulf War: Final Report to Congress, Pursuant to Title V of the Persian Gulf Conflict Supplemental Authorization and Personnel Benefits Act of 1991, 108

Subject: Policy on the Assignment of Women in the Armed Forces, 108
Women in Combat: Report to the President, 108
Women in the Military: Deployment in the Persian Gulf War: Report to the Secretary of Defense, 108
journal articles, 106–8
2 Air National Guard Officers Relieved of Command in Sex Discrimination Case: A Report Says that a Female Fighter Pilot Was Denied Missions that Men were Given, 107–8
63 Women Get Carrier Orders, 107
Army Women, 107
Comment: Beyond the Persian Gulf Crisis: Expanding the Role of Servicewomen in the United States Military, 107
Embattled N.Y. Fliers Face New Era, 107
Feminist Perspectives on Women Warriors, 106
From Women's Services to Servicewomen, 108
Military Culture: A Paradigm Shift?, 106
Our Women in the Desert: Sharing the Duty (and Danger) in a 'Mom's War', 106
Reconceptualizing Sexual Harassment, 108
Sex and the Soldier, 106
Should Women Be Sent Into Combat?, 107
Should Women Go Into Combat?, 106
The Right to Fight: The Taboo on Women in Combat May Finally Crumble as Congress Debates a Bill to Allow Women to Fly Warplanes, 106–7
War and the Second Sex: Women Are Smart and Capable, But Would Battlefield Equality Hurt Combat Readiness?, 106
We've Come a Long Way': NCO's Career Shows Women's Progress, 106
What of the Women Who Want No Combat Role? Supporters Are Not Always the Ones Who Would Fight, 106
Women Have What It Takes: An Army Captain Tells Why Females Should Fight, 106
Women in the United States Military: Protectors or Protected? The Case of Prisoner of War Melissa Rathbun-Nealy, 107
Women's Work, 108
Women Marines, 86
Women's Armed Services Integration Act of 1948, 2, 3, 79–80, 109, 110
World War I, 2
archival sources, 50–51
Charlotte Edith Anderson Monture Collection, 51
Letters and postcards of Rose Heavren, 50
Lilliann Dial Collection, 51
The Signal Corps "Hello Girls" File, 51
books, 44–8
A Heart for Healing: A Memoir of the Life of Elizabeth Campbell Bickford, 45

A History of the U.S. Army Nurse Corps, 45–46
American Women in World War I: They Also Served, 45
Answering the Call: The U.S. Army Nurse Corps 1917–1919: A Commemorative Tribute to Military Nursing in World War I, 44
Black Women in White Racial Conflict and Co-operation in the Nursing Profession 1890–1950, 46
Fever of War: The Influenza Epidemic in the U.S. Army During World War I, 44
Finding Themselves: The Letters of an American Army Chief Nurse in a British Hospital in France, 47
In Uncle Sam's Service: Women Workers with the American Expeditionary Force, 48
Into the Breach: American Women Overseas during World War I, 47
Journal of E. Elizabeth Weaver, Army Nurse Corps, World War I, 47–48
Lamp for a Soldier: The Touching Story of an American Nurse in World War I, 47
Mademoiselle Miss: Letters From a World War I Nurse at an Army Hospital Near the Marne, 44
Mobilizing Minerva: American Women in the First World War, 46
Nurse Helen Fairchild: World War I 1917–1918, 47
Nurses at the Front: Writing the Wounds of the War, 46
Nurses in Action, 45
Nurses of a Different Stripe: A History of Colombia University School of Nursing, 45
Ordered to Care: The Dilemma of American Nursing 1850–1945, 46
Out Here at the Front: The World War I Letters of Nora Saltonstall, 46–47
Pride of America, We're With You: The Letters of Grace Anderson U.S. Army Nurse Corps World War I, 48
The First Enlisted Women 1917–1918, 44
The First, the Few and the Forgotten: Navy and Marine Corps Women in World War I, 44–45
The Physician's Hand: Work, Culture and Conflict in American Nursing, 46
Women Marines in World War I, 46
journal articles, 48–50
A Base Hospital Is Not a Coney Island Dance Hall, 49
A Brand New Vet of WWI, 50
A Certain Restless Ambition: Women Physicians and World War I, 50
A Letter from a Navy Nurse, 48
Experiences of a Navy Nurse, 50
From a Navy Nurse, 50
How Army Nurses Became Officers, 48–49
I Was A Hello Girl, 48
Letters from Navy Nurses, 48, 49

She's In the Navy Now, 50
The Army Nurse Corps, 49
The Army's Forgotten Women, 49
The Experiences of an Ex-Navy Nurse on Recruiting Duty, 50
The Golden Fourteen: Black Navy Women in World War I, 50
The History and Development of the Navy Nurse Corps, 49
The Overlooked Heroines: Three Silver Star Nurses of World War I, 50
What the Navy Gives to and Expects from the Chelsea Nurse, 49
With High Hopes: Women Contract Surgeons in World War I, 49
women volunteers establish parameters of service, 42–51
World War II, 2
  army and navy nurse corps, 54–63
    A Half Acre of Hell: A Combat Nurse in World War II, 61
    Albanian Escape: The True Story of U.S. Army Nurses Behind Enemy Lines, 59
    All this Hell: U.S. Nurses Imprisoned by the Japanese, 60
    American Nightingale: The Story of Frances Slanger, Forgotten Heroine of Normandy, 62
    And If I Perish: Front line U.S. Army Nurses in World War II, 60
    Bedpan Commando: The Story of a Combat Nurse during World War II, 62
    Brave Nurse: True Stories of Heroism, 60
    Chip on My Shoulder, 56
    Combat Nurse: A Journal of World War II, 62
    Combat Nurses of World War II, 56
    Fearless Presence: The Story of Lt. Col. Nola Forrest, Who Led the Army Nurses through the Heat, Rain, Mud and Enemy Fire in World War II, 61–62
    From Nightingale to Eagle: An Army Nurse's History, 56
    From Survival to Arrival, 56
    G.I. Nightingale: The Story of an Army Nurse, 56
    G.I. Nightingales: The Army Nurse Corps in World War II, 62
    Hathaway, 57
    Heads in the Sand, 58
    Helmets and Lipsticks, 58
    Her War: American Women during World War II, 57
    I Have a Story to Tell, 63
    I Served on Bataan, 61
    In Uniform 1936–1946, 58
    Lingering Fever: A World War II Nurse's Memoir, 57
    Long Ago and Far Away, 61
    Mother Wore Combat Boots and Chased Troop Trains, 59
    My Fifty Years in Nursing: Give Us to Go Blithely, 61
    Navy Nurse, 57
    No Time for Fear: Voices of American Military Nurses in World War II, 58
    Reflections of One Army Nurse in World War II, 57
    Reflections on Quiet Adventures and Memoirs of Florence "Flo" Scholljegerdes, 62
    Reminiscing: An Account of the 300th Army General Hospital during World War II, 57
    Thank You Uncle Sam: Letters of a World War II Army Nurse from North Africa and Italy, 59
    The Colonel Was a Lady, 59
    The Way It Was: An Air Force Nurse's Story, 56
    They Called Them Angels, 58
    To the Angels, 62–63
    Unsung Heroes: Combat Nurses and Army Wives, 56
    Warrior in White, 58–59
    We Band of Angels: The Untold Story of the American Nurses Trapped on Bataan by the Japanese, 60
    What a Way to Spend a War: Navy Nurse POWs in the Philippines, 57
    With Love, Jane: Letters from American Women on the War Fronts, 59
    Women Were Not Expected, 60–61
    World War II: A Navy Nurse Remembers, 69
  coast guard SPARS, 71
    The Coast Guard and the Women's Reserve in World War II, 71
    Three Years behind the Mast, 71
  journal articles, 76–8
    American Military Women Prisoners of War, 76
    Beyond Paradise: The U.S. Navy Nurse Corps in the Pacific in World War II Part I, 78
    Beyond Paradise: The U.S. Navy Nurse Corps in the Pacific in World War II Part II, 78
    Christmas Christmas Everywhere! How Army and Navy Nurses Spend Christmas Overseas, 77
    Creating G.I. Jane: The Regulation of Sexuality and Sexual Behavior in the Women's Army Corps during World War II, 77
    Creation of the WAC Image and Perception of Army Women 1942–1944, 77
    Hi-Ho! Hi-Ho! Back to Nurse I Go, 77
    Indians at Work: A News Sheet for Indians and the Indian Service, 77
    Jacqueline Cochran, Trailblazer, Barrier Breaker. A Century of Flight: Military Pioneers Who Made Aviation History, 76
    Naval Hospital in San Diego, 78
    Navy Nurses on the U.S.S. Solace, 77
    Nurse Draft Bill Passed by the House, 78
    Nursing Care in Air Ambulances: Navy Nurses Continue to Meet Many Unique Problems in Air Evacuation, 78

Index

Rugged and Right: That's Teresa James, 78
The Long Flight Home, 77
The Senior Cadet Nurse, 78
Those Unseen, Unheard Arkansas Women: WAC, WAVES and Women Marines of World War II, 76
Transport Duty with the U.S. Navy, 78
U.S. Cadet Nurse Corps: Established Under the Bolton Act, 78
WAVES, WAACs, SPARs and Nurses, 78
What's All the Fuss About? My WAFS/WASP Flying Experiences, 77
Women Airforce Service Pilots of World War II: Exploring Military Aviation, Encountering Discrimination, and Exchanging Traditional Roles in Service to America, 77
Women in Combat: The World War II Experience in the United States, Great Britain, Germany and the Soviet Union, 76
Women in Uniform: The World War II Experiment, 76–77
Women, Combat and the Gender Line, 76
navy WAVES, 68–71
Angel of the Navy: The Story of a WAVE, 69
Cleared for Take Off, 71
Grace Hopper: Admiral of the Cyber Sea, 70
Grace Hopper: Navy Admiral and Computer Pioneer, 69
Improbable Warriors: Women Scientists in the Navy in World War II, 70
Making WAVES: A Woman in This Man's Navy, 70
Making WAVES: Navy Women of World War II, 69
More Than a Uniform: A Navy Woman in a Man's World, 69
Mother Was a Gunner's Mate: World War II in the WAVES, 70
Navy Blue and Other Colors, 70
Navy WAVE Memories of World War II, 69–70
Okay, Girls, Man Your Bunks! Tales from the Life of a World War II Navy WAVE, 69
Old WAVES Tales, 68
Once a WAVE: My Life in the Navy 1942–1946, 69
The Way of the WAVES, 68
Wave Goodbye: A Navy WAVE's Memoir, 70
reports and theses, 78
Oveta Culp Hobby and Her "Lieutenants": Transformational Leadership in Action in the Women's Army Auxiliary Corps of World War II, 78
Women Pilots with the AAF 1941–1944, 78
unit histories, 76
As You Were, the 2629 WAC Battalion, Italy, 76
History of the WAC Detachment 9th Air Base, 76
women airforce service pilots, 72–76

A Wasp Among Eagles: A Woman Military Test Pilot in World War II, 73
Amelia Earhart's Daughters: The Wild and Glorious Story of American Women Aviators from World War II to the Dawn of the Space Age, 74
And Still Flying, The Life and Times of Elizabeth "Betty" Wall, 75
Clipped Wings: The Rise and Fall of the Women Airforce Service Pilots (WASPs) of World War II, 74–75
Flying for Her Country: The American and Soviet Military Pilots of World War II, 75
For God, Country and the Thrill of It: Women Airforce Service Pilots in World War II, 75
Jackie Cochran: Pilot in the Fastest Lane, 75
Jackie Cochran: The Autobiography of the Greatest Woman Pilot in Aviation History, 73
Letters Home 1944–1945, 74
On Final Approach: The Women Airforce Service Pilots of World War II, 74
On Silver Wings: The Women Airforce Service Pilots of World War II, 75
Sharpie: The Life Story of Evelyn Sharp, 73
Sisters in Arms: British and American Women Pilots during World War II, 75
The Stars at Noon, 74
Those Wonderful Women in Their Flying Machines: The Unknown Heroines of World War II, 74
WASPs: Women Airforce Service Pilots of World War II, 76
Winning My Wings: A Woman Airforce Service Pilot in World War II, 74
women general histories and World War II, 53–54
American Women and World War II, 54
American Women in a World at War: Contemporary Accounts from World War II, 53
In Defense of a Nation: Military Women during World War II, 53
Serving Our Country: Japanese American Women in the Military during World War II, 54
Sisterhood of Spies: The Women of the OSS, 54
They Also Served: American Women in World War II, 53
Til I Come Marching Home: A Brief History of American Women in World War II, 53
We're in this War Too: World War II Letters from American Women in Uniform, 53–54
What Did You Do in the War, Grandma?, 54
women marines, 71–72
A Few Good Women: Memoirs of a World War II Marine, 71
Dearest Folks: Sister Leatherneck's Letter Excerpts and World War II Experiences, 72
Marines? Yes!, 72

Our Home on the Hill 1943–1946, 72
Woman Marine: A Memoir of a Woman Who Joined the U.S. Marine Corps in World War II to "Free A Marine to Fight," 72
Women Marine Association Volumes 1–3, 72
Women Marines: The World War II Era, 72
Years of Grace, Days of Glory: The Legacy of Germaine Laville, 72
women's army auxiliary corps and women's army corps, 63–68
A Date with Destiny: A WAC in Occupied Japan 1946–1947, 66
A WAC Looks Back, 67
An Officer and a Lady: The World War II Letters of Lt. Col. Betty Bandel, Women's Army Corps, 64
Battle of the WAC, 64
Call of Duty: A Montana Girl in World War II, 66
Creating G.I. Jane: The Regulation of Sexuality and Sexual Behavior in the Women's Army Corps during World War II, 66
Daughters of Pallas Athene, 68
Eisenhower Was My Boss, 67
Fighting in the Jim Crow Army: Black Men and Women Remember World War II, 66
Girl in a Pink Skirt, 66
Hey Lady, Uncle Sam Needs You, 66
Justice Older Than the Law: The Life of Dovey Johnson Roundtree, 66–67
Lady G.I.: A Woman's War in the South Pacific c., 64
Laugh, Cry and Remember: The Journal of a G.I. Lady, 66

Los Alamos WAACs/WACs, World War II 1943–1946, 64
Love and War: One WAC Remembers World War II, 65
My Mother's Fort: A Photographic Tribute to Fort Des Moines: First Home of the Women's Army Corps, 64
One Woman's Army: A Black Officer Remembers the WAC, 65
One Woman's War: Letters Home From the Women's Army Corps 1944–1946, 65
Our Mothers' War: American Women at Home and at the Front during World War II, 68
Past Forgetting: My Love Affair with Dwight D. Eisenhower, 67
Ruffles and Drums, 67
Skirt Patrol: Women's Army Corps, Army of the United States, 63
Stand in for a Soldier, 64
Stateside Soldier: Life in the Women's Army Corps 1944–1945, 65
The Good Soldier: The Story of a Southwest Pacific Signal Corps WAC, 68
The Lipstick Explosion, 67
The WAACs, 67
The Women's Army Corps: United States Army in World War II Special Studies, 67
Their Day in the Sun: Women of the Manhattan Project, 65
To Serve My Country, To Serve My Race: The Story of the Only African American WACs Stationed Overseas during World War II, 66
WAC Days of World War II: A Personal Story, 68
We Were First! We Heard the Guns at Wewak, 64